Fabricating the People

Public Administration: Criticism & Creativity

Fabricating the People

Politics and Administration in the Biopolitical State

Thomas J. Catlaw

THE UNIVERSITY OF ALABAMA PRESS
Tuscaloosa

The University of Alabama Press
Tuscaloosa, Alabama 35487-0380
uapress.ua.edu

Hardcover edition published 2007.
Paperback edition published 2014.
eBook edition published 2007.

Typeface: Garamond

Manufactured in the United States of America
Cover design: Todd Lape/Lape Designs

∞

The paper on which this book is printed meets the minimum requirements of American National Standard for Information Science–Permanence of Paper for Printed Library Materials, ANSI Z39.48-1984.

Cloth ISBN: 978-0-8173-1572-6
eBook ISBN: 978-0-8173-8018-2

Library of Congress Cataloging-in-Publication Data

Catlaw, Thomas J. (Thomas Joseph), 1973–
Fabricating the people : politics and administration in the biopolitical state / Thomas J. Catlaw.
pages cm. — (Public administration: criticism & creativity)
Includes bibliographical references and index.
ISBN 978-0-8173-5815-0 (pbk. : alk. paper)
1. Legitimacy of governments—United States—Public opinion. 2. Public administration—United States—Public opinion. 3. Political leadership—United States—Public opinion. 4. Public opinion—United States.
5. United States—Politics and government—2001–2009. I. Title.
JK275.C37 2014
351.73—dc23

2014035010

To the many who are, and the many more yet to come

Life itself is neither a good nor an evil:
life is where good or evil find a place,
depending on how you make it for them.
—Michel de Montaigne

Contents

Acknowledgments

A long, rich line of nurturing relationships made possible the composition of this work. It is a pleasure to acknowledge them here.

I am grateful for the many enriching discussions about this project. Thanks, in particular, to Marshall Alcorn, Ami Avitsur, Corey Davis, Michael Dimock, Amy Gignesi, Susan Halebsky-Dimock, Allan Jones, Aaron Kupchik, Elena Kupchik, Victoria Ludwin, Nick Samuels, Brad Snyder, and Andrew Zimmerman.

Of the many colleagues who have offered (and continue to offer) engaging criticisms of my work, I thank Kym Thorne, Louis Howe, Matthew Witt, Patricia Mooney-Nickel, Frank Scott, and Eric Austin. I am also grateful for early discussions about the problem of representation with participants of the 2002 Postmodern Public Administration Study Group of the European Group of Public Administration, specifically Isabel da Costa, Anna Maria Campos, Peter Bogason, and Paul Frissen. David John Farmer and Margaret Stout generously read a draft of the whole manuscript and offered insightful feedback on the text and its structure. I thank H. George Frederickson for his encouragement of this project, and Steven Aufrecht for his early support.

I have been fortunate to have arrived at the School of Public Affairs at Arizona State University during an exciting, even historic time for the state of Arizona, the university, and the school. There is a palpable optimism about the future and an inspiring sense of possibility. This spirit has certainly found its way into this book. I have been supported by an enviable group of colleagues. I should especially like to thank Laura Peck, Khalid Al-Yahya, Barbara McCabe, Janet Denhardt, Joe Cayer, and Heather Campbell—each has given to the completion of this book considerable time, patience, and energy. I would also like to acknowledge the research assistance of Heidi Spann, who was of great help with chapter 4, and Qian

Hu and Greg Jordan, who were invaluable in the final preparation of the manuscript.

I am most grateful to Robert Denhardt for his support of this project and, just as important, for his cultivation of an open, dynamic intellectual environment at ASU as director of the School of Public Affairs. Our school, with the diverse range of methodologies and theoretical approaches it houses, practices precisely the kind of social science of which the world needs more.

At ASU, I have been part of the ongoing dialogue of the TOC group. This venue has proved vital to me in fleshing out many inchoate ideas, and I thank Kelly Campbell, Michael Coyle, Chao Guo, and Heather Stickeler for their discussions and their intellectual and emotional range.

The University of Alabama Press stands as one the important presses in the history of public administration. Publishing many classic works in the field, it continues to support cutting-edge advances in public administration thought. I extend deep appreciation to the staff at Alabama, unfailing advocates of this project; this publication is testament to that advocacy. I am very honored indeed that this book is published under the imprimatur of The University of Alabama Press.

I wish also to acknowledge the kind permission of Sage Publications and *Administrative Theory & Praxis* to use here portions of previously published materials. Portions of chapters 1, 4, 5, and 7 appeared, respectively, in "The Death of the Practitioner," *Administrative Theory & Praxis, 28*(2) (2006): 190–207; "Performance Anxieties: Shifting Public Administration from the Relevant to the Real," *Administrative Theory & Praxis, 28*(1) (2006): 89–120; "Authority, Representation, and the Contradictions of Post-traditional Governing," *American Review of Public Administration* (2006); "Constitution as Executive Order: The Administrative State and the Political Ontology of 'We the People,'" *Administration & Society 37*(4) (2005): 445–482.

I give special thanks to Hugh Miller and Camilla Stivers. Hugh and Cam read the manuscript in its entirety with great care and attention. Their critiques and recommendations dramatically improved the final product, and our exchanges about the text exemplified their own remarkable work on discourse and dialogue. I could not have completed this project without them. I owe the deepest of thanks and appreciation to Lori Brainard and Michael Harmon, who serve as invaluable mentors, friends, and intellectual guides. Orion White is a dear friend and sharp critic. He has "suffered" many iterations of this work and, such is his way, always prompted new thoughts that kept the discourse moving. Words will certainly fail to articulate the manifold ways in which I am grateful to Cynthia McSwain. So I won't try.

My wife, Suzanne, has lived this book with me for many years. Among her many gifts to me, I thank her most for our shared struggle against the insistence of the model.

Fabricating the People

1
Public Administration and Political Ontology

Crisis and Political Ontology

Over the last thirty years, there has been a rising tide of hostility toward government. During the same period, the field of public administration in the United States has been concerned with its own, perhaps more narrow, crisis of legitimacy. But why? Just as skepticism about and mistrust of government is not a recent phenomenon in American political culture, neither is the question of legitimacy new for the field of public administration. Indeed, the very concept of public administration arguably is defined by its ongoing search for an identity and disciplinary coherence; and skepticism toward government is central to the liberal political tradition. Yet since the late 1960s, the question of legitimacy in both domains has been taken up with an impressive urgency. What is at the root of contemporary antigovernmentalism?

Broadly speaking, the field of public administration has offered two explanations for this legitimacy crisis, one normative, the other "performative."[1] The first explanation locates the crisis of government in the absence of the correct value set, be it defined in terms of constitutionally or democratically based values. From this diagnosis, it seeks to alter the consciously held values of the individual public administrator and the field generally from neutrality to an explicit normative position. The latter position conceives of the crisis primarily in terms of government's failure to perform and deliver effective services to the public and so grounds its remedy in the advancement of professional and/or technical knowledge. Though this is a stylized presentation of these positions, naming differences in emphasis more than in kind, the twin deficits of normativism and performance nevertheless mark the dominant theoretical positions in public administration and orient contemporary efforts to enhance both the efficacy and legitimacy of government. Departing from these poles—indeed, arguing that these apparent adversaries share everything of any importance—this text makes a rather different *kind* of argument. It contends that the current crisis of government has its roots in the breakdown of the theoretical plausibility and practical efficacy of a set of foundational assumptions about reality itself. This crisis is caused by the collapse of a distinct *ontological* conception of human life. The very fabric of the world is coming undone.

It may sound strange to talk about a breakdown or failure of an ontology since, in philosophical terms, ontology is the inquiry into, fundamentally, *what is*—what it means *to be,* what objects can be said to exist, and what assumptions we make about them and their relations to other entities. Can *what is* really fail or break down? Can the meaning of being change? Philosophical and theoretical developments, ones that have unfolded and gained prominence during the same period as our legitimacy crises, have challenged radically the simple givenness of objects and our ontological commitments to them. That is, assessing *what is* can no longer be viewed simply as a matter of common sense, given experience of the world.[2] Rather, the basic assumptions we make about the nature of our reality substantively create that reality as well as our subjective and collective experience of it.[3] Ontological commitments are the basic ideas or principles by which we make up our worlds. As I will elaborate over the course of this text, the ontological crisis of the current period refers to the breakdown in the plausibility of the supposition that there is an ultimate, given unity behind appearance to which all differences in the final instance reduce. I name this ontology *representation.*

We have come to understand, further, that ontologies are political. Our basic set of commitments and assumptions about the world implies specific ways of organizing politics and specific political forms. According to Adrianna Cavarero (2002), "each political form implies a political approach to the question of ontology. In other words, since politics, however one understands it, concerns itself with human beings, each conception of politics raises the ontological question, or rather, it presupposes a political ontology" (p. 513).[4] Political forms, in other words, imply distinct ontological commitments, and an approach to ontology implies an account of politics, political form, collective life, and what it means *to be.* Applying this to our own political context, the institutions of representative government and the modern presuppositions of democracy—namely, the idea of a popular sovereign or People—themselves are linked to a distinct set of ontological commitments. Approaching from the other direction, ontology implies a political form and establishes certain requirements for a theory of knowledge (epistemology) and the organization and constitution of instituted authority.

Much concern has been expressed about social fragmentation and how people appear to be less inclined to sacrifice for the common good. I will argue here, however, that the core problem of the contemporary world is less that we all see the world from our own narrow individual perspective or interests and so fail to work toward a common good (a position sufficiently accommodated by political liberalism and positivist epistemology), but rather that we can now appreciate that we may live in and hold fidelities to the truths of different worlds. The objects that count as real to us, what we can know about them, and what it *means to live a meaningful life* can vary in fundamental ways that are not simply superficial misunderstandings. These differences are, furthermore, not amenable to empirical or phenomenological resolution since the very terms and criteria of judgment and adjudication of, for example, the good are internal to those worlds (Badiou, 2006/1988; Kuhn, 1996/1962).[5] Nor can these differences simply be reduced to a humanist presumption about a universally shared, unconstructed trait or characteristic of humanity. In other words, the world can no longer plausibly be thought to exist as a given unity, nor can it be conceived as being something we all have in common. It is not simply the case that the world is so complex that, when aggregated, our particular concepts and consciousness cannot capture the whole (Miller, 2002, p. 62; Simon, 1997/1945). Rather, there simply is not a whole world to represent. Indeed, the world is now presented increasingly in the full force of its multiplicity. In the domain of the political, the unity of the People, the popular sovereign's presumptive We, fragments into proliferating categories of group identity, interest, and enclave—seemingly possessing neither a common cause nor a common adversary.

The breakdown in representation may be thought of as what Karl Weick (1993) calls a "cosmology episode." "A cosmology episode occurs," Weick writes, "when people suddenly and deeply feel that the universe is no longer a rational orderly system. What makes such an episode so shattering is that both the sense of what is occurring and the means to rebuild that sense collapse together" (p. 633). Though I would resist pointing to a single traumatic event that ruptured the world of representation, Weick's idea captures something crucial—not only are we struggling to make sense of our worlds and those of others, but both the theoretical assumptions and institutional arrangements we have relied on previously to make up worlds and to create sense itself, such as representative government and the presumptions of popular sovereignty, no longer seem to work (Castells, 2000). They seem less effective in helping us to construct a stable, rationally ordered world. With the eroding efficacy of the presupposition that a single view can "represent" social, political, or personal reality, political orders that are founded on this ontological commitment, including liberal democratic government, and that have been constructed to reproduce these presuppositions find themselves on ever more tenuous footing.[6]

Consideration of these problems from the perspective of public administration, the field of study today most intimately acquainted with the everyday work of governing and the reproduction of this ontology, reveals an additional dimension of the relationship of political form and ontological commitment, namely, the practical difficulty of disentangling different understandings of ontology. Colin Hay (2006) describes a standard philosophical distinction between two distinct, "albeit closely related" understandings of ontology.[7] "The first, and more abstract, is concerned with the nature of 'being' itself—what is it to exist, whether (and, if so, why) there exists something rather than nothing and whether (and if so, why) there exists one logically contingent actual world. The second sense of the term is concerned with the (specific) set of assumptions made about the nature, essence and characteristics (in short, the reality) of an object or set of objects of analytical inquiry. . . . [P]olitical ontology is a 'regional ontology' " (p. 80). Hay's lucid account restricts itself to the study and inquiry into, first, the nature of being and, second, a more specific, "regional" approach to objects or specific domains of objects. Whereas philosophy may concern itself with being in general, he writes, political analysis cannot proceed without making decisions with regard to its assumptions (which may vary considerably) about a set of more narrow matters, for example, "the relationship between structure and agency, context and conduct" or "the nature of the human (political) subject and its behavioral motivations" (p. 81).

The everyday work of governing presents a case in which this division of ontological labor will not hold. As Cavarero (2002) suggests, governing implies an answer to the ontological question "What does it mean to be?" insofar as politics broadly defined can be said to consider the question of "the good life" (Waldo, 1948). That is, while ontological commitments speak to the nature and scope of entities that can be said to exist (White, 2000), as in the regional ontologies of social science, commitments in the realm of government also answer, even if only implicitly, the question of what it *means to be* in the world. As critics of technicism and rationalism have long argued, governing cannot be reduced to the status of a science and the manipulation of objects. It cannot be only a regional ontology (or constellation of regional ontologies) precisely because governing provides an answer to the question of what it means to be and, in doing so, itself establishes a general array of objects, relationships, and properties that orient and organize the regional worlds. When we consider in this text, then, the question of "the People," we are thinking about *both* a posited entity *and* a certain way of being-together in the world, about the status of particular entities as well as how we take them to be in the world, about the status of *human* entities and how we take ourselves to be in the world.

From this answer to the question of being itself, certain dispositions for order and human existence emerge to inform and guide theories, practices, and techniques of governing. What we will see is that the fundamental commitment of representation is to a *unity* behind appearance and differences or, in the language of philosophy, that *being is One* (Badiou, 2006/1988). Our world has been built on this foundation, and this is a foundation now beyond reconstruction. The challenge for administrative thought is to consider the contemporary crises of governing from these densely interwoven dimensions—being, political form, epistemology, and governing practices. The task, in other words, is to illuminate the dimensions, limits, and possibilities of *representation's political ontology*[8] and to consider how else we ontologically might construct our worlds.

Waldo and the Obstinate Constellation of Public Administration

There are good reasons to begin an inquiry into the contemporary condition of governing from public administration. Public administration's ever-present legitimacy question makes it especially close to the problems at the heart of this breakdown in the political ontology of representation. In addition to its role in reproducing a specific political ontology (a point to be demonstrated in chapter 5), the appearance of the administrative state (or at least a self-conscious public administration[9]) marks a distinct moment in the ontology of representation. The administrative state is a symptom of sorts, and during its history, there has been considerable theoretical development that will assist in formulating the contours of representation. However, public administration has not been fully able to confront the problems and opportunities that this failure of our political ontology poses.

The reasons for this are complex and hinge on the field's self-construction on and within representation itself. A few reasons are clear enough now, though. First, the field's thought has been limited by historical misconceptions and, in no small measure, by a not infrequently defensive posture before more "mature" academic disciplines (e.g., political science and economics). Second, it has been unnecessarily deferential to an image of the "real world" of administrative practice (Catlaw, 2006b). Third, and no doubt conditioned by the previous two points, public administration has largely ignored the question of ontology, its fundamental understanding of reality (McSwite, 1997a), viewing such "academic" or "theoretical" pursuits as insufficiently practical or useful to the labors of governing.[10] These factors have circumscribed the field's internal critical discourse and theoretical exploration.

Paradoxically, the field's development has been restricted most seriously by the parameters established by perhaps its greatest, certainly most prominent critic, Dwight Waldo. In *The Administrative State,* Waldo (1948) famously wrote: "Any political theory rests upon a metaphysic, a concept of the ultimate nature of reality" (p. 21). (We can read the word *metaphysic* here as *ontology* [White, 2000, p. 1].) Waldo held that the ontology upon which public administration was founded was "a verdict of science." Scholars and practitioners of public administration had uncritically accepted a "scientific" attitude that, by virtue of its understanding of reality as being governed by fixed, discoverable social laws, conditioned an unhealthy preoccupation with efficiency, technical expertise, neutrality, and the self-evidence of the facts. The articulation of this "value-free" scientific position, as Waldo noted, in actuality concealed a fully fledged political theory of government. Far from public administration being merely a technical enterprise, its language of technique and neutrality concealed a robustly developed political philosophy. Articulating a position that would be demonstrated ably by others in the following decades, Waldo went on to argue that the insistence on a rigorous distinction between politics and administration was simply untenable.[11] His was among the earliest salvos in the ongoing assault on the "politics-administration dichotomy."[12] Most important, Waldo's critique exposed the theoretical and historical relationship between the objectivism of modern science and the administrative state. He showed that the administration was not and could not be "neutral" because it was a product of a distinctive historical period and, more fundamentally, because, normatively, it relied on that "verdict of science."

The threshold that Waldo did not cross, however, was to link this verdict and the emergence of administration with the particular form of modern politics, namely, political representation and the problems generated by depositing sovereignty in "the People." Whatever critique Waldo mounted, politics remained self-evident and, as I shall suggest here, by necessity, so did public administration. This is not to say that Waldo's own body of work lacks traces of another line of analysis. Waldo raises the question of the foundations upon which American democracy is constructed in his discussion of the nineteenth century's preoccupation with notions of "higher" or "fundamental law." The linkage between a faith in a higher, religious law and scientific law and faith in (a certain kind of) democracy is made clearly: "Yet it would be a serious mistake to suppose that American students [of public administration] have escaped the influence of 'higher law' notions widely accepted by the American community. Faith in democracy . . . is just such an idea. To the extent that democracy has been thought superior and ultimate as a form of government and way of life, it has itself served as the higher law to which everything else must be referred; we have seldom permitted ourselves to doubt that democracy accords with the moral constitution of the universe" (1948, p. 17).

This discussion continues in Waldo's rich examination of what he calls "cosmic constitutionalism" and its "conflation, a fusion and confusion, of the ideas of moral and physical necessity" (1948, p. 155).[13] Many years later, Waldo (1980) asks a more precisely formulated, if seemingly only rhetorical, question: "With regard to *democracy* the problem of definition is severe. *Democracy* of course means 'rule by the people'—but what does that mean? Who are the 'people'? How and by what means can they 'rule'? What are the limitations, in principle or practice on their rule? What about the contention that rule by the people is impossible, that the word itself reflects confusion?" (p. 84). Elsewhere, he provocatively notes (Brown & Stillman,

1986, p. 61) that the emergence of the administrative state marked a turn toward *democracy* and away from the representative republicanism constructed by the Federalist Constitution. Thus, in various places in Waldo's work, there are traces of a different line of analysis. Here, we pick up and follow these traces.[14]

Administration, the Suspect Enterprise

Whatever other lines of inquiry Waldo's work adumbrates, in the decades that followed the post–World War II debate on the politics/administration dichotomy and epistemology raged on. Criticized from myriad perspectives and on empirical, normative, historical, and philosophical grounds, the battle-weary dichotomy has "died a thousand deaths, by a thousand cuts" (Fox & Miller, 1995, p. 3), which need not be rehearsed here. Similarly, the objectivism of science has been exposed thoroughly; the socially constructed (or at least paradigmatically mediated) nature of the facts are well documented in many literatures and even incorporated into mainstream perspectives in the field (e.g., Ostrom 1989/1973). The possibility of simply representing reality has become an increasingly difficult intellectual position to defend. Still, these two elements remain as the essential coordinates of public administration discourse, and the terms of the dichotomy remain the predominant view of public administration among the public and, generally speaking, academics outside of public administration. Having spent the good part of his life criticizing it, in the last years of his career Waldo (1980) himself concluded, "I do not believe it is possible to 'solve' the problem of relating politics to administration in any way that is systematic and generally acceptable, in and for the United States, under present conditions and in any foreseeable future" (p. 77).

Precisely why has it proven so difficult to resolve the matter of the relationship of politics to administration? Many answers have been advanced to account for its durability. The dichotomy is, perhaps, "partially accurate" as a description of the relationship between career civil servants and elected officials and, arguably, it provides a "normative base, rooted in democratic theory, for assessing the appropriateness of [administrative] behavior" (Svara, 1985, p. 221). Functionally, the dichotomy may also serve to insulate administrators from the demands of "particularistic politics" (Montjoy & Watson, 1995), thereby creating both a professional standard and an incentive for administrators to reproduce belief in the dichotomy. No doubt, the dichotomy also has the commonsense appeal of folk wisdom insofar as it appears to map onto everyday dualisms, what Goodnow (1900) called the psychological necessity of formulating and carrying out or deciding and acting. It replicates an everyday notion of the giving and taking of orders. In the style of Waldo's own historical approach, recent intellectual histories of the development of public administration in the United States suggest another set of explanations (e.g., McSwite, 1997b; Stivers, 2000). From these vantages, the dichotomy can be seen as part of the strategy for legitimizing the nascent field of public administration. This legitimizing unfolded through an attachment to the language of scientific neutrality and objectivity and, by extension, its authority. The possibility for administration necessitated the creation of what I shall call in chapter 2 a "domain of sovereignty" for public administration, and this sovereignty was founded on this verdict of science, regardless of whether we accept weak or strong versions of the dichotomy.

Compelling though these accounts are, they do not address an obvious question. Why was such a strategy and discourse necessary in the first place? In other words, what were the underlying assumptions that produced the dichotomy (even if only in a weak form) as a "reasonable" solution? What are these "conditions" to which Waldo alludes? The infamous, insoluble dichotomy—and the concomitant epistemological problems that attend to the questions of values and facts and the possibility or desirability of a science of administration—is a symptom of the deeper dilemma noted above—*the legitimacy problem.* The very question as to whether administration is either value-free or value-laden and the matter of its relationship to politics emerge only under conditions within which administration is a suspect enterprise and must seek firm ground to justify itself. The legitimacy question, I further suggest, is the portal to the political ontology of representation and to understanding the dynamics of the contemporary world.

So, another question: Why, then, is administration suspect? We will consider this question in depth in chapter 6 but, briefly here, within the liberal democratic American context, administration has been held as suspect insofar as it portends the installation of a powerful, unelected, and ostensibly unaccountable cadre of bureaucrats.[15] This, so it is alleged, constitutes a grave threat to the defining premise of democracy—government according to the will of the sovereign People.[16] Within this form of the political, the administrative state, potentially, is parasitic on the body politic of the People. Interestingly, where this political form is operative, the dichotomy is, in fact, a rather moot point because the question of politics is effectively bracketed. In other words, when squabbling over whether a value-free administration is or is not possible and/or desirable, we do not concern ourselves with the status of the sovereign to whom administration is beholden. The People as the origin of authority and the self-evidence of the representational mechanisms that purport to express the People's will are assumed. The full dimensions of our political ontology are never considered; the field's discourse remains hermetic.

Indeed, when we examine disagreements in public administration, we see that disputes have raged most heatedly (e.g., Friedrich-Finer, Waldo-Simon, new public administration and social equity, the Blacksburg group, the contemporary criticisms of the new public management, etc.) on matters concerning the question of what *kind* of administration or administrator is best for this liberal democratic People. This is all the terrain of the dichotomy. With partial exceptions to be discussed later, the sovereignty of something "out there" called "the People" is simply assumed and, as such, the functional distinction between politics and administration—between expressing the People's will and carrying it out—is always maintained. The dichotomy is unavoidable.

Waldo's Unfinished Project

Waldo's insistence on posing the question of the "metaphysic" of administration was, in principle, correct, and *The Administrative State* justly remains an ongoing inspiration for critical discourse in public administration. The overall effect, though, of Waldo's directive—intended or not—to contest the "verdict of science" and call into question the "sovereignty of the facts" grounded theoretical development in public administration on something of an epistemological jetty. It turned theoretical development toward regional questions of knowledge and the status of "facts," with the implicit or explicit task of demonstrating the political, value-laden dimension of administration, and distracted from the considerations of a general ontology within public administration.

My point is not that Waldo was an inessential moment in the trajectory of the field's development; nor does raising the limitations of Waldo's critique dismiss the turning point it marked. Quite to the contrary. However, this focus on the metaphysics of *science* and the problem of the dichotomy deflected from an inquiry that would have linked a fundamental conception of reality (ontology) with a specific epistemological position (the verdict of science) with a distinctive form of the political (the People). At the same time, this emphasis deflected from a different historical understanding of the emergence of a self-conscious public administration that would have pointed to precisely such an inquiry.

Modalities of Politics

To appreciate the dimensions of the endgame in which public administration and modern political thought about governing generally landed itself, let us begin by observing the doubling of the term *political.* There are at least two senses of the "political" at work in public administration's discourse. First, let us call "*P*olitics" the process of representing the will of the People, the possibility of which the field takes for granted; and second, there is the question of the *p*olitical dimension of administrative action, which has been contentious as both a theoretical and practical matter. (There are still other meanings of politics circulating in public administration. I will consider these in the discussion of Frank Goodnow in chapter 2.) The importance of this formulation is how the two politics imply one another. As I shall show in subsequent chapters, the rough-and-tumble world of politics (small p) depends upon the stability of Politics (big P). *P*olitics acts as a categorical boundary on the play of *p*olitics; it constitutes the latter's commitments and relations. The presuppositions of "the People" both enable and delimit the visible (its objects) and speakable (what can be known and said about those objects) world of politics. In effect, Politics is an answer to the ontological question of what it means to be.

Public administration avoids the first, Politics, and so never actually addresses the conditions of the dichotomy and the dimensions of the Political. Rather, administration lets Politics remain self-evident, leaving only administration to be problematic, and *not only* for itself but for politics as well.[17] It remains regional and disciplinary in its focus, even when engaging in its own theorizing. Indeed, the field's silence with regard to the Political reflects a timidity that is actually *reinforced* by its concern with self-legitimacy, since this issue serves to efface questions surrounding Politics. The legitimacy problem puts administration in a position, so to speak, of holding a debt to the People that it can never repay. The field constantly strives to live up to the People's expectations and demonstrate its legitimacy and usefulness. To call into question the Politics of the People would seem to be a gesture not merely impolitic but suicidal. It would be an invitation to the People to call in all debts, to settle all accounts, and seemingly to confirm the very worst suspicions of the cruel intentions of the bureaucrats of the administrative state.

Fabricating the People

The conditions of the contemporary world, however, require that we extend public administration's understanding of our political ontology and representation and cross the threshold to call fully into question the status of the People and attempt to formulate a theoretical framework from which to contemplate governing beyond this political form and the modes of institutionalization and organization that have developed in its service. It requires that we directly confront the political form of public administration and attempt to bring its tacit understanding of the Political (i.e., the presuppositions of the basic efficacy of the representative medium, the plausibility of a represented referent, and the assumptions made about that referent) into question. As we will see, there are two central dimensions of representation and the People.[18] Against the backdrop of its basic commitment to unity and oneness, the People is produced through the deployment of (1) a rather specific *biopolitical relationship;* and (2) a distinctive *logic of exclusion.*

In elaborating, first, the dimensions of representation's biopolitical relationship, I rely on a distinction drawn by Giorgio Agamben (1998/1995) between two Greek terms for life, *zoë* and *bios.* As Agamben writes, zoë is the simple fact of biological existence; bios names a qualified form or way of life. Beginning from this distinction, I argue that within the ontology of the People, a *single,* qualified bios is imposed as the categorical definition of zoë. In turn, that imposition (bios) purports to derive its force as a representation of the natural (be it defined biologically or culturally) way of life itself (zoë). There is a fundamental presupposition that the People has *a* way of life, and furthermore, that this way of life rests upon a positive, "natural" foundation. In other words, not only does the answer to the ontological question of what it means to be rest upon a presumptive unity of which all differences are ultimately derivative, but the authority to impose and create a unity acquires its force from an association with the naturalness of a way of life. Modern politics essentially is concerned with the imposition of specific, presumptively unified political forms onto life, and it justifies those impositions implicitly in naturalistic terms. It further generates standards of judgment (the normal, the correct, the neutral) on these bases. This political ontology renders our small-p politics within the dominion of the People a *biopolitical project* in which life itself is literally at stake (Foucault, 1991/1979).[19] This project attempts to create the unity presupposed by the People and its ontology.

The core contradiction, though, of this biopolitical project is this—the People, rather than being a universal category or unity, in fact, is characterized by a logic of exclusion; it creates unity through exclusion. These exclusions are necessary because the term *the People* is actually empty or devoid of content; it is given content solely by virtue of some element being excluded. By maintaining the exclusion and policing the boundary between the inside and outside, the content of the category remains temporarily stable. It is through this logic of exclusion and the institutions and practice that emerge to execute it that the People is *fabricated* (cf. Neocleous, 2000). I use this word rather than other terms such as "imagined" (Anderson, 1991) or "invented" (Morgan, 1988) to capture the factitious or "made-up" (Hacking, 1999/1986) quality of the People and ontology itself. I also use it in order capture the way in which presuppositions, symbols, fictions, and images are put to work in the creation of objects and technologies, the manipulation and manufacture of bodies and meaning, and the constitution of individuals. Thus this text does not aim simply to do to the People what others have done to the public interest (e.g., Schubert, 1960) and show that the idea is simply a metaphysical illusion. *To fabricate* combines this understanding of how fictions, images, and symbols are put to work with Nietzsche's (1967/1887) insight about the nexus of creation, violence, and "the state," which "went on working until this raw material people and semi-animals was at last not only thoroughly kneaded and pliant but also *formed*" (p. 86; emphasis in original). In our political ontology, the work of fabrication produces the referent or object of political representation, the People. As chapters 3 and 4 will show, the identification, production, and maintenance of exclusions through vast technical apparatuses and locations across society *fabricate the People* by putting the symbol and fiction of the People to work and by constituting a *particular* kind of collectivity.

Public Administration, Representation, and the People

For public administration, interrogating the status of the People creates a new vantage from which to understand its legitimacy question, its emergence as a field, and its role in maintaining social order. If the era of the field's founding indeed was a search "to save democracy" (Waldo, 1948, p. 75), we can ask: What was it, exactly, that needed saving? What precisely had come undone? These questions aim to assess the functionality of the limits of the ontology itself and to illuminate how public administration and the administrative state were political solutions to a specific Political crisis. In this light, the very plausibility of the administrative state is brought into question, and its objects of concern and action are revealed to be effects produced by a particular crisis-induced, historical reconfiguration of a Political constitution. This field's "problems" can be shown to be effects of the ontology of representation and its People. The problems that define public administration qua public administration can be shown to be symptoms, which have been treated for a century without diagnosing the underlying pathology: the category of the People.

Ultimately, the rereading proposed here aims to displace the political ontology upon which public administration rests and, consequently, to prepare a theoretical space for a new set of questions and concerns around which a new identity for "public administration" and governing might be formulated. By tracing the logic of the People, we will begin to see how governing exceeds our traditional "political" institutions and patterns of social organization and interaction. Government can be seen to be a generic "conduct of conduct" (Foucault, 2000a/1983) that permeates the whole of the social field in various ways.[20] This formulation displaces the question of Politics/politics–administration and its concomitant public-private division of labor. "Governing" becomes located in every space, actualized through every interaction. It can no longer be plausibly delegated to either side of the dichotomy or any traditional institution; it cannot be held apart or distinct from the People.

The account of representation gives us a way of talking about a kind of governing that is detached from divisions of sphere and sector and focuses us on the specific relationships and orders being reproduced across heterogeneous social spaces. This move constitutes a critical step toward theorizing a workable theory of governance that supersedes representation and the administrative state-form and, more immediately, engages in the collective project of articulating an alternative that challenges the reigning hegemony of neoliberal governance captured under the term new public management.[21] Indeed, in many respects, we face a task comparable in scope and significance to the sixteenth century's invention of "public power" in the secular state, a time that saw deep interpenetration of ontology, politics, practices of governing, epistemology, and the invention of a new conception of collective human life (Hardt & Negri, 2000; Israel, 2001).

The Status of Democracy

Let me be clear about the project undertaken here. This work is an attempt to theorize democracy beyond the People and its ontology, in particular via public administration, for the reasons noted. I must emphasize, however, that this effort to move beyond the People is *not* an attempt to move beyond *democracy,* if by democracy we mean something generic like self-governing or self-conducting of conduct. Indeed, it is the primary argument of this text that the concept of the People, by virtue of its peculiar construction, puts democracy on tenuous footing by foreclosing lines of thinking and acting under the auspices of a naturalized form of life and its presumptive unity. The crisis of representation requires disentangling these associations, practices, and relationships and articulating a different kind of biopolitical relationship. If governing is the conduct of conduct, to rethink governing is to reconsider the ways in which we conduct ourselves.

2

Public Administration and Sovereignty

Doing the Unstuck

Scholarly enterprises typically attempt to identify a "gap" or hole, as it were, in our knowledge of a field, and subsequently explain how the author intends to "plug" it. Here, I propose to reread the intellectual history of public administration and in doing so to identify what has *not been said,* not in order to plug a hole but to examine how a certain unspoken element, a *nonknowledge,* in fact has constituted the very ground for the possibility of the theory and practice of public administration and representational governing. It is an *omission* or exclusion from the field of knowledge that produces the coherence and stability of that field and the problems to which it attends. The social effectivity of the discourse of public administration, in other words, is sustained so long as its logic escapes it and remains unthought, implicit, and in the background (Zizek, 1989, pp. 16–21). Thus, in reviewing the field's most prominent thinkers and writers, we find that each author has *not said* the same thing. As such, while this chapter does, in part, indulge in the traditional, perfunctory "cartographic" exercise in which, arguably, straw men are successively slain, it is more than this. It is through this mapping of the unsaid that the subject of study emerges.

I encourage those who may feel that they have little interest in this parade of public administrationists to persist in their reading of this chapter. For while the literature of public administration may be viewed by the academy as being cut from a less dear and sophisticated cloth (Goodsell, 2004; McSwite, 2002) and by practitioners as lacking "relevance" to the everyday labors of governing (Bolton & Stolcis, 2003; Catlaw, 2006d; LaPorte, 1971; Streib, Slotkin & Rivera, 2001), the richness of public administrative thought lies in how it compels an encounter with the inadequacy of the "folk wisdom" of government. It is rather remarkable how the discourse of public administration challenges everyday understandings of governing: making public administration, again, an auspicious location for critical thought about governing. As Waldo (1947) was a half century ago, I, too, am impressed by its auspiciousness.

What I hope to demonstrate here is that all previous attempts to "resolve" the legitimacy question in public administration are, by virtue of their presupposition, theories of sovereignty. While my understanding of sovereignty will receive further analytic exposition in chapter 3, I will say here that this conceptualization of sovereignty involves, at its core, a relationship between a bounded domain, an excluded element, and a particular ground for determining what will be excluded legitimately. I will outline the intellectual history of public administration in terms of three distinct formulations of sovereignty. These are moments or streams of inquiry, though they should be not viewed as chronologically distinct; I am not proposing to periodize the field. The appearance of each theme at a particular sociohistorical instant does mark a disjuncture, but certainly not a displacement of the antecedent moment I seek to describe.

All three moments conceive of theories of sovereignty that are "below the bar" of the People (see figures 1–3). The first moment of the field runs from Frank Goodnow through Herbert Simon, Vincent Ostrom, and Laurence Lynn. I will contend that this stream advances "a theory of dual sovereignty" within which a domain distinction is asserted to support the functional and analytical distinction between politics and administration. This means that justification for the separation of politics and administration is based on the sovereignty of each over distinctive domains of knowledge—political knowledge and factual or technical scientific knowledge. Concomitant with these realms of sovereignty, the theory of dual sovereignty draws a clear relationship between the *formal structure* of scientific and political rationalities. Politics possesses a legal or legalistic rationality that expresses the will of the People; administration exercises a scientific rationality over a body of facts. Government is subsequently split into the expressive (politics) and executive (administration) functions, which assumes an institutional division. This division is predicated upon dual sovereignty with regard to a body of knowledge. Dual sovereignty, however, does not raise the status of the People in any way. The existence of an objective, third position logically and chronologically prior to both politics and administration is assumed.

The second movement, which distinctly emerges with Dwight Waldo

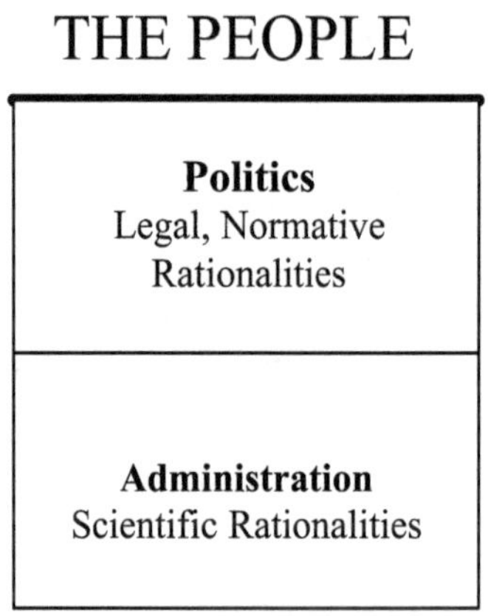

Fig. 1. Theory of Dual Sovereignty

and subsequently includes innovative exemplars Emmette Redford, John Rohr, Gary Wamsley, H. George Frederickson, and Michael Spicer, attempts to craft a "unified theory of sovereignty." This stream denies the domain distinction, yet retains the functional differentiation. In the case of unified theorists, rationality assumes an "integrated" character beneath which both political and administrative rationalities are subsumed. Administration's strict sovereignty over the facts is rejected, as is politics' privileged exercise of political rationality. However, the sovereignty of the People is asserted above politics and administration. Both politics and administration can be considered "political" insofar as both are involved in the expressive function.

Finally, the third position, to date theorized most completely by Michael Harmon, O. C. McSwite (O. C. McSwite is the pseudonym of Cynthia McSwain and Orion White), and Ralph Hummel and Camilla Stivers, brings the sovereign relation itself into question, but within a trajectory largely mapped by the unified theories. What is under scrutiny in this third stream is the structure and functionality of one-dimensional rationality. This stream reveals that rationality stands in relation to an excluded element; rationality and its representations are *not whole,* and it is on the basis of this not-wholeness that rationality is itself possible.

The objectivity of the People, however, is not considered by theorists of this stream. The critique of rationality remains below the bar of the People. That is, the logical analysis of the relationship to the exclusion does not ex-

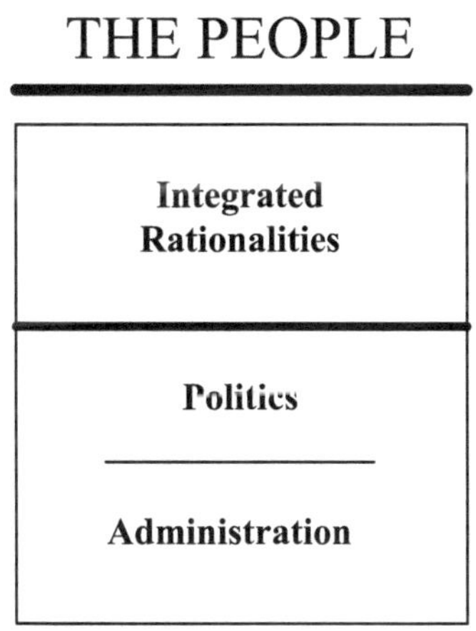

Fig. 2. Theory of Unified Sovereignty

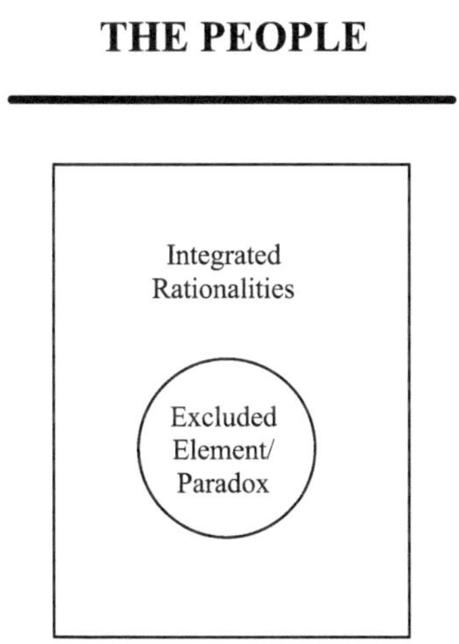

Fig. 3. Sovereignty in Question

tend to political form and, therefore, does not bring the Political itself into question. I will use the limits of this third position as my point of departure to describe in chapters 3 through 5 the general structure of sovereignty and its effectivity in and beyond public administration via an analysis of democracy's popular sovereign, the People.

This chapter considers fourteen key texts in the intellectual history of public administration. While such a selection, inevitably, is partial (in the double sense), the texts have been chosen according to two general criteria. First, at its core, each text is explicitly or implicitly concerned with analyzing the problem of administrative legitimacy and with offering a significant resolution to it. Second, the texts were selected so as to suffice as a survey of the major intellectual positions and debates within the field of public administration over the last century. No doubt many readers will contest my terminology and employ different names, but for present purposes we will call these positions orthodoxy (represented by Frank Goodnow), traditionalism (Emmette Redford), positivism (Herbert Simon), Waldovian heterodoxy (Dwight Waldo), new public administration (H. George Frederickson), public choice/new institutionalism (Vincent Ostrom), new public management (Laurence Lynn), neoconstitutionalism (John Rohr, Gary Wamsley, Michael Spicer), critical postpositivism (Michael Harmon, O. C. McSwite, Ralph Hummel and Camilla Stivers).[1]

The Theory of Dual Sovereignty

Frank Goodnow, *Politics and Administration* (1900)

Goodnow posits a prepolitical entity beyond both politics and administration. This is a position of judgment, which Goodnow calls the "will of the state." Consider, first, that Goodnow uses the term *state* as a synonym for *sovereign* (pp. 2, 9). Thus, in societies with democratic governments, the "state" is a *popular* sovereign, that is, a People. When Goodnow uses the term *will of the state,* he is not, strictly speaking, concerning himself with the will of a *government.* Rather, he intends the will of the *sovereign,* or, in the case of democracy, the will of the People. He makes this clear when he writes that "the constitution-making authority, that is, the people, expresses the will of the state as to the form of the governmental organization and the fundamental rights of the individual" (p. 16). Then, later, he writes, "the people, the ultimate sovereign in a popular government, must, however, have a control over the officers who execute their will, as well as those who express it" (p. 98). The People exists as a constitution maker. It is an entity *prior* to the constitution of a political order and the forming of a government, and thus is the origin of political authority. Government in this scenario is a kind of contingent overlay and not a generative modality. This notion has remained virtually uncontested in public administration.

Second, Goodnow famously identifies two basic political functions of the government. He writes, "the action of the state as a political entity consists either in operations necessary to the expression of its will, or in operations necessary to the execution of its will" (p. 9). Goodnow will identify these two political functions of the will as politics and administration. "Politics has to do with policies or expression of the state will. Administration has to do with the execution of these policies" (p. 18). Care is required here because there are a number of senses in which Goodnow is using the term *politics.* First, politics is one, perhaps the primary, dimension in the life of the People. Politics is divided into two functions, politics and administration: an expressive and an executive (in the sense of to execute or carry out) function. Politics, consequently, concerns "the determination of who ultimately and who secondarily and derivatively shall express the will of the state" (p. 27) and "the determination of the methods in which this will shall be expressed" (p. 35). These are matters of the "organization of the formal government" (p. 27). Finally, Goodnow acknowledges the use of politics "in the sense in which it is used by most people in ordinary affairs" (pp. 18–19), that is, a way of organizing to influence the action of government and/or public opinion. If there has been confusion regarding "politics" in public administration, Goodnow may well be its source.

Nevertheless, it seems clear enough that Goodnow identifies several different moments in this architectonic, though he confuses matters when he gives them all the same name. First, there is the People (state). The political life of the People is fundamentally characterized by two functions: the expression of its will and the execution of that will. Constitutions, second, concern the creation of a general governmental framework that outlines who will express this popular will and how. This is the organization of formal government structures and procedures, and it is a creation of the People. It must be stressed that constitutions, in this schema, do not *constitute* the state or its will. They are themselves an *expression* of that sovereign will and create the organization through which that will is expressed. Finally, there is politics, the process by which individuals and groups influence and interact with government.

Administration would appear to be more straightforward. It appears in the single sense of the *execution* of the will of the People and the determination of the technical means through which execution might occur. But, in fact, it is not so clear precisely because the notion of politics is unclear. Thus, if politics is to have control over administration, the difficult question is *which* politics has control over administration? Or, when Goodnow writes that "administration has been subjected too much to the control of politics in the United States" (p. 43), which politics is the culprit? Which politics is administration subordinate to, and does its status change depending on the mode of politics in question?

For Goodnow the matter of concern is politics in the second or third sense. Either constitutions are corrupted representations of the real People, or politics qua parochial interest impede fulfillment of the will. What has not been in question in the field is the status of the People and the functional distinction between expression and execution, regardless of the media of either. I write this nonknowledge upon which the organization of the other modes of politics depend as *Politics/politics–administration,* where Politics is the sovereignty of the People and its governmental apparatus delegates in two dimensions, to politics/expression and administration/execution below the bar of the People.

These two dimensions define the terms of a theory of dual sovereignty, which relies upon an epistemological distinction (see Harmon, 1989b). First, administration is sovereign over the realm of "facts." Goodnow writes, "No control which a political body can have over a body intrusted [*sic*] with the acquisition of facts and the gathering of information can result in the gathering of more facts or the acquisition of more information" (pp. 80–81). These are activities engaged in the impartial "pursuit of truth." This "semi-scientific, *quasi*-judicial, and *quasi*-business" dimension of the executive function "has little if any influence on the expression of the true state will" and so should be "absolutely free from the influence of politics" (p. 85). Politics (lowercase p) accesses a different truth, the knowledge of the will of the People, that is expressed through representations facilitated by a constitutional arrangement and, ultimately, law. Legal and legalistic rationalities operate in politics. It is this dual sovereignty that makes it possible to articulate the requirement for a functional harmony as the condition for the most approximate fulfillment of the will of the People.

Herbert Simon, *Administrative Behavior* (1945)

Herbert Simon's classic text would appear initially to be resistant to incorporation within the framework in which I propose to examine the political ontology of the People. His work is not explicitly a political treatise, and concepts like sovereignty and "the People" are not to be found in *Administrative Behavior,* a text concerned with "the process of choice which leads to action" (p. 1). However, if Simon is conceived as a theorist of dual sovereignty and *Administrative Behavior* as a major intervention in "administrative constitutional" theory, he can be easily integrated.

In this framework, though, we must be cautious not to overestimate Simon's innovations. Harmon (1989b, p. 440) notes that Simon's innovation was to employ "fact-value" as an epistemological justification for the dichotomy between policy and administration. This distinction, though, was already made explicit by Goodnow a half century earlier; and, moreover, despite Simon's disparaging assessment of the "proverbs of administration," Simon, of course, concludes: "Can anything be salvaged which will be useful in the construction of an administrative theory? As a matter of fact, almost everything can be salvaged" (p. 42). I propose that this intention be taken seriously and that Simon be viewed, to use Kuhn's (1996/1962) formulation, as engaged in straightforward "normal science," a project of working through and extending the dual sovereign theory, which is given clear expression in the famous fact-value dichotomy. Indeed, Simon's transposition of the dichotomy explicitly onto what was in any case a division grounded in epistemology provides a useful accommodation for the mingling of politics and administration found in Goodnow.

In this context, Goodnow engages in a variety of "revolutionary science" that displaces the party-judicial political order of the nineteenth century described in chapter 4 (see also Goodnow, 1900; Skowronek, 1982), with Simon engaged in the puzzle-solving activities characteristic of normal bench science. While Simon views himself as engaged in a "salvage project" and not, as Kuhn puts it, in "mopping-up operations" (Kuhn, 1996/1962, p. 24), the end result is the same. His text calls forth no new phenomena and merely intends to solidify the science of administration by elucidating its epistemological foundations. He aims to clarify the sovereignty of the facts in the domain of administration.

The novelty of Simon's argument lies in his use of the decision as the basic unit of analysis, which allows him to formulate a "micro-physics" of administrative behavior. This allows him to describe not only the domain of the facts but also the behavior of those who are, so to speak, *subjects of the facts* (i.e., "Satisficing Man"). Simon sees administrative behavior as being more difficult and complex than orthodox thinkers let on, and he deftly attempts to describe and account for analytically the nature of organizational complexity. He develops and deploys a battery of paradigmatically appropriate concepts to diagnose the dimensions of these administrative situations. Thus there is novelty and import in Simon's classic text sufficient to justify canonical status. But as an object of anathema and critique, its dangers have been exaggerated. *Administrative Behavior* was pregnant in Goodnow's formulation. As Kuhn (1996/1962) wrote, "normal science seems to progress so rapidly [because] its practitioners concentrate on problems that only their own lack of ingenuity should keep them from solving" (p. 37).

Vincent Ostrom, *The Intellectual Crisis in American Public Administration* (1973)

Vincent Ostrom's remarkable text diagnoses the intellectual crisis in public administration as a failure of professional knowledge. "The practice of any **profession**," he writes, "depends upon the knowledge its members **profess**" (p. 3; bold in original). He raises the possibility that the knowledge taught by those who teach and used by those who practice public administration may not be improving human welfare and, worse, that "the contemporary malaise in American society may have been derived, in part, from the teachings of public administration" (p. 4). The thrust of Ostrom's criticism is analogous to Simon's—public administration does not really *know* anything. His proposed remedy is also the same—to reassert the sovereignty of public administration over a body of facts. Ostrom, however, contends that the original boundary of the domain, the traditional *bureaucratic paradigm* (which includes Simon), of public administration has broken down. Public administration, Ostrom writes, is in need of a new paradigm. He proposes Public Choice, writing, "When the central problem in public administration is viewed as the provision of public goods and services, alternative forms of organization may be available for the performance of those functions apart from an extension and perfection of bureaucratic structures" (p. 16).[2]

Concomitant with this paradigmatic shift within public administration is a realignment with politics and reassertion of *law* as the "basis of a rational social order" (p. 82). It is possible to see this as a harmonizing project in the manner of Goodnow. Administration establishes its new domain and in doing so brings itself again into its subordinate position vis-à-vis politics. Indeed, Ostrom states that public administration mistakenly began from a basis in management rather than law (p. 127). With the return of administration to its natural roots as the executive function, its expansion is halted, allowing politics to return to its proper expressive function.

Critical to this discussion is Ostrom's consideration of "factual" sovereignty and his reproach of Woodrow Wilson for advancing a Hobbesian unitary conception of sovereignty with "ultimate authority over all governmental prerogatives" (p. 89). It is from this conception of sovereignty that Wilson rejected the constitutional doctrine of separation of powers. What concerns Ostrom is that a "sovereign cannot have the last say and still be accountable to others" (p. 145). The sovereign is above the law. This notion is, he suggests, foreign to the American system, which is characterized by "a system of positive constitutional law which is enforceable as against those who exercise governmental prerogatives" (p. 90). In this brilliantly constructed text, Ostrom appears to sidestep the problem of sovereignty itself.

But there is a problematic asymmetry in the design of Ostrom's argument that singularly demonstrates the importance of the People in sustaining the field. While criticizing Wilson for his unitary sovereign problem, the very term *sovereign* disappears in his discussion of the American political system, and he posits a questionable correlation. He asks, "Must the science of association used in public administration be built on the Hobbesian theory of sovereignty? Or can a science of association also be built on a theory of limited constitutions on the assumption that political structures can be devised in which those who exercise the extraordinary prerogatives of government are subject to the rule of constitutional law?" (p. 94) Something is amiss here. A unitary sovereign is not conceptually incompatible with the separation of powers, of *governmental authority.* Arguably, this is precisely the formula of the American political system. The People, a popular sovereign, skeptical of government, divides its authority. It is by virtue of that very separation that the popular will is expressed. It is indeed on the basis of its formulation by that popular will (via its representatives) that law derives its force. Ostrom conflates unified authority with unitary sovereignty in an effort to parallel his criticism of the bureaucratic paradigm's harmful preoccupation with "unity of command" and centralization. However, Ostrom *must* rely on a sovereign People in order to sustain the coherence of his argument: most important, the necessity of administration's "return to law." If there is no popular sovereign, there is no ground upon which to accept the legitimacy of the federated system from which public administration deviates or to lament its departure from law.

Laurence Lynn Jr., *Public Management as Art, Science, and Profession* (1997)

Laurence Lynn's text is quite close in purpose, approach, and content to Ostrom's *The Intellectual Crisis in American Public Administration.* Lynn summarizes his project clearly:

> The argument of this book is that the field of public management, conceived of as the executive function in government, will have a stronger, more enduring, and more useful identity as a domain of scholarship and of professional identity if its contributors and practitioners (1) establish intellectual foundations in those scholarly fields and subfields that can illuminate the executive role in government; (2) develop habits of reasoning, intellectual exchange, and criticism appropriate to a scholarly field; and (3) apply their intellectual skills in a distinctively useful way to answering the central questions of public management. (p. 7)

He is, however, rather more literal and explicit about the origins of political authority. In an overreaching statement, Lynn writes, "Unique among the world's democracies, American government is accountable to the freely expressed will of The People; popular sovereignty is more than myth, elections more than ceremony" (p. 9).

What warrants further commentary, however, is Lynn's placement (and, perhaps, public management in general) in the company of Goodnow and Simon, given the number of factors that might lead one to conclude that Lynn is a unified theorist. For instance, Lynn says that public management brings together public *administration* and public *policy.* He believes that "public administration is about politics, and politics is about citizen control of the state" (p. 19), and he identifies public management as an effort "to define and legitimate a sphere of authority and a repertoire of behaviors for a formally undefined and politically suspect collection of public actors" (p. 23). The reason Lynn is a dualist is because, most basically, he is concerned with public management as domain of knowledge. Public management proves its worth by virtue of what it *knows.* Public management does, though, profess to know more than technical facts. Lynn writes, "Preparation for learning on the job, rather than poor simulations of the job itself, is the proper mission of professional education" (p. 101).

While emphasizing that much of public management cannot be taught and consists in a certain "artistry," Lynn is nevertheless critical of the strong normativists in public administration (e.g., Gary Wamsley, John Rohr, Robert Denhardt, and H. George Frederickson [pp. 52–54]), who rule out or are dismissive of "instrumental or technical rationality as a dimension of effective practice" (p. 105) and deny that the public manager is "a designer of order" (p. 107). They have nowhere to go but "toward the managerial Heart of Darkness" (p. 105). This can be avoided, Lynn contends, if the field takes an appropriately broad view of executive leadership and the appropriate body of knowledge is created and applied that mixes "the technocratic and artistic in ways that lead to effective management" (p. 114).

A "Unified" Theory of Sovereignty

Dwight Waldo, *The Administrative State* (1948)

Dwight Waldo's 1948 *The Administrative State* examines the vision of government and political philosophy that underlies the conceptualization of public administration as technical expertise in possession of neutral competence. In raising this issue, Waldo contests the position that "democracy" ought to be confined to its "proper sphere, a decision on policy" (p. 14) and so "could only apply to the deciding phase of a two-fold governmental process" (p. 75). As noted in chapter 1, Waldo's insistence on exposing the "metaphysic" of administration (p. 21) was a critical one, but his approach to this question, which contested the "verdict of science" as a way to surface and confront this metaphysic, was deflective and steered criticism of and within public administration into an endgame. The manner by which Waldo challenged orthodoxy's doctrine of "dual sovereignty," that is, the "sovereignty of facts" in administration and the "sovereignty of the People" in democratic politics, in fact, further concealed the conditions for the division itself.

The trajectory on which Waldo sets critical discourse in public administration is one that accepted the sovereignty of the People and the presence of a governmental apparatus or set of institutions that was separate and distinct from the People. Indeed, it is through proximity to the People (either through a doctrine of equity, citizen participation, constitutionalism, or post-teleocratic governance) that the administrative state can become a fully legitimate part of American democratic government. It is critical to appreciate the disjuncture *and* continuity that Waldo's text inaugurates. The importance of administration asserting itself as political hinges on the presupposed expressive function of politics—expressive, that is, of the will of the People. Administration asserts itself as inextricably political in order to establish itself as possessing legal and representative, as well as scientific, rationalities. It is access to the People that is at stake in this parallel vision, not the status of the People itself *nor* the functional distinction between politics and administration.

This is the beginning of a line of inquiry that attempts to formulate a unified theory of sovereignty, that is, one that unites the People with the facts, the creation of a "popular science," so to speak (Siegel, 1999). It seeks an integration of legal and scientific rationalities. This is not to assert that this line of inquiry inexorably would result in criticism of rationality per se, though some thinkers certainly would undertake this project (e.g., Farmer, 1995; Harmon, 1995; McSwite, 1997b; Stivers, 2000); others close to Waldo would not (e.g., Stillman, 1991). Rather, the question is one of the domain of administrative action and the nature of administrative behavior as well as a refusal to accept the notion that the functional distinction between politics and administration demanded an epistemological division. The price to be paid for this access to Politics, however, is a ritualistic acknowledgment of its subordination to politics and, paradoxically, an exacerbation of the legitimacy problem. Why would a political public administration exacerbate the legitimacy problem? For the simple reason that an administrative apparatus functionally subordinate but now no longer distinct from politics would be exposed, in time, to the charges of distorting *both* functions from the untouched, pre*political* objectivity of Politics—a stunning upending of Goodnow's initial critique. The effort to "reharmonize" politics and administration by limiting political interference in administrative questions culminates in a critique of administration as overextending itself into the domain of politics. Yet conditions are not what they were one hundred years ago, making the assertion of political control and the neutralization of the bureaucracy dubious strategies in the contemporary search for order.

Emmette Redford, *Democracy in the Administrative State* (1969)

Redford's text is important for his selection of a certain word and his rejection of another, more obvious one. Redford's text is called *Democracy in the Administrative State.* The title announces its rejection of the distinction implicit in the typical phrase "democracy *and* the administrative state" (Hyneman, 1950). Redford's classic analysis works through the logic implicit in the theory of unified sovereignty, which he calls a "workable democracy" normatively rooted in a democratic morality. Redford notes that some observers "may think of [the administrative state] as a Frankenstein monster extracting too much of national resources and threatening people's liberties. Others may look at the services performed by it with concern that these be effectively rendered, and perhaps expanded" (p. 4). Redford aims to reconcile the behavior of the administration with the American ideal of democracy. This reconciliation is to occur within a single domain—democracy *in* the administrative state. The efficient and factual dimensions of administration coexist with administrative-political interest brokering. Administration, Redford concludes, is an instrument for "two types of service for society" (p. 195).

Aside from a few scattered mentions, the standard ritualistic invocations of the People or of its sovereignty are absent in Redford's subtly crafted text. Nonetheless, there are important detectable traces of the People in his formulation of workable democracy. Workable democracy, he says, has two dimensions, macropolitics, which is politics in the traditional sense of voting and elections, and micropolitics, which is administrative politics. The analytical levels reflect a hierarchy of function. "Administration is the servant of politics" (p. 143). Redford, however, makes clear that this analytical distinction is one not simply of normative priority but also of chronological necessity since "administration begins when the initial direction is given and it never escapes from its subordinate role" (p. 194). In classic fashion, expression precedes execution. However, something also *exceeds* the expressive function. This is evident when Redford asks, "Can we legitimize the administrative state through democratic control?" (p. 196) This question implies a power beyond conventional *political* control since we know, according to Redford, that democracy is possible for both the political and administrative functions. Something exceeds these functions. Redford comes close to naming this "something" when he writes, "We look nevertheless for means of realizing the democratic morality (which assumes the supremacy of the will of the governed) in the administrative state (which makes men subject to the decisions of others)" (p. 197). What Redford calls the democratic morality, a set of ideals from which democratic processes derive, itself assumes the supremacy of the will of the governed. This is called the will of the People, the popular sovereign.

John Rohr, *To Run a Constitution* (1986)

John Rohr's 1986 text is well known and well respected for its meticulous and learned inquiry into the constitutional arguments in favor of the administrative state. No one has dared challenge either Rohr's scholarship or his admirably modest conclusions, and this is not my intention, either. The position I take here is that, for all its erudition, Rohr's textual exegesis is largely beside the point. Characteristically, Rohr anticipates this response to his project. He writes, "What does worry me . . . is the critical reader who thinks that what I am doing is not worth doing at all" (p. 178). Rohr's concern prompts him to ask that customary standards of evidentiary judgment be lowered in order that the novelty of his argument be permitted its complete exposition.

The argument, of course, is to justify or legitimate the administrative state in terms of constitutional principle, to demonstrate that "The Public Administration is part of a constitutional *order* that was chosen by The People in the great ratification debate of 1787/88" (p. 185).[3] Again, to challenge Rohr's project is not my task. Neither, however, is it to call his project into question simply by arguing that the Constitution is itself not legitimate. These two maneuvers rely on the same logic, merely proposing competing representations. Rohr believes that the administrative state can be justified by recourse to constitutional principles because the Constitution is the creation of a sovereign People, itself the origin of all authority. Critics of the Constitution dismiss it merely as an inauthentic or corrupted expression of the People. The Founders were biased and did not represent the true interests of the *whole* People.

What is under examination here, though, is precisely the status of the People and how the legitimacy question emerges within and is symptomatic of a specific form of the Political. Indeed, the reason Rohr's analysis is beside the point is because what I understand to be the problem is everything that makes his analysis possible, namely, the ontology of the People and its constitutive exclusion. It is the People that create, to use Rohr's words, "certain limits" that close "off many possibilities that were open to other societies" (p. 180). The constitutive affectivity of those limits is my interest.

Rohr writes, "The Constitution is the symbol of our common life as a people who are organized for action in history" (p. 192). For Rohr, it is clearly the Constitution's status as the expression of a sovereign People that both stands as prima facie evidence for its legitimacy and forms the crux of his case against the intellectual founders of public administration, Woodrow Wilson and Frank Goodnow. Both Wilson and Goodnow, he claims (quite erroneously in the case of Goodnow), denounce popular sovereignty and wrongly locate sovereignty in institutions of government and not with the People (again, Goodnow simply does no such thing) (p. 85). Thus it is not the well-intentioned straying of Goodnow and Wilson from the Constitution qua constitution that brands public administration as illegitimate but public administration's deviation from what is held to be the definitive political judgment of a sovereign People. The Constitution is not merely a document; it *is* an expression of the "real life of the People."

This is an important point for Rohr, since "legitimacy means more than legality" (p. 5). He believes that public administration's legal status is settled, but its legitimacy remains uncertain (p. x). To rephrase this, legality is a function of law, while legitimacy emanates from the transcendent—or, in a democracy, the People. The Constitution is thus a materialization of the will of a sovereign People. Departure from it, therefore, exceeds mere contractual violation and careens into desecration of the sacred. There is, as it were, a profound distinction between a covenant and a contract. Rohr's formulation reminds us of the divinity of the People and, by extension, the struggle for power within which the People was invented to counter the ungodly politics of another divine representative, the king (Morgan, 1988).

To his credit, Rohr carries the logic of his argument to its conclusion and affirms the functional and hierarchical distinction between politics and administration (pp. 183–184). His formulation, of course, does not concede so readily to politics but rather affirms the subordinate independence of the discipline within the unified sovereign realm of the People. In giving public administration the power to choose among its "several masters," public administration emerges as the arbiter of the People's will in spite of its subordinate status. Here, Rohr deftly exploits the Politics/politics–administration formula to elevate public administration to the level of politics while retaining its subordinate position vis-à-vis Politics. Sometimes politics is Political, other times not. Sometimes administration is Political, sometimes merely political. What is retained is a neutral third position from which either political or administrative claims might be adjudicated and from which the public administration can judge among its various constitutional masters.

Gary Wamsley, "The Agency Perspective" (1990)

In the manner of Rohr, Wamsley's piece is a clear attempt to "empower and constrain" (p. 115) public administrators' actions via a general subsumption within the "common good." Wamsley, too, relies on the same formula, Politics/politics–administration, to develop his "agential perspective." This is quite evident in Wamsley's charge to the agency to perform a series of metaphysical functions, most critically "mirroring of manifest and latent representation of interests" (even if it must "go beyond" such conventional interest group liberal tasks) and pursuing "a common good—one that is distinguishable from what a society (even one faithfully represented) thinks its wants" (p. 117). To accomplish these ambitious social goals, Wamsley recognizes, "we need a social construct that is valued for more than itself." He calls this regulative ideal a "required transcendence" (p. 124). Ultimately, this means the People. He asks, "Who is the principal? The president? Congress? The courts? Clientele? Interest groups? . . . this is a difficult question that admits of no ready answer. Ultimately, the answer must come close to being metaphysical in nature: the public interest or 'The People'; for although the Constitution created a republic that did not make them the 'firsthand' principal, today it is they who must ultimately be seen as principal by the Agency in our system" (p. 127).

He equivocates slightly later in the essay, writing that "agents must respect their principal(s) whether that means 'The People,' voters, the legislature, the president, or some other constitutional superior" (p. 132). However, the concern here is the persistence of a posited background against which claims to the common good could be assessed. Indeed, the point is that politics may fail to produce the necessary *Political* outcome. Administration exists as an empowered but constrained function and a necessary "backup" system in a unified domain to realize the good of the required transcendence, the People.

H. George Frederickson, *The Spirit of Public Administration* (1997)

The matter of concern in H. George Frederickson's *The Spirit of Public Administration* is his examination of the "public" in public administration and his maintenance of a functional and normatively hierarchical distinction between politics and administration. Frederickson identifies several "requisites" for any general theory of the public in public administration, the first of which is that an understanding of "the Public" be grounded in the Constitution. Frederickson writes, "The principles of popular sovereignty, representative government, the rights of citizens contained in the Bill of Rights, procedural due process, the balance of powers and other aspects of both federal and state constitutions are the foundations of such a theory, and that foundation *must* be firmly and fastidiously adhered to" (emphasis added). It is the acceptance of the constitutional founding that makes up the "wellspring of legitimacy" of government. Echoing Wamsley's required transcendence, Frederickson notes that "each generation of citizens *must* return to that original debate to confirm the Constitution's legitimacy," for this is how a "sovereign people" breathes life into the document (p. 44; emphasis added). For Frederickson, the constitutional order is the originary and founding act of a sovereign People that establishes the Political context. This point establishes Frederickson as a unified theorist.

In an engaging, insightful section, Frederickson writes that political history produces various "publics" (i.e., representations) and, by extension, some publics may, in fact, be in conflict with the founding values, with the People's order. Majorities can be wrong. Frederickson makes this clear when he writes that public administrators are "controlled by a higher principle than that of majority decisions: the constitutional order" (p. 45). As Frederickson insists, the Constitution *must* be affirmed and legitimated. It is on a taken-for-granted basis that constitutional values express the authentic will of the sovereign People and thus can be justifiably enforced. Recalling Wamsley's "manifest and latent representations" (1990, p. 117), Frederickson suggests that it is against the backdrop of the Politics of the People that collective public (interest groups) and "inchoate" publics appear. His formulation thus relies on a doubling of "public" that is homologous to the Politics/politics distinction I have outlined. Here, it is articulated as Public/public. It is only with a concept of the Public that the claims of these various publics can be judged and, if necessary, excluded as insufficiently Public. Constitutional values give specificity to this Public, and indeed it is on this basis that "[t]he citizen *must* believe that the values of the American regime are true and correct and not just ideas that are psychologically gratifying or accepted by the majority" (p. 45; emphasis added).

Frederickson's adherence to a functional distinction between expression and execution is based on the same logic as is Goodnow's. Just as Goodnow argued that politics had been burdened by administrative responsibilities that frustrated the political function, Frederickson suggests that administration should not be unduly burdened with political duties that inhibit its own functions. Excessive involvement of either in the affairs of the other frustrates the fulfillment of constitutional, popular values. Yet it is the very positing of a supra-Public that exists beyond both politics and administration that allows administration, in rare moments, to "resist, thwart or refuse to implement policy that runs counter to the founding documents or to American regime values" (p. 229). It is through functional harmony that the will is fulfilled.

Michael Spicer, *Public Administration and the State* (2001)

Michael Spicer's text is a sophisticated attempt to synthesize the postmodern critique of representation, identity, and intention with the "legal turn" in public administration exemplified by neoconstitutionalism. The crux of Spicer's argument is that postmodern conditions, rather than threatening the viability of the constitutional order, in fact provide a fertile ground for its recovery. It is a deft rhetorical move. In key ways, Spicer's overall project—a critique of "teleocratic" or purposive government—shares much with the present work, though its approach and conclusions are quite different. The difficulty with his text is that the nature of his attempted synthesis undermines the important point he wishes to make. He goes one better than even Rohr and effaces the *normative* dimension of constitutionalism and law, embedding the Constitution within the terms of the Lockean notion of *natural* law. His critique of purposefulness in administrative behavior (teleocracy) culminates in an advocacy of the Constitution as merely the undirective and undirected "rules of the game." This stands in direct contradiction to the grounds he provides for rejecting teleocracy, namely, the violence inhering in purposive actions taken under the auspices of a "We."

Spicer holds that all visions of administration express a tacit conception of politics, a "purposeful" view of the state within which public administration becomes an instrument of state organization for the execution of that vision. Spicer does not need to choose sides in these debates since there are no sides—everyone is implicated in teleocracy (that is, government concerned with and conditioned by a purposive vision of the state). The problem with these visions is that purposiveness depends upon political centralization and epistemological privilege. In other words, power must be centralized within the instruments of government to ensure coherence in vision and realization, and government must have superior knowledge of its policy objects in order to predict outcomes. Both of these requirements, Spicer says, are rarely, if ever, met in practice. "Rather," he writes, "for most of our history, our political practice has reflected a vision of the state as something more akin to a 'civil association'" (p. 71). Moreover, postmodern social conditions probably make such teleocratic action impossible in the future.

Postmodern conditions also make the practices of a purposive state violent because "in a state that is organized around a particular set of substantive purposes or ends, meaningful political discourse can take place only within the context of a particular language game" (p. 96). "In other words," Spicer states, "political discourse in a purposive state will not and cannot reflect much, if any, in the way of universal values" (p. 96). Purposive action necessarily excludes a host of other opinions and discourses, an act that is increasingly clear as postmodern fragmentation continues, and in effect compels a self-consciously heterogeneous social field to conform to the purposes and ends of a single language game or definition of the common good. Indeed, nothing "good" can come of saying "We" in the midst of postmodern multiplicity. Spicer concludes that it is only when no particular language game prevails that society is just (p. 104).

Spicer proposes thinking "about public administration in terms of a state as a civil association" (p. 108). He is, though, not ringing the "citizen participation" bell, which itself might be classified as purposive administration. By civil association Spicer means a vision "in which individuals recognize themselves as essentially free to pursue their own particular interests and their own particular values within the framework of a set of rules of conduct that limit the harm that they can do to each other." These rules by themselves are thought to be without purpose and, quoting philosopher Michael Oakeshott, do "not secure a substantive relationship in terms of common action (1975, 201)" (p. 71). Rules limit the harm members of the association can inflict upon one another and constitute a system of spontaneous order. He continues, "Given a state constituted in this fashion, the role of government becomes largely that of elucidating, protecting, and enforcing the rules of conduct that govern individual and group actions and their interactions" (p. 72). The rules themselves do not advance any order in particular or protect any one group. Government simply adjudicates and does not manage.

But there is a problem with Spicer's call for a civil association that draws from constitutional tradition amid postmodern multiplicity. It is the first phrase of the Constitution and the ostensible legitimizing ground for American government: "We the People." If Spicer's advice is taken, his own argument ought to be rejected based on the terms of his argument. Spicer does not specify what it is about law that lends to it this "purposelessness." What quality does it have that allows it to function as a "spontaneous order"? Spicer is advancing a classic liberal myth here, and he retains the Politics/politics–administration formula. Law emerges from the natural, organic, and self-regulating life of the People, and government exists merely neutrally to adjudicate that law, to administer justice (David Hume) and make life more calculable (John Locke). However, the *ordering* of a legal order is denied, and the position of objective evaluation is reasserted in strong terms. In effect, what Spicer asserts is a modified version of the formula Politics/(politics)–administration. Competing visions of the state and political collectivity, even within the brackets of the People, are denied under the auspices of a natural legal order.

Sovereignty in Question

Michael Harmon, *Responsibility as Paradox* (1995)

Harmon's work constitutes a major theoretical breakthrough in the study of administrative ethics, but the import of this study for public administration exceeds that subfield. Harmon begins with the self-evident, but virtually ignored, observation that "responsibility" necessarily entails a certain duality—that "the belief that people's actions *cause* events to occur . . . is a precondition for their *answerability* to others for those action" (p. 2; emphasis in original). That is, people must be responsible for an action (they must be its cause) before they can be held responsible (or morally culpable) for its effects. What underwrites traditional, or *rationalist,* ethics is thus a particular theory of human agency and a belief "that responsible action is synonymous with morally or legally *correct* action, and that the purpose of moral discourse on government and of laws and other guidelines regulating administrative action is to preserve or restore a state of moral innocence." Paradox, however, throws a wrench in the rationalist machine. It "describes the condition of innocence lost irretrievably with the dawning of consciousness" (p. 4) and "both foils rationalism's logical claims with unpredictable revelations of counterexamples and mocks its moral exhortations with continual reminders of the ambiguity inhering in situations that demand action" (p. 68). Thus, the rationalist conception fails on *both* logical and empirical grounds, largely as a consequence of its one-sided preoccupation with the objective, external dimension of experience.

Paradoxes entail opposing and/or contradictory forces, but these forces are linked or connected and so constitute necessary and inevitable elements in social life (p. 73). Paradoxes thus lurk in the very logic of everyday situations; they are not anomalies. Harmon goes on to distinguish between *schismogenic* paradoxes, the bad or vicious kinds, and *antinomial* paradoxes, the good, complementary variety. The former, Harmon writes, are "evidence of something going awry in our understanding of antinomial ones"; something has gone out of balance. They are "at least analogous to, if not deeply rooted in, attempts to recapture lost innocence; or in the language of contemporary psychology, . . . such situations reveal the existences of 'avoidances' or even neuroses" (p. 77). Bringing to light the paradox in a schismogenic situation is difficult because it often entails surfacing the constitutive suppression and runs up against the problem of self-reference—"the tendency to use current definition of the problem as the only basis for reflecting on what needs to be redefined or reframed" (p. 79).

In this reading of Harmon, it is the failure to acknowledge the constitutive moment of self-reference that precipitates the slide into the schismogenic, or pathological, dimension of paradox (p. 80). The schismogenic is itself a relation between a principle and its opposing pathology (say, self-reflexivity and confluence) that will not admit of its constitutive opposition. Thus, just as the moral subject becomes isolated in the rationalist schema from the other and, consequently, his or her authentic individuality, so, too, is the correlative moral principle severed from its countervalence, thus impeding moral action and responsibility.

The central element in Harmon's text that places sovereignty into question is his analysis of how the ontological implications of the constitutive effectivity of paradox challenges the myth of a pure origin. Paradox is not simply an epistemological fall from grace, a lamentable side effect of positive knowledge. Rather, in paradox there is an element that is heterogeneous to the situation yet also *constitutive* of it. It is both within and without. In denying this constitutive moment, rationalism is a discourse that denies the conditions of its own possibility, treating them as contaminates—and in one sense, then, generating a self-annihilating dialectic.

A limitation of Harmon's analysis within the framework of sovereignty outlined here is that he treats rationality one-dimensionally, and he confines his analysis to the manifestations and constitutive effects of paradox in facts and consciousness, a disposition generally consistent with the unified theorists. Strictly speaking, Harmon remains concerned with administrative behavior and does not broach the subject of the Political form of administration or the affectivity of paradox in the Political.

O. C. McSwite, *Legitimacy in Public Administration* (1997)

McSwite's text echoes Harmon's themes but provides a broader context within which to conceive them. McSwite locate public administration within a trajectory of American political thought that has its origins in Anti-Federalism, which, they write, has been a persistent counter subtheme to the order created by the 1789 Constitution. McSwite, however, do not surface the Anti-Federalist narrative in order to recover a more appropriate or correct representation of the People. Rather, the Anti-Federalist narrative is discussed as an account of government that asserts itself as *another* People, another version of the People. This is a critical point, and indeed it is perhaps not worked out as fully in *Legitimacy* as it might have been. The Anti-Federalist position is recovered not as a better version of the People but as a People that has been repressed. McSwite suspend judgment (that is, comparison and evaluation of the representations of these two People to the true People) and elide representational objectivism. McSwite deny such logic and in doing so deny the liberal mythology of a neutral prepolitical position of judgment.

Herein lies the importance of McSwite's defense of the Articles of Confederation as a workable and work*ing* governmental framework. Both the Federal and Anti-Federal positions arise from *within* an order, from within a *constituted People.* McSwite do not indulge any criticism of the "failures" of the Articles that might justify the conclusion that the "real" interests of the People were being poorly served. The debate over the Constitution evokes two tensed, if not antagonistic, Peoples, one Federalist and one Anti-Federalist; "the People" is not a *whole* People. Rather, the assertion of the constitutional People depends upon a basic or constitutive exclusion of the Anti-Federalist representation.

Like Harmon, McSwite deploy this dimension of the analysis toward a critique of technical rationality. Certainly, it is explicitly political insofar as it rises to question the "deferential attitude" conditioned by the "Man of Reason" order, but the emphasis remains on instrumental, or what McSwite call modernist, rationality. Nevertheless, the culmination of *Legitimacy*'s analysis, "Beyond Reason," explicitly formulates the dialectic of inside-outside that is implicit in Harmon. This problem is approached via the notion of boundary and its relation to reason. McSwite write, "Boundaries are also *intrinsically* problematic. If we are going to have a reasoned approach to reality, this approach must apply to *all* reality—that is, to the universe itself. . . . The rub is this: The idea of a boundary means that something is left out—on the other side—so how can 'everything' be bounded?" (p. 243; emphasis in original). There is a limit to limits, which reason, by virtue of its very constitution, denies. The ontology of rationality is, therefore, established in a dialectic of denial and absorption with the excluded element that gives its coherence. Having surfaced this dialectic, McSwite begin to conceptualize social organization in a way that allows for the creation of meaning and generation of identity without relying on the idea of a boundary, or constitutive exclusion.

If there is a limitation in McSwite's text it is its overemphasis on critique of *scientific,* technical rationality, the sovereignty of fact, as the fulcrum of social change: an effect, perhaps, of Waldo's initial critique. Indeed, while there is extensive analysis of the pathological dialectic between reason and that which exceeds its boundary, *Legitimacy* remains basically unconnected to the latent critique of the concept and structure of the People suggested above. The domain of the People is left untouched, and it leaves the critique somewhat detached from larger political questions. A second limitation is that other than the actions of particular public administrators, the functionality of *public administration* within the general discourse of rationality and ontological boundaries is not explored.

Ralph Hummel and Camilla Stivers, "Government Isn't Us: The Possibility of Democratic Knowledge in Representative Government" (1998)

Grounding their analysis in the philosophy of Kant and Heidegger, Hummel and Stivers explicitly connect contemporary hostility toward government with problems of knowledge and politics via the concept of *representation* and, most important, the *failure* of representation. This failure is not a technical problem but concerns the question of whether there is something that, in fact, *cannot be* represented, something that remains outside of or excluded from representation.

Hummel and Stivers argue that contemporary antigovernmental sentiment "has deep roots in the knowledge structure of the political system" (p. 29), namely, representation. "*Representation,*" they write, "*produces alienation*" (p. 33; emphasis in original). As in similar arguments advanced by Harmon (i.e., the face-to-face encounter) and McSwite (critique of reason), the root of the problem is that the system of representation deals with citizens only as abstractions; we are only represented in government, never actually present. As a consequence, "laws are crafted and policies administered to fit all, or the average; they therefore fit none of us" (p. 29). Government, in turn, becomes primarily an enterprise of instrumentally administering these ill-fitting rules and abstractions through the "technical-logical operations of reason" (p. 33). Government, literally, is *not us* because an "originary knowledge gap" opens up between the lived, actual, and particular experience of the citizenry and public officials (p. 30). This gap is reflected in the actions of government, actions in which citizens *necessarily* do not see themselves.

Provocatively, and most relevant to this discussion, Hummel and Stivers then problematize the very idea that interests in society can be *represented.* They ask, "How can what people are and what they want be known, much less represented in the processes of legislation and administration?" Following Heidegger, they note that many human experiences, like love, well-being, or a late evening conservation, simply cannot be represented in language or rationally reconstructed in formal conceptual language (despite Heidegger's own formidable efforts to do so). In relying on the mechanisms of representation, government is denied an understanding of the nature of human or being. In advancing this argument, they open "again the question of publicness, or the nature of the political" (p. 30). In other words, they question the alienating, detached mode by which the world is opened, the way in which "the public" comes into the world (Hummel, 2002).

A different politics would open or reveal the public in a new way and close the gap between people and the government. This might be accomplished by "opening the processes of implementation" and creating democratic, collaborative knowledge in administrative contexts (p. 32). Ultimately, the creation of these contexts requires the admittance of personal, experiential *knowledge* in order that it reconnect with the abstract, depersonalized world of representative government. Opening to the world of experience then shifts the focus of government and governing. Unlike the purposeful, instrumental practices of representation, a "politics of care"—the process of world making, of creating something-in-common—assumes primary concern. "The point of politics," they conclude, "is not the answers it gives, but the process, connections, and arguments it makes possible. This does not mean that real issues cannot be dealt with, only that as long as we put the rationalist search for final answers in the driver's seat, we ensure that the process is on track to a dead end—to the obliteration of public life" (p. 45).

Several points are critical. First, Hummel and Stivers draw an explicit link between the problematic of epistemology and the very idea of representative government, the political form. Yet this innovation is not fully exploited; rather, the move seems to legitimize the administrative state as a privileged locus for creating democratic, collaborative knowledge and remains (at least in this text) "state-centered." Significantly, they follow Heidegger in intimating that the ultimate horizon of being cannot be represented, only evoked. However, and in connection with point one, the Heideggerian thesis about representation is not generalized or explored as a general problem of social fabrication and reproduction, and their critique, in this respect, seems more a unified theoretical approach concerned with closing the gap of representation than an analysis of the gap or how the gap works. Finally, they offer an instructive distinction between representation and the politics of care in terms of different modes of world making or opening up the public. In my terms, I would say that the People names one way (the way of representation) of opening the experience of collectivity; Stivers and Hummel do not, however, raise the question of the People per se or consider the People as a response to the ontological question of what it means to be in the world. Above all, though, they lucidly show why the very heart of our modern democracy, *representation,* portends the obliteration of public life. As we shall see in the subsequent chapters, this is precisely what is happening today.

Conclusion

This chapter explored the intellectual history of American public administration through the lens of the field's "unsaid," the presumption of the People. Public administrative discourse takes place, is made possible, and is constructed by virtue of being *below the bar of the People.* What "the People" presumes, ultimately, is that that there is a "positive" (i.e., possessing given content) outside to representational appearance that serves as a firm referent for *both* politics *and* administration. Public administration has assumed this position and its positive content, and on this basis, developed three distinct approaches to governing below the bar, three theories of sovereignty, that attend to the broad project of legitimizing the administrative state in American democratic government. We turn now to the basic relations and practices that this elementary, seemingly innocuous, commitment sets into motion.

3
Representation

If the general thrust of the continental critique of knowledge and philosophy that followed in the trajectory of Nietzsche and Heidegger[1] may be identified, broadly, as a *critique of representation* (May, 1994, 1995), public administration has yet to fully examine the implications of this critique for the technologies and institutions of *political representation.* By and large, the insights of phenomenological, critical-theoretical, and poststructuralist thought have been conceived as strategies for improving the efficacy of representational media and for closing the gap between representation and its referent. We have employed epistemologically based critiques of representation in an effort to remedy the deficiencies of political and social givens and (mis)representations, grounding the case for improving the techniques of political representation in an epistemological critique of the possibility for representation itself.

We do not, however, extricate ourselves from the problems of representation by undermining them at the "micro" level of scientific and administrative practice in order to remedy the "macro-objectivity" of representational politics. In other words, exposing or de-reifying the "ideological" content of any taken-for-granted objectivity (such as a fact, instrument, proposition, or identity) does not perforce serve to make representational politics itself *more objectively* representative or inclusive. Indeed, we are confronted with a paradox in the contemporary social world: if the effects of "inclusion" on our system of political representation are examined, we find, as Lowi (1969) was perhaps among the first to note, that faith in the overall political system actually seems to have declined as participation and inclusion have increased, that is, as the terms of representation (the predicates that define the People) have expanded and as more members of the polity "count" as part of "the People." It would appear, then, to be untrue that representativeness or correspondence between government as representation (representative) and the People as the object of representation is at the heart of the contemporary legitimacy crisis of government.

The tactic proposed here is to conceive of the contemporary legitimacy crisis as a problem of the People, as a problem generated by a particular formulation of the Political. In my view, this is what is entailed in shifting from an epistemological to an ontological inquiry. It is a tactical approach that attempts to understand the logic of political representation—the very idea of representation itself—more thoroughly. What logic is put to work in the invocation of the People? What objects and relationships are posited? On what objective basis (in the sense of object as *both* thing and purpose) are authoritative claims to speak based? How are we to be-together in the world of representation? This set of questions raises the issue of the status of subject and object of representation and proposes the thesis that the core problem of our contemporary moment is the historical exhaustion of particular conceptualizations, technologies, and practices of *inclusion* rather than the persistence of political, economic, and social exclusion (Sørensen & Torfing, 2005).

In preparing the way to consider these questions, this chapter proceeds in three main sections, moving from the highly abstract to the more concrete. The first part considers the range of thought in public administration that has considered the question of representation. We will examine the problem of representative bureaucracy, critical enterprises that challenge the givenness of everyday representations of the world, and arguments that have challenged political representation and the question of the People. This discussion is distinct from the analysis of the previous chapter, which focused on the general structure of the field in order to demonstrate that virtually all of public administration's discourse took place below the bar of the People. Here, I will consider how the field has taken up the question of representation in order to better situate this analysis and its own formulation of representation. This begins in earnest in the second section with a recounting of Richard Rorty's (1979) outline of representation as a problem of epistemology as it emerged in modern philosophical thought, in particular in the work of Descartes (White, 1999). I employ this account to shift to a description of a general theory of representation in order to propose a framework within which both political and epistemological representation might be conceived as, most basically, a relationship of model and copy. This is an outline of representation at its most formal, abstract level. Within this framework, I draw from the work of philosophers Gilles Deleuze and Michel Foucault to illustrate how representation comports itself toward difference and exclusion and how the model of representation relies on the presumptive organic processes of life (zoë).

The third part of this chapter attempts to locate the nexus of the general economy of representation and political sovereignty. It "descends" from the abstract model-copy relation to show how content for the models, in general, is produced. This is considered in terms of the notion of the exception and the act of judgment that decides on the exception. This part begins with a formulation of difference that attempts to shift from conceiving difference as an epistemological category to thinking about it in terms of "serial heterogeneity" in order to displace the search for correspondence between model and copy to consideration of a qualitatively different mode of relating. Representation proposes to ground a relation, fundamentally, as one of organic necessity and sameness through the positive determination of the ideal terms (predicates) of the model. At an elementary level this requires the bounding out or exclusion of some predicates, which generates a materialization of the *constitutive exclusion.* This is an element whose very exclusion is required in order to create the content of the "inside" or the model of representation. In subsequent chapters, we will see how this exclusion becomes the target and grounds for government.

In addition to the primary decision regarding ontological commitment, representation conceals the decision that establishes the positive determination of the model. The next section shifts from the general idea of the origin of content to show how this content is produced *in general* in situations. This is an act of judgment that I then link to the core of *sovereign authority.* I turn to the German legal theorist Carl Schmitt to elaborate the connection between sovereign authority and the materialization of the exception and to suggest how representation attempts to arrest the relations of serial heterogeneity precisely by positively and organically grounding one of the two in the other. The name for this mode of the political, in which the political definition of the organic model is at stake, is *biopolitics.*

Representation in Public Administration Theory

Thought in public administration about "representation" has focused on two historically intertwined matters: representative bureaucracy and the status of scientific and sociopolitical representations of reality—representative bureaucracy and challenges to "the given." A third line of thought considers representation in a different, more critical manner. This line of thought surfaces possibilities for linking problems of political representation to ontology and to the replication of that ontology across diverse contexts of politics and society. My analysis of representation will bring together these critical positions with the sovereignty in question theories in order to elaborate a general theory of representation and its logic of exclusion.

Representative Bureaucracy

The first axis of public administration scholarship on representation concerns the question of representative bureaucracy and the composition of the professional civil service. As Rohr (1986) has shown, the question of the representativeness of American political institutions is not new; it has been with us since the nation's Federalist founding. During the ratification debate, Anti-Federalists (and many Federalists) worried that the small number of representatives in the Congress would make it impossible for that body to be a "microcosm of the society as a whole" (p. 41) or "to reflect (to *re-present*) the society as a whole" by possessing the same "interests, feelings, opinions, and views, which the people themselves would possess, were they all assembled" (p. 42). Rohr inventively uses this "defect" in congressional representation to ground, in part, a case for the legitimacy of the administrative state. The administrative state, Rohr writes, allows "millions of its employees the opportunity to fulfill the aspirations of citizenship—to rule and be ruled. . . . the administrative state has the capacity to increase and multiply public spiritedness and thereby infuse the regime with active citizens. This could bring government close to the people and thereby heal a defect in the Constitution that has been with us from the beginning" (p. 53).[2]

As the dilemma of the representativeness of government generally has been with us since the founding of the Republic, so, too, are more narrow questions concerning the representative nature of the civil service longstanding. Concern over representativeness lay behind Andrew Jackson's spoils systems, and the Pendleton Act of 1883 provided for proportional geographical representation in the civil service (Cayer, 1975, p. 26; Chandler & Plano, 1982, p. 220; Mosher, 1982, pp. 12–13). Emerging from the demands of the civil rights movement in the 1960s, advocacy for a representative bureaucracy centered not on geographical representation but on racial, gender, and ethnic identity categories and, for this reason, suggested aspirations to representativeness in a double sense. First, much in this literature (see Dolan & Rosenbloom, 2003) expresses the Anti-Federalist concern for approximating the popular will in public organizations by making those institutions "look like" the people they serve; government represents those on whose behalf it governs in the broadest possible terms. As society becomes more inclusive, so, too, must government and its representation. This is, moreover, an explicitly normative conceptualization of the public administrator, one at odds with the model of neutral competence and merit principles (Mosher, 1982). Not merely a servant of an anonymous public, the representative bureaucracy begins from the specificity and historically situated experiences of particular groups, yet nevertheless operates through a *representative.* Second, it is postulated that individuals, as representatives of those groups, will hold certain views, interests, or preferences and advocate for them within the bureaucracy, though the relationship between these "passive" and "active" (Mosher, 1982) forms of representation is not entirely clear (Dolan & Rosenbloom, 2003, p. 79). More generally, representative bureaucracy is, as Mosher (1982) writes, "itself an implicit acknowledgement that administration is involved in policy matters" (p. 13) and, further, is a paradigmatic case of individual public administrators acting from their own personal life experiences and beliefs (see Lipset, 2003/1971; Maynard-Mooney & Musheno, 2003).

Representative bureaucracy raises two interesting issues. First, we see that since the Federalist founding the content of political representations has always been a concern. This is expressed as the desire for government to "mirror" the People in a rather expansive sense—mirroring views, identities, sentiments, affects, and so on. This qualifies modestly Hummel and Stivers's (1998) argument that the personal is not admitted into political representation. The personal or experiential is admitted—indeed, it is often demanded—but it enters as a *general* representation of particular persons and experiences. Differences reduce to an implicit categorical unity behind personal appearance. The admittance of the personal is, furthermore, guided by the logic that as more and more experiences and particularities are accumulated and included, the representation will be more accurate and full. However, these admissions, again, can be made only as general, abstract categories since to admit the personal *as belonging to an actual person* would collapse the distinction between representation and representative. It seems, then, that this view rejects not the personal per se, but rather can countenance the personal and experiential only as an abstraction or representation of the personal. By extension, it must reject a dynamic and malleable view of the self and experience since any dynamism undermines the stable "fit" between the representative and represented (McSwite, 1997b, p. 50). There is, then, a deep tension between the drive to identify the representation (government) with the represented/referent (the People) and the attempt to maintain the distance that distinguishes the two positions.

The second issue follows from this. Since we are not in government but only represented, how will we come to see ourselves in that representation? Will we recognize what we see in the mirror as us? Will we like it? Representation's commitment to a static ontology suggests a particular strategy for addressing these questions. Since experience changes people in unpredictable ways, experience itself must be narrowed in order to arrest the possibilities for thought and action that follow from dynamic engagement with others and the world. This needs to occur on the side of both the referent and the representation in order to ensure the fit between representation and the recognition of that representation as ours. As we will see, exclusion, discipline, and control emerge as essential strategies for arresting and narrowing experience in order to achieve this fit.

Critique and the Myth of the Given

Critical enterprises that challenge the assumptions and practices of epistemological representation and scientific positivism constitute the second prominent axis of public administration's study of representation. Like the demand for a representative bureaucracy and a normative public administration, this challenge was inaugurated in the 1960s and was characterized by the infusion of critical theory, existentialism, psychoanalysis, social constructionism, and phenomenology into the field's theoretical discourse (e.g., Denhardt, 1981; Harmon, 1981; Hummel, 1994/1977; Marini, 1971; Ramos, 1981; White, 1969). Though the heterogeneity of the research and the provocative commentary produced within these sometimes antagonistic philosophical traditions defies easy categorization, we can generalize cautiously to say that the scholarship clustered around normative questions concerning the possibility and *desirability* of a value-free, value-neutral public administration and, as Jay D. White (1999) writes, a broad dissatisfaction with explanatory modes of research like behaviorialist positivism (pp. 26–27).

I want to focus on how these critical perspectives (critical, that is, of mainstream, dominant positivist approaches, rather than in the technical sense of German critical theory) were unified in their assaults, in myriad ways, on the "myth of the given" or "the belief that something must exist independent of science itself that serves as the ultimate basis for all claims to knowledge. That 'something' was once construed as the realm of objective facts. This elusive realm was to serve as both the object of inquiry and the basis for accepting one theoretical formulation over another" (White, 1999, p. 88). As these critical approaches demonstrated, theory was found to play a far less passive role than was assumed. Theories, we learned, rest on different ontological foundations; they produce different objects and relationships among others; and they produce what-counts-as-fact in different ways. Language and theoretical frameworks, in other words, do not neutrally represent a given reality but help to create and mediate our experience with the objects of our attention.

Myths of givenness were also revealed and critiqued beyond the domains of social science. Since the world was not simply given, it was to be theoretically and socially constructed. Denhardt's (1981) *In the Shadow of Organization* is a powerful example of linking critiques of scientific epistemologies (e.g., positivism) with broader social, institutional critique. Akin to showing how positivism organized the realm of science and our relationship with it in specific ways, Denhardt showed how the impersonal and hierarchical rational model of organization, too, was not neutral. It embodied and reproduced a specific ethic of alienation, deference, and control. In critiquing this ethic, Denhardt challenged the dominant representation of our organizational lives, which, he argued, "not only mold our work life, but also our political and even religious involvements" (p. 16).

Like "organization," categories of identity (Alexander, 1997), organizational roles (Stivers, 1993), laws, rules, and regulations (Yanow, 2003) have been explored, challenged, and shown to be not *simply given.* Rather, they are artifacts of human creation and invention, only some of the possible representations of reality, and all are open to contest. To this point, Dvora Yanow (2003) writes at the end of her important analysis of state-defined categories of race and ethnicity, "There is nothing natural about the concepts or the categories, but various 'common sense,' everyday practices (re)present and treat them as if they were, thereby making them appear to be so" (p. 206). Nevertheless, as with many of our artifacts, we continue to endow them with a "misplaced concreteness" (Berger & Luckman, 1966), and lose "sight of the 'as if' quality of both" (Yanow, 2003, p. 207). Here, we see in a limited sense how the narrowing of experience can occur: through a mistaken assumption that representations of reality are natural and given. In a way, these critical enterprises ask us to look in the mirror of representation and say, "That's *not* me. That does not *need* to be me and my world. Something else is possible."

The Problem of Minimal Distance

There is much to be said about these two rich streams of scholarship. I want to call attention, however, to a concern common to them. As in the sentiment expressed by the Anti-Federalists, we can see in the requirements for a representative democracy a desire for a mirroring, mimetic, or *representing* relationship between the bureaucracy and the People. This demand extends beyond mere identity or categorization to include sentiment, sensibility, and preference. It is through this mirroring that government becomes closer, literally and figuratively, to the People. The aim of politics is to narrow this gap between representation and referent, although there may be various "empirical questions" as to whether this is occurring. I considered some of the problems of this project above.

Along different lines, a similar effort to "close the gap" of representation animates de-reifying critical projects. This takes the epistemological form of the closing or narrowing of the gap between subject and object. The object, the reification, is seen as—improperly—something apart from the subject, distant from him or her, as "having legitimacy independent of the intersubjective processes people actually use in creating, sustaining, and transforming them" (Harmon, 1981, p. 6). In leaving things as given, we become alienated from our own artifacts, including those artifacts that represent us to ourselves. This problem generally has been confronted by arguing for the cultivation of a nonreified, other-regarding, self-reflexive consciousness. As Harmon writes, "*non*reified thinking implies a cognitive ability to suspend temporarily, to stand apart from, one's usual categories of meaning in order to see and appreciate the problems and situations as described by others" (p. 134). This is a paradoxical dynamic, though. For while the reified consciousness mistakes the world as given, objectified, and apart from itself, the nonreified consciousness actually seeks to create distance such that critical reflection is possible.

The chief limitation of these critical efforts is itself the question of limits and the danger that these critical enterprises potentially turn into their opposite. The general problem that challenges to the myth of the given encounter is that such challenges are inexhaustible and do not know any "proper" boundaries. There is no ground or necessity to stop critique; it can continue relentlessly with no stoppage, though "justice," "responsibility," or some kind of warrant may be introduced ex post facto to arrest this critical process. Critical discourse itself may come to resemble the "deterritorializing" logic of capitalism (Deleuze & Guattari, 1987/1983, pp. 452–454), which eviscerates all stabilizing social codes—the "good" and the "bad." Practically speaking, this leaves us with no means for arresting this deterritorialization through the "legitimate" imposition and defense of some particular reification or mythical given. This can create intense feelings of insecurity and vulnerability that can generate a desire to affirm strong identifications rather than a desire for emancipation from the given and for exploring new possibilities and relationships. (As I will suggest later, insecurity is a particularly challenging problem today.) The practices of dereification can also turn into its opposite, becoming techniques for rejecting the (inherently) incomplete scientific record and promoting "artificially maintained controversies" (Latour, 2004, p. 226) (e.g., of global warming) rather than techniques for compelling certain inconvenient realities to be considered in the public realm. As Fox and Miller (1995) suggest, the reasoned and scientific bases of critique "have turned back in on themselves and have eroded their own bases of confident assertion" (p. 50). The dereifying impulse can become a tool for arresting change and for promoting suspicion and cynicism of any and all claims, reducing all belief to fetishism.

Raising these problems does not entail abandonment of critical intellectual projects or the broad hopes expressed in representative bureaucracy. Rather, it aims to surface the limits of these approaches, their shared background of representation, and to consider the conditions for new tactics. New tactics must think anew the question of the gap, this minimal distance, and our relationship toward it. The practical task today is twofold—one, to push the limits of critique to encompass the taken-for-granted ontology of representation and the People; and two, to reconsider how these reifications and artifacts are created, maintained, and changed. What we are seeking is a fundamentally different modality for the creation and sustaining of human worlds that somehow moves us beyond both the appeal to the brute facts of the matter and the reactionary pathologies of the critical, de-reifying impulse that threatens to leave us without any world at all.

Representation and the Fading Referent

In addition to the "sovereignty in question" theories outlined in chapter 2, several texts theorize representation and related themes in ways that are important to this tactical project—McSwite's (1996) "Postmodernism, Public Administration, and the Public Interest," Fox and Miller's (1995) *Postmodern Public Administration,* Frederick Thayer's (1973) *An End to Hierarchy! An End to Competition!,* and Eva Sørensen's (2002) "Democratic Theory and Network Governance." In various ways, all raise the question of the "referent" of representation and connect this matter to broader political, epistemological, and social relational concerns, yet do not consider—with the exception of McSwite—the question of the exclusion as the third theory of sovereignty did. I will begin with McSwite.

McSwite's text marks an attempt to resuscitate the notion of the public interest, long thought dead and buried by its critics (e.g., Schubert, 1960), and legitimize the place of public administration in American governance in postmodern conditions.[3] "From our vantage point," they write, "as strong advocates of a positive role for governance in society, the conditions of postmodernism create an opportunity for revitalizing the idea of the public interest and for defining clearly a role for public administration in the structure and process of American governance" (p. 199). These postmodern conditions are characterized by a radical "*rejection of the possibility of representation*" or, more precisely, a "denial that representations actually represent phenomena that exist objectively apart from the system of representation" (p. 207). Discourse "denies the existence of a superordinate term [e.g., God, Truth, the Good] as an anchor with which it can ground its rhetorical manipulations" (p. 212). As such, reality loses a stable referent, and so judgments become ultimately self-referential, and the modern understanding of meaning fades, lacking any authoritative mechanism outside of representation for arresting linguistic signification.

How does this help to revive or reconceptualize the public interest? From the perspective of postmodernism, traditional contests over the content or meaning of the *P*ublic *I*nterest were destined to become ideological because different interests advanced themselves as discrete representations of it. Failure to represent one's position in this way was a sure way to guarantee that one's voice would not be heard—who would listen to the non-Truth? To adjudicate various claims on the public interest, an institutional "fix" was required, a fix that McSwite call the Man of Reason, who oversees "ideological squabbling and resolve[s] it by considered objective judgment" (1996, p. 217). Yet under conditions of postmodernism, this fix no longer works. As the discussion of the limits of critique suggested, "we all know" that facts are socially constructed, that experts disagree, and that power is implicated in knowledge. McSwite, however, see these conditions as an opportunity to conceive of little-t truths as being concretely and contextually assembled "in a tentative pattern through a group process grounded in authentic communication" (p. 219). These public interests or, probably more precisely, public*s*' interests would name the "guidance and support" (p. 223) of truths grounded in specific contexts and specific groups that "forfeits, of course, the heroic possibility of superordinate judgment and a vision of heaven generated by mortals that can be held out as a collective goal" (p. 221). The task becomes the creation of contexts rather than producing accurate representations.

The limitations of McSwite's general position were presented in chapter 2, and the particular limitation of not calling into question the People itself is evident here. First, in McSwite's discussion, we can observe an affinity with Frederickson's discussion of multiple publics. Frederickson's discussion, however, takes place against the background of the Constitution and the unity it supposedly represents. McSwite's discussion of multiple publics, despite the radical rejection of representation (where representation is defined as "phenomena . . . exist[ing] objectively apart from the system of representation" [p. 207]), nevertheless takes places against the implicit background of the People, and so maintains the fundamental condition that permits the ongoing reference of publics' interests to the public interest, to the single, unified, body politic. Nevertheless, what we can take from this discussion is the explicit rejection of representation itself as well as a clear "disaggregation" of the public interest into discrete zones in which the interests of various publics' are invented and maintained, and in which relevant scientific knowledge is incorporated into the situation.

Similar themes are pursued in Fox and Miller's (1995) discourse-based approach to public administration. They begin their account from the premise that the "*representative democratic accountability feedback loop* model of democracy . . . does not work in any way that can be called democratic. The procedural democratic theory—which begins with individual preferences that are aggregated to popular will, codified by legislation, implemented by bureaucracy, and evaluated by attentive voters—lacks credibility" (pp. 4–5; emphasis in original). Efforts to reform the political system continue to assume the loop and wrongly locate blame for the widely perceived failure of government at the doorstep of the bureaucracy. The actual causes of the failure of "democratic will formation" (p. 7) lay in broad and profound changes in society and culture which, like McSwite, they identify as postmodernity.

Of central concern to Fox and Miller is the postmodern "thinning" of reality and the eclipse of shared metanarratives—e.g., the public interest or the People—that once organized a common sense and capacity for stable judgment. In postmodernity, we experience the breakdown of representation as signs "begin to float away from any 'real' referents" (1995, p. 50); representations detach from their objects. Experience of a broad "macroculture" fades, and where robust discourse communities develop they do so "only in enclaves or subcultures (a tendency referred to as *neotribalism*)" (p. 7). Politics, for its part, now traffics in symbols, images, and sound bites rather than substance; the gap between words and deeds grows. "Postmodern politics," they write, "is the simulated politics of symbol manipulation" (p. 64).

Fox and Miller point to the *political* problem caused by the failure of the democratic representative loop, one that will not be remedied, as they cogently argue, by increased control over the bureaucracy, constitutional moral exegesis, or nostalgic incantations of community. They are also correct in their suggestion that the "goal" of public administration scholarship need not be the often self-serving, navel-gazing enterprise of legitimizing the administrative state, and this powerful statement suggests that public administration need not be taken for granted. Further, they productively situate the problems of government today "outside" of public administration and away from bureaucracy; it hinges (at least in part) on the broader postmodern sociopolitical context within which government is embedded.

Yet Fox and Miller's discourse-based approach to public administration, despite the deconstruction of bureaucracy and intriguing replacement of it by "public energy fields," itself still operates on the terrain of the loop and political representation. A desire for a reality "out there" to represent is evident the text in spite of their efforts to reject "something external called sovereign." We see this, first, in the quiet shift of the referent of representation to a phenomenological terra firma of the body[4] and "our shared and indubitable experience of life" (p. 80), an ontological claim in unaddressed tension with the text's empirical assertion of macrocultural thinning and tribalist incommensurability; a unity behind appearances is asserted as "experience." As we will see in chapter 6, this move is itself symptomatic of the current regime of biopolitical production, which trains attention on the individual body. Second, the persistence of a constitutive, positive outside is evident in their persistent rejection of the apathetic, "fools, gadflies, extremists, plotters, ego trippers, or the greedy hiding behind sophistry" (p. 40). As if these are unproblematic judgments. Here we see the operation of a dividing strategy that is generative of a split between authentic and unauthentic representations of the referent (see Campbell, 2005; McSwite, 2005b, 2005c). Still, as in McSwite, we find in Fox & Miller an attempt to formulate an account of governing "inside" appearances.

Frederick Thayer's (1973) text is critical because it suggests a formal way of linking the microdimensions of primary concern to McSwite with the macroanalysis advanced by Fox and Miller[5] through a kind of generalized structural relationship that connects diverse political, organizational, and familial relationships (pp. 43, 58, 126).[6] This approach provides a way of conceiving "governing" in the broad, pervasive sense of the "conduct of conduct" proposed here: one beyond the conventional domains of politics and administration. For Thayer, this basic relationship in our society is hierarchy, and hierarchy, in turn, serves to sustain both the institutions of representative government and economic competition. I will focus here on what Thayer believes to be the alienating effect of hierarchical relationships and on his critique of representative government.[7]

Alienation, Thayer argues, occurs when "the world, society, or organization does not respond to the individual member, and subjects him to forces he can neither comprehend nor influence in a meaningful way" (1973, p. 47). People ultimately become mere things, distant from themselves, the people around them, and the products of their labor. The full dimensions of an alienated existence are realized in modern organizational life, which is formalized and impersonal and emphasizes the neutrality of technique, impartiality, and objectivity. For reasons that are not fully elaborated in the text, Thayer argues that hierarchy is the root cause of alienation since it institutes, to import Foucault's phrase, a dividing strategy between "*ruling* and *being ruled, issuing commands* and *obeying them, repressing* and *being repressed*" (p. 52). Through these divisions, hierarchy fundamentally alienates us from one another and the work of building the world.

Thayer argues that we can see this alienation clearly in our representative system of government. Representation succeeds only in limiting the power of the rulers, not in abolishing the distinction between the ruler and the ruled. Rehearsing criticisms of electoral and bureaucratic politics, Thayer writes that these activities are inherently alienating insofar as they do not let people speak for themselves (1973, p. 191). Indeed, the only aim of these processes is "victory" and "the turning of some people against others and the victory of some people over others" (p. 57). Representative government, in the phrase of sociologist Ulrich Beck (1992, p. 191), is actually "democratic monarchy." Only the faces of the king change; the basic *P*olitical structure does not. Rather, as in the case of representative bureaucracy, the tack we take is to make the king more representative of the People; we attempt to perfect the apparatuses of voting and to close the gap between government and constituency. There is no move to change the underlying hierarchical relationship, and so, close to the point made by Hummel and Stivers (1998), by virtue of the distancing, divisive hierarchy on which it depends, our representative system actually *produces* alienated citizens by design. Thayer believes that changes in contemporary society enable a different kind of social relation of "structured non-hierarchy" that would create an ethos of mutual support and collaboration (pp. 7–43) and eliminate distinctions between politicians, citizens, and administrators (p. 130).

As noted above, Thayer's analysis is a formal one, like McSwite's (1997b) analysis of the Man of Reason, in that it concerns less the particular content of representations and faces of hierarchy than the general relationship of hierarchy. Hierarchy is primary to any *particular* hierarchical relationship. Like Hummel and Stivers (1998), he intimates that governmental (il)legitimacy is not a function of representativeness. Indeed, it is precisely the reverse: representational hierarchy is the cause of alienation and, ergo, illegitimacy.

The limitations, though, of Thayer's provocative argument are twofold. First, we need to know more about the relationship between hierarchy and representation than Thayer provides. As he notes, hierarchy is not a new phenomenon. Modern representation, however, reconstitutes the hierarchical relationship in terms of impersonality and neutrality. We need to know more about how the construction of this impersonality works and how the content of neutrality is produced. Second, and perhaps more important, we need some way to understand the "mental" and cognitive hierarchies that constitute and structure us as subjects of language and discourse. Thayer seems to suggest that once formal hierarchy is done away with, an ethos of mutual support and collaboration would emerge. However, "flat" informal collaboratives might still replicate certain forms of hierarchy, as Thayer himself suggests in the case of the household. Similarly, the logical inverse could also be true: relations of formal hierarchy could be developmental and nondominating (Smith & Berg, 1997/1987; White, 1990). We need to theorize a relationship that is actually more generic than hierarchal.

Finally, in an analysis that recalls Fox and Miller's critique of representation's feedback loop, Eva Sørensen (2002) writes that Western liberal democratic political systems are gradually changing from "hierarchically organized, unitary systems of government that govern by means of law, rule, and order, to more horizontally organized and relatively fragmented systems of governance that govern through the regulation of self-regulating networks" (p. 693). While many theorists have construed the challenge of networks to be one of accountability (e.g., Grant & Keohane, 2005), Sørensen pushes further, arguing that networks challenge the "political ontology" of liberal democracy, that is, its assumptions about social reality itself.[8] Networks challenge four presumptions of this reality: (1) that the People is a pregiven, prepolitical subject; (2) that representation is the link between the People and authoritative decision making; (3) that administration is a "nonactor" or mere instrument in a democracy; and (4) that there is a separation between society and the political system (pp. 693–694).

From this theoretical setting, Sørensen moves to rethink representation not as a mirroring or mimetic operation but as a generative or aesthetic one. Representation "is the means by which the abstract notion of a sovereign people is transformed into a concrete sovereign capable of governing society" (2002, p. 697). The People is not the prerepresentational sovereign that expresses its will but a sovereign produced through processes of representation. Reading backward from Sørensen's work, we can find at least two notable and related discussions in the public administration literature. Interestingly, we find that Woodrow Wilson (1887) considers the disaggregated nonexistence of the People. Popular sovereignty, he writes, significantly complicates the work of governing by displacing power from the single body and opinion of the royal sovereign to the "multitudinous monarch of public opinion," and "this other sovereign, the people, will have a score of differing opinions" (p. 207). This sovereign is different, too, by virtue of its disembodied nature: the "sovereign's mind has no definite locality" (p. 208). This dispersed, disembodied quality makes government coordination difficult and leaves would-be reformers without a single ear to whisper into, without a single mind to change. Public opinion becomes the "first principle" of government (p. 208). The argument about the constructed, nongiven nature of the People was also advanced in Mary Follett's (1998/1920) *The New State.* In a passage similar to the earlier excerpt from Waldo, she writes, "Who are the People? Every individual? The majority? A theoretical average? A compromise group? The reason we go astray about public opinion is because we have not as yet a clear and adequate definition of the 'people.' We are told that we must elevate the 'people.' There are no 'people.' We have to create a people. The people are not an imaginary average, shorn of genius and power and leadership. . . . The people are the integration of every development, every genius, with everything else that our complex and interacting life brings about" (p. 220). "When public opinion becomes conscious of itself," she concludes, "it will have a justified confidence in itself. Then the 'people,' born of an associated life, will truly govern" (p. 226). As she (1951/1924) writes elsewhere, "genuine authority is not a matter of 'will,' even of the 'will of the people'; it is an interweaving *activity*" (p. 254).

Where in *The New State* Follett saw the neighborhood group (as well as the group in the formal workplace) as the potential realm for creating the People, today, multilayered horizontal networks expand the scope of those who can participate in the contest to construct the People. Sørensen writes, "Political representation in a system of network governance can therefore best be understood as a process in which an actor through political battles obtains the legitimate right to construct the identity of the represented, and to make political decisions with reference to this identity" (2002, p. 698). In this context, new challenges arise that are, similarly, fourfold: (1) how can the construction of the people be democratized; (2) how can representation be democratic when representatives are coproducing the representation rather than, say, mirroring the will of the represented; (3) how can democratic control be ensured when administrators are coproductive governance actors; (4) how can equality and liberty be protected without clear boundaries between the political system and society (p. 703).

Sørensen goes a long critical distance beyond the ontology of liberal democracy and indeed brings into question the prepolitical status of the People in a way that is nearly unprecedented in public administration. However, she retains the category of the People; indeed, she is explicit about this. Referring to the work of political theorist William Connolly (1995), she (2002) writes, "Some theorists of democracy go so far as to question whether it still makes sense to talk about 'a people.' . . . My answer to this question is both yes and no. . . . If there are no images of commonality there is no basis for acting together. However, it is no longer possible to build democracy on pre-given images of 'a people" (p. 705). While it may seem that I am pushing this point well beyond the threshold of usefulness, I want to insist that in retaining the category of the People the central problem remains. First, Sørensen takes rather too seriously the very idea of a pregiven image of the People. That is, all images of the People have *always* been the creations of representation, yet none are ever imposed as "merely" creations or aesthetic representations. Rather, to speak for the People is to acquire the authority to impose and command something in the name of that People. This qualifies significantly the "payoff" of recognizing that the People is "just a social construction." When we shift from congresses and parliaments to networks but retain the logic of the People, the essential, structuring logic of a politics of the One remains in place just as it does in McSwite's publics' interests.

But the more important point is this—the fundamental problem is *not* the pregiven images of the People but *the People as the pregiven image of a collectivity and the ontological commitment to the One that inheres in this image.* Not only are all representations partial representations of a disembodied, constructed People-as-One, but *the People itself* is a partial way of imagining and constructing reality. We need to understand not merely *that* the People is a construction but both *how* this relationship is constructed and the consequences of retaining this political ontology of the One.

Representation: The Insistence of the Model

Epistemology as a Problem of Representation

In his classic critique of epistemology, *Philosophy and the Mirror of Nature* (1979) Richard Rorty begins with an exploration of Descartes' "the invention of the mind," which inaugurated a fundamental disjuncture between the world of objects and knowledge about them.[9] In the Aristotelian (and Thomist) conception, the "intellect is not a mirror inspected by an inner eye. It is both mirror and eye in one." Critically, the split proposed by Descartes produces a third position, "mind," that inspects the images produced by the eye. The position of the intellect is something like a solitary person in a private screening room, watching successive images of reality flash across the screen. For Descartes, the mind reviews and assesses *representations* of reality. Rorty writes, "The Inner Eye surveys these representations hoping to find some mark which will testify to their fidelity" (p. 45). A great rift is created between the inner world of representations and the outer world of things. This is a rift that must be "healed" through the development of an apparatus of judgment. The question becomes: How will true representations (or, more modestly, more accurate or "better" ones) be distinguished from inferior ones? How well is reality "mirrored"? This "problem of knowledge" is called epistemology.

This "epistemological turn," Rorty continues, also initiated a shift from a concern with living to one of science in philosophy (1979, p. 61), and, more particularly, "provided a field [i.e., the human mind] within which *certainty,* as opposed to mere *opinion,* was possible" (p. 137; emphasis in original). However, while Descartes had established the dimensions of the basic problematic of epistemological certainty, it ultimately fell to Kant to work through its challenges. It was Kant's "Copernican Revolution" that established the grounds for a nonempirical epistemology by moving the outer "inside" in and establishing the position of the transcendental subject. Kant argued that we can only have a priori certainty about objects (that is, knowledge of them antecedent to any sensual, "pathological," or empirical experience of them) if our minds "constitute" the objects themselves. The comparison therefore would be made among two sorts of representations—formal ones (concepts that create the objects) and material ones (intuitions of the representations of those objects). "A judgment is a representation of a representation, a putting before the mind of a putting before the mind" (Hacking, 1983, p. 133). The search for these foundational formal concepts of the mind (e.g., linguistic, structural, neurophysiological) would, in turn, become a philosophical project and, moreover, make possible a scientific morality grounded in foundations that establish the conditions for all possible experience.

All this, it bears noting, took place in a political context. Rorty writes, "The 'epistemological turn' taken by Descartes might not have captured Europe's imagination had it not been for a crisis of confidence in established institutions" (1979, p. 139). Indeed, as Jonathan Israel's (2001) *Radical Enlightenment* meticulously details, in the wake of the collapse of the political and theological nexus of scholastic Aristotelianism, "the most pressing priority . . . it was universally acknowledged, was to overcome the growing fragmentation of ideas and, by means of solid demonstration and convincing arguments, restore stable and enduring structures of authority, legitimacy, knowledge, and faith" (p. 9). Analogous to the crisis that a science of administration much later served to address (see McSwite, 1997b; Stivers, 2000), Cartesianism emerged as a potential answer to the search for order that oriented itself, first of all, with regard to the mechanistic philosophy that emerged in Galileo's New Science, which had called into question the Thomist-Aristotelian cosmology.

A General Economy of Representation—The Model and Copy

As Rorty's comments about political context and the discussion of representation in public administration suggest, what comes to the fore is the need to ground a critique of epistemological representation *and* political representation in a common framework that might displace the "objectism" of each, or rather the shared preoccupation with the representation givenness of an object, and orient ourselves toward another political ontology that could define a different axis of politics and knowledge. Perhaps more critically, this move might define a Political form that is not itself based in problems of knowing an object or in reproducing an image of a unified collectivity. This would be a politics that would give us something different *to do,* some other regime of practices, something other than representing, and open us to the articulation of a different political ontology. I will now attempt to outline a common framework within which to understand both these modes of representation as manifestations of a common logic and the replication of a specific kind of relationship.

Following Gilles Deleuze, let me now make a first cut at specifying a general economy of representation in order that I might return to the explicit question of the Political. In essence, representation can be understood as a relationship of model and copy (Deleuze, 1990a/1969, 1994/1968). That is, a model is posited that expresses a generality connected with a posited real objectivity of the world. The model-copy relationship can be thought of as akin to the general and particular or, more specifically, a general that grounds and forms the particular that is encountered. Particulars, in other words, are held to be manifestations of the general and are related to one another based upon their relationship to the general, to some underlying, fundamental element held in common among them. This element marks them as common insofar as they possess something in common.

Consider the example of the term *human.* The term is the general category within which a particular set of entities are collected. The criterion for inclusion is the possession of some property or characteristic that is common to a set of entities—call it "humanity." Humanity is the universal possession of entities designated as human. The challenges of category making immediately become evident. First, the term itself needs content or to be specified beyond the emptiness of humanity or being-human. In representation, as will be argued below, the temptation is to see these descriptors in naturalistic, organic, and purely descriptive terms. However, categorization rests on a *decision.* This is evident in the racist, sexist, and highly discriminatory practices that have excluded by definition certain beings from the human by determining the human in specific terms—e.g., whiteness, male, heterosexual, able-bodied—or by defining certain humans in non-human terms—e.g., as property or "animals."

The word *model* is used here because these categories are not used only to organize, catalog, and describe. Rather, they are used for judgment among the various "copies" or representations out in the world; they define criteria for judgment and, further, permit or discourage certain lines of action. For example, when African slaves or white women are categorized as non-human or property a determination is made, in the case of slaves, that they are categorically distinctive; white women (in restricted instances) may be included as human but make "poorer" copies of a model of humanity defined in terms of maleness. Certain actions, such as the legitimate infliction of violence, may also be permitted in a political community by virtue of the categorical decision to *exclude* entities from a given grouping.

Three points can be emphasized. First, modern political struggle can be defined largely in terms of a struggle for recognition within or inclusion into given models of representation. Second, the models are without given positive content. This content is produced through struggle, contest, and decision but, nevertheless, the models are asserted and gain their legitimacy as natural, normal, or neutral. And third, models (and therefore representations) are inherently exclusionary because *all* content cannot be included in the model without the model failing to differentiate and permit judgment among its subsets, and, therefore, produce content for the model itself. That is, if "human" encompasses all entities, it ceases to conceptually differentiate. Representational models include and exclude, and this originary constituting decision on the exclusion is made through reference to a positive object whose content is allegedly represented in the model. As we will see, central to representation is the denial of this initial exclusionary dividing moment. This becomes particularly problematic for supposedly universal categories like the People that assert their Oneness and must somehow "manage" the multiplicity and internal difference that is excluded from the representation and the terms/predicates of the model.

Quantitative Order of Equivalence

Models of representation operate in two modes—the qualitative order of resemblances, or of order, and the quantitative order of equivalences, or of measurement (Deleuze, 1994/1968, p. 1; Foucault, 1970/1966, p. 53). For public administration and policy, cost-benefit analysis and efficiency (see Morçöl, 2002) may be the paradigmatic technique and terms that rest on the quantitative order of equivalences. The quantitative order of equivalences is also something experienced every day when, for example, we use money. It is the logic of a comparison in which some element is identified to serve as a standard by which two heterogeneous elements can be evaluated. Thus the comparison always already implies a third term that inheres in all the objects of comparison; indeed, for the compared objects, their value is only realized through the third term, the general equivalent. These objects differ in quantitative terms. Historically, gold was the commodity that established the basis for the comparison of all other commodities and served as a model of equivalence, though it is no longer.[10]

In his famous "Chapter on Money," Marx (1973) makes this point apropos of the realization of the commodity form. He writes, "in order to realize the commodity as exchange value in one stroke, and in order to give it the general influence of an exchange value, it is not enough to exchange it for one particular commodity. It must be exchanged against a third thing which is not in turn itself a commodity, but is the symbol of the commodity as commodity, of the commodity's exchange value itself; *which thus represents, say, labor time as such*" (p. 144; emphasis in original). The full implications of the mapping of representation onto the money relation (which is the precondition for capital) cannot be pursued here, but nevertheless it is useful to observe how the definition of the common or shared qua exchange value arrives already "cooked" in the money relation, thus concealing precisely that which value itself already represents, namely labor time. Thus it is the representation of objectified labor that not only establishes the terms of exchange (the model), arrays and distributes commodities (the copies), but also produces an element (about which I shall say more in a moment)—the constitutive exclusion, which in capitalism is called surplus value. What is capital's surplus value but an internal *and* external excess or difference produced by a replication of the circuit of capital, a circuit that requires the continual production of the excess. In *Capital,* Marx (1967/1867) wrote of this paradox: "It is therefore impossible for capital to be produced by circulation, and it is equally impossible for it to originate apart from circulation. It must have its origin both in circulation and yet not in circulation. We have, therefore, got a double result" (p. 163).

This argument concerning capital's relationship to the general mechanisms of representation has been elaborated thoroughly by Jean-Joseph Goux (1990/1973). Analogous to the project undertaken here, Goux attempts to "bring to light the common process by which the major symbolic elements accede to hegemony as general equivalents." That is, he is interested in the historical processes through which one particular element or symbol becomes the general arbiter and designee of value to other particularities. Certain values attain a "privileged representativeness and even a monopoly on representativeness within the diverse set of which they are members" (p. 10). These "exceptions" become the rule (p. 31) and, so to speak, also the ruler in the double of sense of sovereign and measurer. Following Marx, Goux argues compellingly that the money relationship is the paradigmatic manifestation of representation—" 'genesis of the money form' is the story of a universal process: the ascension to a power of *representative* and the institutionalization of its role" (p. 11). The money relation "casts light upon all *centristic* tendencies, upon all notions of radiation from the center, the process of centralization" (p. 44; emphasis in original). Goux calls this science of money a *theoretical numismatics.*

Then, drawing primarily from Lacanian psychoanalytic theory, Goux establishes homologies or isomorphisms among other domains of market society. For example, he shows how the role of universal equivalent "is played by gold in the world of commodities; by the father in the world of others [i.e., social relations]; and by the sexual organ, becoming a phallus, in the world of part objects [of desire]" (p. 23).[11] Goux, further, suggests that the monarch and the word (p. 39) serve as universal equivalence and, in an instructive phrase, he calls the hegemonic positioning of these various terms "accessions to sovereignty" (p. 24). These ascensions serve, ultimately, the end of unification, or "the subjection of the many to the sovereignty of the one" (p. 39). This displaces "the diversity of relationships among elements in a univocal, exclusive relationship to the general equivalent which *magnetizes* or *funnels* towards its ideal center all value relationships, making them its tributary ways" (p. 45).

Goux's text, however, does not examine the unique problem that the People poses in this logic of the general equivalent. His discussion of the political is limited to a discussion of the monarch and, more precisely, absolutism. But this is not the form that popular sovereignty and representative democracy follows. As suggested earlier in the discussion of public administration's examination of representation, and as I will consider in further detail in chapter 4, the "democratic invention" (Lefort, 1986/1980) entails the emptying of the monarchical throne, the inauguration of a nonlocalizable source of political power, and a rupture between state and sovereignty. It appears to usher in a new order, precisely the "*decapitated*—polymorphic, acephalous social organization that would challenge the monopolies on representation" (Goux, 1990/1973, p. 47). These questions need closer attention. More broadly, I see no necessity in asserting the science of *money* as the basis for a general theory of representation. This actually seems to replicate the substitutive logic Goux criticizes. Nevertheless, Goux's text is a critical link in (1) establishing a structural homology between the political ontological critique of representation advanced here and the core of the capitalist economy; (2) evincing, like Frederick Thayer, the importance of showing how formal relations can replicate themselves across heterogeneous contexts to produce the effect of order; and (3) demonstrating the underlying homology between qualitative and quantitative orders of representational valuation.

Qualitative Order of Resemblance

The second mode is the qualitative order of resemblances. It is exemplified in the taxonomy of species and was outlined above in the discussion of humanity. A single "essential" characteristic or a cluster of them is identified that comprises a definitional model of a particular species, class, or category. Particular instances of the species are related back to the model, and particularities themselves enter into a relation with one another through the terms of the model. That is, they do not relate to one another directly but rather enter into relation by virtue of the formal category that organizes them. The qualitative mode of order does not require external reference. Rather, criteria for identity are established internally by the model, whose difference itself is marked externally from its position in a series of other models. Of course, the particulars "inside" are nevertheless marked off and distributed according to the external positing of the model itself. We see in this example the double exclusionary movement of representation. First, an originary exclusionary decision is made that defines the positive content of the model through representation of the object. Next, hierarchies and secondary exclusions are made so as to be able to array and distribute the differences that must be managed in order to conceal the original decision on the exclusion that constitutes the category itself.

Along different lines, the qualitative dimension of representation can be seen in Slavoj Zizek's (1991, 1993) analyses of the "Nation-Thing" that highlight the particular problem that representational models inevitably come up against. Zizek (1993) writes that "the element which holds together a given community cannot be reduced to the point of symbolic identification: the bond linking together its members always implies a shared relationship toward a Thing, toward enjoyment incarnated." This materialized enjoyment is what constitutes the kernel of a nation's "way of life," that which essentially distinguishes Us from Them. The Thing is experienced as ineffable, beyond words or definition. "All we can do is enumerate the disconnected fragments of the way our community *organizes its enjoyment*" all the while We know and sense that there is always "something more" that defines Us in excess of the determined predicates (p. 201; emphasis in original). In other words, our Thing ultimately cannot be reduced to the specific terms of the model. It remains ineffable and only tacitly apprehended. A critical question that we will explore is how this recognition and its concomitant differentiations are produced and maintained internally in the face of the category's universality.

How, then, is this like taxonomy? The plausibility of species differentiation fundamentally rests on the same in-excess of the predicates. That is, all the qualitative characteristics of two species of birds can be listed and identified, yet this itself does not exhaust *both* their intraspecies similarity and interspecies difference. Here, too, identification relies on something excessive that similarly points toward a shared some-*Thing*. Identification of "our Thing" is not, of course, a matter of internal identification, though there is certainly the dimension of belief; identification of who has our Thing—i.e., who's in and who's out—is made externally. The distinction between determinations of nations and birds, of course, is that while our Thing is incarnated in material practices (such as national rituals, customs, etc.) and is inaccessible to Them, the impossible fullness of our Thing is nevertheless always threatened by an other's Thing and their enjoyment. It is the excess of the other's Thing that paradoxically provokes the experience of loss or deficit, or of, as Zizek says, the "theft of our enjoyment."

It is important to appreciate how interdependent these decisions and exclusions are in reproducing representational relations. The originary decision on the exclusion purports to represent the positive object and, in doing so, to produce content for the model. This content, subsequently, permits judgment and the distribution of differences within the category. Internal contest of the model logically will produce disruption of the capacity for judgment and differentiation and, furthermore, destabilization of the originary division between the "internal" content of the model and its "external" exclusion. Similarly, disruption of that originary boundary will cascade through the *socius,* producing disturbances in the terms of the model and so problems in the recognition of judgment and the arraying of differences. Crisis and breakdown are endemic to this world by virtue of its foundational ontological commitment.

To summarize: representation is a relationship between a posited model and various derivations or copies. Representation operates in two ways—one qualitative (resemblance), the other quantitative (equivalence). We are sometimes tempted to see these as opposed to one another, as in public administration's normative and positivistic discourses, but they operate in identical manners. Representation also establishes a specific relationship to difference. Differences exist (1) between concepts; and (2) as deviations from the established terms of the model. With regard to the second difference, there are, further, "better" and "worse" (in both the qualitative normative sense and the quantitative sense of measured accuracy) copies depending on the degree to which particulars are capable of representing the terms of the model. Insofar as differences relate to one another, they do so either across abstractions or as deviations. Epistemology emerges as the central practice of judgment, as the *political science* of arraying, distributing, and recategorizing copies; deciding who is in and who is out; and for arranging rank and order for the better and worse approximations of those "inside" the model.

We can see that representation establishes a set of formal, abstract relationships. These relations are "empty sacks" (Verhaeghe, 2001) into which content is poured in various domains—the economy, taxonomy, identity. Representation also posits an object beyond itself; something must be represented to the mind even if the mind itself is closed off in a world of representations. What is the status or nature of this object? The object is conceived as substantial, present, and as a unity. Behind the "many" representations and copies there is a One defined either as "transcendental limit (a One *beyond* being, or God) or as all-inclusive immanence (a cosmos or Nature)" (Hallward, 2003, p. 4). That is, even if the human subject is shut off in a world of appearances, as Kant and Descartes say, there is still a positive order of Being behind appearances that grounds the *reconstruction* of the object in representation and, subsequently, judgment in representation's preferred naturalistic terms. This is basically how political representation proceeds. Government is to be the rational reconstruction of the object, the People. Thought and representation do not fabricate this substantial unity even if one concedes the active construction of knowledge. The being of beings within categories is defined essentially as identification with and replication of a given model of representation; collectivity is a conceptual abstraction and focused identification with our Thing, differentially articulated from Theirs, and disputed internally as a matter of contest over the predicates that (over)determine Us.

This is the political ontology of representation.

Representation and the Model of Life: Unity Behind Appearances

I have claimed throughout that the models of representation rest on a fully present unity that is specified in naturalistic terms. For this reason, the modern political project is biopolitical. I will now more specifically describe how and why this is the case.

Representational models are specified as a model of Life (zoë), the all-inclusive immanence. It is a model grounded in substantial, unified organic processes of Life that constitute a ground for politics. Here, I will draw on Michel Foucault's (1970/1966) examination of the breakdown of the classical world of representation that he provides in *The Order of Things*. Foucault's archaeology describes the *episteme* of the classical age and its rupture in the last years of the eighteenth century by the modern or anthropological age. Without rehearsing the whole of his complex argument, I wish to emphasize Foucault's demonstration that, whereas the classical age was organized around an analytic of order, of identities and differences and of universal characterization, in the modern age we find

> an area of organic structures, that is, of internal relations between elements whose totality performs a function; . . . these organic structures are discontinuous, . . . they do not, therefore, form a table of unbroken simultaneities, . . . certain of them are on the same level whereas others form series or linear sequences. So that we see emerging, as the organizing principles of this space of empiricities, *Analogy* and *Succession:* the link between one organic structure and another can no longer, in fact, be the identity of one or several elements, but must be the identity of the relation between elements (a relation in which visibility no longer plays a role) and of the functions they perform; moreover if these organic structures happen to be adjacent to one another, on account of a particularly high density of analogies, it is not because they occupy proximate places within an area of classi-

> fication; it is because they both have been formed at the same time, and the one immediately after the other in the emergence of the successions. Whereas in classical thought the sequence of chronology merely scanned prior and more fundamental space of a table which presented all the possibilities in advance, from now on, the contemporaneous and simultaneously observable resemblances in space will be simply the fixed forms of a succession which proceeds from analogy to analogy. (p. 218)

This passage makes several critical points. First, we can see how representation is manifest in these organic structures. The structures themselves do not occupy the realm of the visible but now shift to a domain "out of sight" and behind appearances. We can see this clearly in the example of taxonomy (the qualitative mode of representational distribution). Foucault writes, "To classify, therefore, will no longer mean to refer the visible back to itself, while allotting one of its elements the task of representing the others; it will mean, in a movement that makes analysis pivot on its axis, to relate the visible to the invisible, to its deeper cause, as it were, then to the rise upwards once more from that hidden architecture towards more obvious signs displayed on the surfaces of bodies" (1970/1966, p. 229). The origin or source of the representational model moves "inside" into organic structures of Life (zoë). That is, the authority of the model is gained by virtue of its depositing into the all-inclusive immanence of Life. This allows for the conflation of the correct and the natural.

Second, reference to "facts" constitutes a de facto appeal to the natural and organic, that is, to that which *is not humanly constituted* but purely a neutrally-as-naturally corresponding (mimetic) representation of the ever-displaced model. Thus we no longer merely categorize according to correlations captured by the eye—resemblances—but rather now take the visible to be a representation of some deeper, embedded organic, invisible model or structure that regulates or resonates with Life's rhythms (hence Foucault's persistent concern for surfaces and suspicion of depth). There is a disruption in the presumptive referentiality of words to things that is akin to the rupture described by Rorty. "There is talk of things that take *place* in another space than that of words" (Foucault, 1970/1966, p. 230). Words and things become torn from one another, and the "real" becomes invisible and shifts to another place, one beyond the representations produced in the mind and its symbols. This also generates the dilemma of the gap and turns our attention to how the tearing of words from their referents is not a postmodern phenomenon but one at the heart of modernity itself, insofar as the referent or real is displaced into the domain of the invisible.

Third, to the general abstract model-copy relation we now add the important fact that the model is not merely the position from which representation can be judged, but in its objectivity, also that which makes representations possible. In other words, it is by virtue of the fact that there is a natural, content-emitting "real" that allows for representational copies, that there is thought plausibly to be a stable and objective position from which these representations can be arrayed, distributed, and decided upon. This introduces a profound shift in the grounding of authority since the authorization to speak and the products of those who stand to speak for the faithful representation of the model now speak on behalf of the mute self-regulating processes of Life itself; and, as is well commented upon, authority becomes for this reason impersonal. We can see the ground for the bifurcation of authority into the dual normative (speaking for Us) and positive (speaking for things) dimensions that characterize the administrative state.

Fourth and finally, there is an important temporal, historical point. The rupture of the classical world does not occasion a displacement of the discourses of the classical age. Indeed, in a certain sense, the contemporary moment cannot be made sense of until it is viewed in terms of the simultaneous presence of the classical discourse of universal order and the anthropological, modern discourse of organic structure. This is important because this sedimentation allows for the possibility of thinking the juridical discourse of unified sovereignty on the organic terrain of Life in the form of the popular sovereign. This finds its nexus in the notion of "law," which allows for the positing of an autochthonous political order based on the rule of law (in the dual scientific and normative, often teleological, senses). Moreover, it is also for this reason that the opposition of the popular to the royal sovereign can be grounded in a critique of the arbitrary exercise of power. The distinction is fundamentally one of law and its origins. A space is now created for a political order governed by a law (e.g., the Constitution) as natural as those of philology, economics, and biology and for those "regional" laws to be projected onto the domain of society. This is an order rigidly opposed to the embodied "exceptional" position of the royal sovereign and the apparent arbitrariness and dangerous exercise of power such an exceptional position above the law portends.

Most basically, it is this copresence that allows for the conflation of zoë with the qualified bios and the emergence of the biopolitical project of fabricating the People.

The Precipice of Representation—Materializations and Exclusions

As suggested above, representation's models always leak. There is always some element that, in various ways, is slipping away from or is excluded from the model; some element resists and cannot/will not be assimilated to representation, though the necessity of this exclusion is always denied. The unity can never be what it claims; it can only be not-All (Lacan, 1999/1975). No quantity of representations will ever add up to One. Representation is always running a deficit. Given this problem, it will become the practical task of representation to establish techniques for managing, organizing, and taming the "leak." These techniques are the topics of chapters 4 and 5. I want to draw initially on O. C. McSwite's (1997b) presentation of the constitutive paradox of boundaries to illustrate in another way why representations always leak.

The general attitude of representation toward the exclusion is to attempt to manage it and to bring it under control somehow through an act of *materialization.* That is, the ontologically constitutive failure of representation to maintain itself in (impossible) fullness, completeness, and self-perpetuating regularity is materialized in the social field through the production of an internal representation of its external limit. The materialization of the exclusion materializes the impossibility of the posited unity. McSwite (1997b) note that this can be the particular identification of "people we just don't like," the fabrication of an Other.[12] As Zizek suggests, this excluded element has two paradoxical dimensions. First, the exclusion is an object of both attraction and loathing because it represents a seemingly limitless excess that is inaccessible. It is also the element that impedes or undermines the calculated stability of the positively determined model and the unity behind appearance. This move, thus, banishes the "origin" of reality and establishes, at best, an ambivalent, though often violent, attitude toward the exclusion. The exclusion is seemingly both the threat to and wellspring of life in the modular world of representation, which feeds off the exclusion like a vampire, all the while struggling to eliminate it through either actual bodily annihilation or integration into the determined model.

The second paradox concerns how the exclusion is both the element that seems to undermine objectivity and the holder of the place of the objective point of view itself. In representation, there are three positions—the object(-cause)-of-representation (model), representations (copies), and the position of judgment (place from which to assess the fidelity of correspondence to the model). To assess and distribute representations, the judge perforce requires a position "outside" the field of representation. However, it is more exact to say that the judge requires possession of criteria by which the accurate and inaccurate representations can be identified. In other words, the judge requires the determination of the terms of the model. This is a critical point, for what representation profoundly *denies* is the act of judgment that has *already been made* (perhaps even the very decision to judge) prior to the secondary judgment of differentiation and assessment. This denial takes the form of the invocation of neutral, naturalistic, or normalizing language.

What I mean is this—the positing of the object of representation as a *positive* object demands the determination of the predicates of the model. What *is* the object? It is only this explicit determination that permits the identification and judgment of representations. But these predicates are *selected* from the field of immanence itself even if they are subsequently elevated to the transcendent (in either the theological or naturalistic modes noted above). A judgment concerning the criteria of judgment already has been made antecedent to the judgment concerning the fidelity of the various representations. And these criteria attain their force by virtue of being marked by the natural (thus commonly shared within species), the organic and, finally, the good. Thus the objective position of the model is, in fact, *particularly* occupied as the universal. It is this doubling that allows for the representational act of judgment itself.

We can see that there is an initial moment of exclusion that positively defines the predicates of the model by virtue of their marking by the real object. We saw this in the example of "human." By necessity, certain predicates *cannot* be included in the model. However, given the positing of the naturally occurring structures of Life in the model, this exclusionary moment is effaced. Next, some accounting for difference, deviance, and disturbance must be made since a universal model has been posited. This accounting (which, as argued in chapter 4, is accompanied by mode of technical correction) is the *materialization of the exclusion.* The problem, outlined in the discussion of critical de-reifying projects in public administration, is that in representation the terms of the model cannot be extended infinitely such that the exclusion might become fully incorporated into the model. The model itself requires exclusion. Indeed, the infinite extension of the terms of the model merely destabilizes it by disrupting the boundaries. Why, then, is the exclusion both the element that seems to undermine objectivity and the holder of the place of the objective point of view itself? The exclusion undermines objectivity because it is always the element that is slipping away from its bounds, yet it is simultaneously the place holder for the objective since it is constitutive of the stable object of representation itself. It materializes the exclusion in the social field as the necessary failure of the model to fully embody the real which, in turn, subsequently becomes the object of representational instrumentality to "bring in" the exclusion.

Between Words and Things: The Sovereign Decision

In raising the problem of representation, a critical—if by now commonplace—criticism of a crude "correspondence theory" of truth emerges, one shared by the various critiques already advanced in public administration theory. The correspondence theory of truth poses the possibility via the model of establishing an identity between the object of representation and the representation of the object, between things and words, between the real object and the object-of-knowledge. The criticism of this view of knowledge has been the target of assault for much of the twentieth century (Heidegger, 1977; James, 1977; Saussure, 1972). Concomitant with this has been a pronounced assault on the integrity (moral, structural, etc.) of the knowing subject.

In raising the question of the "correspondence" of these two poles or directions of human existence, the status of what "holds" them together is simultaneously raised. In other words, if, for instance, a simple correspondence between the word and the thing to which it allegedly refers cannot be assumed, then what is the nature of the *relationship* between the two? Attention shifts from acts of corresponding positivities to an analysis of the in-between. The core problem of representation is the manner in which this relationship is conceived—most basically, a relationship of models and copies, predicated upon a naturalistic fullness and relations of the Same. These models necessarily exclude, and this exclusion is projected into and materialized in the social field. Critiques of the very idea of representation insist on the *gap* between the two elements. To continue with this example, words and things are *not* homogeneous. Rather, they are, in the phrase of Deleuze, heterogeneous series. Relations are extrinsic to heterogeneous elements, or series. Thus, for example, consider Foucault's conception of power/knowledge. In his historical studies (i.e., *Madness and Civilization* [1988/1961], *The Order of Things* [1970/1966]) Foucault demonstrates that the "determination of the visible [things] and the articulable [words] features unique to each age . . . goes beyond any behaviour, mentality or set of ideas, since it is what makes these things possible" (Deleuze, 1988/1986, p. 49). There are two heterogeneous elements, words and things, the articulable and the visible. What Foucault emphasizes in the heterogeneity of these two series is that, as a consequence of their division, they refer to two *different objects.* The object of the statement is *not* the same object of vision. It is not a question of the interaction with the object being mediated by language, but the more radical position that the objects of language and the objects of the domain of the visible are different objects.

It is the case that the concrete object of the eye and the abstract object of the statement or of consciousness are disjointed, but it is not because one is more or less "out of line" from the other, but rather because these two series have as their object *different objects.* It is the temptation to collapse one into the other, to elevate one as the "real" of representation that poses the problem here. Rather than attempting to account for the primacy of one over the other or effect some sort of "balance" or synthesis, we might turn attention toward the gap in between and the process that interlaces or bridges the gap between series. We have seen how representation constructs this relationship. A different political ontology could begin with the assertion, then, not necessarily of the impossibility of similitude, but that all similitude or unity is contingently produced or created on the ground of this nonreferential internal *difference* between a double series of, for example, signifier or signified. The world is doubly articulated and an irreducible, unspecifiable gap or excess, this minimal difference, inheres in any articulation. To follow Alain Badiou (2006/1988), we can assert that the most that we can say about the gap of being itself is to call it "empty set" (∅) or void.

This is the difference that representation denies and cannot countenance, a denial that is reinforced by the language of the People. The regime of representation endeavors in any situation to reduce one series to the positivity of the other, which not only generates the consequence of the materialization of exclusion but also advances an overall strategy of authoritatively arresting the potential reconfigurations of any situation in the cause of rendering a broader calculability and regularity under the auspices of the naturally occurring, self-perpetuated givenness of Life (zoë) and fixing the relationship between representation and representative. That is, localized, situational disarticulations, an unweaving of seriality and opening to a new configuration or composition, is impeded precisely because the survival "needs" of the situations are always already produced "outside" of it in the form of the materialized exclusion and, therefore, the preservation and extension of the representational economy.

To this act of arrest and imposition under representation, the name *sovereignty* can be given. Sovereignty acts in the gap of difference to create the modern representational order. Sovereignty attempts to represent that gap, to positivize the ground, the unrepresentable gap that makes possible the coherence of the world.

Sovereignty: Carl Schmitt and the Political

"Sovereign," the German legal theorist Carl Schmitt (1985b/1922, p. 5) famously wrote, "is he who decides on the status of the exception." Since Schmitt is virtually unknown to public administration in the United States, a word about him and his contemporary relevance is in order. Infamous for his role as a leading legal theorist in the Nazi regime, Schmitt is increasingly recognized as one of the most original and quietly influential political and legal thinkers of the twentieth century (Balakrishnan, 2000). He lived and wrote in the epicenter of European political and legal thought and was a direct or indirect "adversary or interlocutor in the writings of figures such as Georg Lukacs, Walter Benjamin, Karl Mannheim, Leo Strauss, Friedrich Hayek, Norberto Bobbio, and Jurgen Habermas, to mention only a few, more familiar and perhaps more sympathetic names" (Balakrishnan, 2000, p. 1). Arguably, Schmitt's influence on American politics has been particularly powerful via Leo Strauss, a number of whose disciples, including former deputy secretary of defense Paul Wolfowitz, populated the G. W. Bush administration (Postel, 2003). Though his reactionary views are evident,

Schmitt was not ultraconservative in any straightforward manner, having been called "the Lenin of the bourgeoisie" (Preuss, 1999, p. 159). His concept of the political "essentially called for the maintenance of the cardinal institutions of bourgeois social order: private property, the right of inheritance, the freedoms of trade, commerce, contract and investment" (Preuss, 1999, p. 159). Schmitt is increasingly recognized as a trenchant analyst of the intrinsic technicism and irrationalism of modern politics, including its liberal democratic incarnation, and his work is particularly relevant now.

In his criticism of liberal democracy, Schmitt points directly to its "blind spot," namely, first, its tendency toward the neutralization and depoliticization of politics and law, not to mention vast spheres of social life (e.g., the economy and private realms) and, second, its desire to reduce the inherently conflictual, antagonistic nature of political engagement to technique or self-reflexive ethics (Mouffe, 1999, p. 2). This is an argument familiar to public administration. Politics itself becomes irrational and falsely perceived as being the practice confined to the relatively narrow band of electoral activities intended to produce in political society the unity its ontology presupposes. Falsely, I say, because mass democracy tends, in fact, to *politicize* vast domains of social life. As Paul Hirst (1999) writes, "Mass politics means a broadening of the agenda to include the affairs of all society—everything is potentially political. Mass politics also threatens existing forms of legal order. The politicization of all domains increases pressure on the state by multiplying interests demanding action; at the same time, the function of the liberal legal framework—the regulating of the 'private sphere'—becomes inadequate. Once all social affairs become political, the existing constitutional framework threatens social order: politics becomes a contest of organized parties seeking to prevail rather than achieve reconciliation" (p. 10).[13] Much of this is, of course, well known in public administration; these are criticisms advanced across the field's many theoretical perspectives. Nevertheless, the field (with partial exceptions as noted above) has tended to conceive of these problems solely in terms of instrumental rationality, finessing the question of how the problems of technicism may lie in our most cherished political ideas. Schmitt's particular critique adds to this discourse a focus on the problematic nature of political liberalism and popular sovereignty in light of the problem of instrumentality. That is, the issue of instrumentality is not only a problem of depoliticization but also a problem of a particular form of politics. The political order of representation, rather than actually limiting governing and politics, politicizes the whole of social life and, indeed, by making the People both the object and subject of governing, renders Life itself as the object of politics.

The issue that Schmitt frames directly and productively is the nature of sovereignty. "Sovereign," Schmitt (1985b/1922) writes, "is he who decides on the exception" (p. 5). Sovereignty has less to do with the representation of a popular will than with a decision concerning the imposition of order, a decision rendered complex by the disembodied, invisible locus of the popular sovereign. By the "exception" Schmitt refers specifically to emergency powers of the state—that is, the authority to suspend the law in the service of preserving order. "The exception, which is not codified in the existing legal order, can at best be characterized as a case of extreme peril, a danger to the existence of the state, or the like. But it cannot be circumscribed factually and made to conform to preformed law. It is precisely the exception that makes relevant the subject of sovereignty, that is, the whole question of sovereignty" (p. 6). The fundamental characteristic of sovereign authority is both inside and outside of the established or constituted political order—it essentially operates on those elements outside the established order but *within* the ring of sovereignty.

Schmitt (1996/1932) writes further that "the concept of the state presupposes the concept of the political" (p. 19), and "the specific distinction to which political actions and motives can be reduced is that between friend and enemy" (p. 26). The political is defined in terms of an antagonism and, in particular, the power to differentiate friend from enemy, to decide on who or what constitutes the outside. There is a spatial demarcation in which the existence of any state depends upon the distinction between an inside and outside, a friend and an enemy. This is not necessarily a territorial division as much as an existential one. Indeed, Schmitt writes that "every state provides . . . some kind of formula for the declaration of an internal enemy," the essence of which takes the "form of a verdict on life and death" (pp. 46–47). The point I wish to emphasize is that, in Schmitt's account, both sovereign authority and the existence of a political community depend upon the determination of an exceptional element—either the enemy (an existential exception, which need not be a geographical "outside") or the state of emergency (a temporal and historical exception), which suspends the law (the political order). The fundamental political distinction in turn determines the conditions that both identify the exceptional moment and inform the direction and dimensions of sovereign action.

How is Schmitt's account of sovereignty useful in this discussion of representation? First, it provides a productive position from which to understand the conventional conceptualization of sovereignty, but one that offers something other than agonizing analyses that search for the locus of sovereignty in physical bodies, formal constitutional schemas, or institutional arrangements. Schmitt's innovation lies in his assertion that the essence of sovereignty is a *decision* that is itself *groundless.* It is essentially self-referential. That is, it comes from outside the recognized and legalized institutions of social and (small-p) political practice and can be grounded in nothing other than the decision to maintain a particular order. Of central concern is the *act,* the decision, which determines them. Second, Schmitt's analysis also points to a particular problem of representation, namely, the displacement of the *internal* difference onto the materialized, external exclusion. This internal difference is represented "empirically" in terms of the friend-enemy, Us-Them distinction.

There is also a central, illuminating paradox in Schmitt's presentation. Slavoj Zizek (2000c) calls attention to how Schmitt reveals the groundless act of the pure decision and how "it is not possible to pass directly from a pure normative order to the actuality of social life—the necessary mediator between the two is an act of Will, a decision, grounded only in itself, which *imposes* a certain order or legal hermeneutics (reading of abstract rules)" (p. 114). For Zizek, Schmitt's decisionist formalism signifies the decision *for order itself* and *not* the decision for any positive, normative order. Under cover of Schmitt's sympathies appears the radical abyss of subjective freedom, the pure decision without recourse to reasons—which themselves are only a selection among the a priori alternatives of the established (willed) order. This is an important insight for the possibility of a different political ontology.

The ambiguity in Zizek's use of Schmitt suggests the complexity of making analytical and tactical use of Schmitt's (and Zizek's) decisionism. There is an open question concerning the *level* at which the sovereign decision is made, and this resembles a classic problem of public administration—the politics-administration division. As we shall see, the question has central importance for rethinking politics beyond the People and representation.

Consider two statements from Zizek. In the preface to the second edition of *For They Know Not What They Do* (2002), he writes, "Marx's old notion of the 'dictatorship of the proletariat,' reactualized by Lenin, points precisely in this direction, trying to provide an answer to the crucial question: *what kind of power will there be after we take power?*" (p. lxxx; emphasis in original). In *The Ticklish Subject* (2000c), he writes, "there is none the less something inherently 'terroristic' in every authentic act . . . a proper political act unleashed the force of negativity that shatters the very foundations of our being" (p. 377). There are two different tactical approaches to the exception implicit in these statements. In the first, there are intimations of the Leninist model of the vanguard party that refuses to wait for the "revolutionary moment" and in its act suspends the symbolic network of the existing political order. The vanguard seizes the conventional apparatuses of state power. In the second statement, the political act seems to acquire the level of subject constitution and marks these processes with profound political import *as processes.* The intervention and transformation is at the "micro" level of human interaction.

The question turns on the relationship and/or distinction between these two events or conceptions of the sovereign act. More precisely, we need to inquire as to the domain of the Political as such and the locus of its production. On the one hand, if the Political act proper concerns the revolutionary event of seizing state power, the question of the status of the external "universal" imposition of order as an arrest on subjective transformation must be confronted. If, on the other hand, the subjective act is the proper Political act, it is possible to conceive of the seizure of state power (e.g., in the name of "the People") as an act that arrests transformation (the suspension of the predicative Good of the model) at the level of the subject since the post-act project of the revolutionary seizure becomes consolidation of the regime. Subsequent "exceptional moments" are thus defined through the lens of regime preservation and representation, extension and/or reproduction and *not* the "authentic act"; social production would seem to take the form of social *reproduction* of the "sovereignly" established model.

There is rich potential in situating the decisionism suggested by Schmitt/Zizek in Foucault's microphysical materialist conception of power and normalization (which will be seen most explicitly in chapter 5) and then analyzing this through the model-copy theory of representation outlined above. In shifting the site of the sovereign decision on the exception, it is possible to conceive the decision on the exception in a less dramatic, *conventionally political* manner. This illuminates how the microdecisions on the exception work to reproduce a regime of *representation* that sustains the macrocapacity to recognize and decide on the exception at the level of the state, such that the state (or government) properly "represents" and protects the social (i.e., natural, self-regulating processes that define the model). In effect, this also serves to de-reify the administrative state and public administration insofar as it allows us to see both representation as other-than-governmental representing of a popular will and governing beyond the domain of the governmental.

Constitutionalism and the Hole in the Law

Is this a plausible way of conceiving sovereignty? What questions or problems should be posed to Schmitt's argument? Let me note two important points of criticism. John McCormick (1997) argues in his study that Schmitt's insistence on making the exception the whole question of sovereignty "is patently false and as [Schmitt himself has suggested] a dangerous position. The exception does not reveal anything, except perhaps that eighteenth- and nineteenth-century liberals were politically naive about emergencies" (p. 153). McCormick's point is that there is no *necessity* for elevating the provision for emergency to the categorical definition of the sovereign, the constitutional provision that trumps all other provisions, as Schmitt does. Certainly, constitutionalism's "metaphysical bias" (p. 155) against contingency does not perforce render it an untenable juridicopolitical system. Along similar lines, Chantal Mouffe (1999) criticizes the friend-enemy distinction as reductionist and not "permitting of a differential treatment of this conflituality" (p. 5). Pluralism becomes impossible if there can be no legitimate dispute among friends who share the same symbolic space. For Schmitt, all difference is necessarily antagonistic; democratic association is impossible.

I want to suggest that the problem of the exception in constitutionalism, however, is not merely a matter of surviving the truly "exceptional" instances at which the constitutional regime is in peril, but more commonly and pervasively, in smaller, exceptional instances that permeate the general terrain of governing and replicate the logic of a political ontology. It is at this level of analysis that the fundamental issue lies. Beyond the "existential crisis" of the regime manifested in states of emergency, Schmitt calls attention to the inherent "gap" in the law. This, of course, is nothing new. To take but two classic statements of the indeterminacy of the law within the (more or less) liberal tradition, consider these statements by John Locke and Thomas Hobbes. In the *Second Treatise,* Locke (1988/1689) writes

> Many things there are, which the [law] can by no means provide for, and for those must necessarily be left to the discretion of him, that has the Executive Power in his hands, to be ordered by him, as the publick good and advantage shall require: nay, 'tis fit that the [laws] themselves should in some Cases give way to the Executive Power, or rather, to this Fundamental Law of Nature and Government *viz.* That as much as may be, *all* the Members of the Society are to be *preserved.*
>
> This power to act according to discretion, for the publick good, without the prescription of [law], and sometimes even against it, *is* that which is called *Prerogative.* (§§159–160)

In *Leviathan,* Hobbes (1991/1651) made a similar point:

> The bounds of that Power [i.e., authority], which is given to the Representative of a Bodie Politique, are to be taken notice of from two things. One is their Writt, or Letters from the Soveraign: the other is the Law of the Common-wealth. . . .
>
> And because such Limitation is not alwaies easie, or perhaps possible to be described in writing; the ordinary Laws, common to all Subjects must determine, what the Representative may lawfully do, in all Cases, where the Letters themselves are silent. (p. 156)

However, Schmitt's criticism, analogous to his point regarding the constitutional exception, is that liberal constitutionalism seeks to conceal the subjective dimension of a judicial decision beneath legal formalism, the naturalness of the judgment. Law in the liberal constitutional setting is conceived as merely technical or mechanical. In Schmitt's view, the tendency toward legal formalism is connected to the dominance of scientific thinking. "The general validity of legal prescription has become identified with the lawfulness of nature, which applies without exception. The sovereign, who in the deistic view of the world, even if conceived as residing outside the world, had remained the engineer of the great machine, has been radically pushed aside. The machine now runs by itself" (1985b/1922, p. 48). The shift Schmitt identifies is, in a manner of speaking, from transcendence to immanence. The break from the monarch as sovereign to the People as sovereign relocates the origin of divine order and embeds it in the all-inclusive immanent plane of natural and physical process; an analogous argument was advanced via Foucault above. At the same time, sovereignty, consistent with Foucault's arguments, also becomes "mute" and in need of representation.

What Schmitt attempts to convey in his emphasis on the indeterminacy in the heart of the law is, at one level, the moment of human subjectivity that adheres in the moment of *decision.* The judicial is both more and less than the mere application of a general legal rule. Here Schmitt's critique of constitutionalism and legal formalism join at the question of the decision of the exception, the problem of the political. There is a moment of existential decision not simply in the decision to stand in a relation of enmity to another nation-state but potentially in every act of judicial decision making. To this we can certainly add *administrative action* as well. This is the dilemma of administrative discretion and why so much hinges on it. For what is determined in the moment of discretion is not simply the discrete act but the ontological condition of the state itself, which is *made up* in an infinite number of "decisions" on the exception and the replication of a specific relation or logic. Representation, again, seeks to arrest those decisions by regularizing and homogenizing thought and action. When this "works," societies are stably produced and politics is afforded a limited "common sense." When representation breaks down (as it inevitably must), social orders must account for their failure and disintegration against the background of unity and rethink the way in which the decision on the exception will proceed.

Properly speaking, it is the existence or *Life* (zoë) of the state, or, to follow Goodnow, the People, that comes into question with the exception as it manifests itself in moments of administrative and legal decision. Yet the gap of the decision that is exposed in this exceptional moment is merely conceived through the insistence on fulfilling the popular sovereign will, adherence to the law rather than being a condition beyond all prescription of law; the subject is effaced beneath technique. It is referenced to the (proliferating) predicates of the model of representation, which insists by virtue of its status that it be replicated. What is at stake in modern politics is this exception, zoë or Life itself, which is conceived as homogenous and representing a common form (bios). Following Giorgio Agamben's (1998/1995) elaboration of Michel Foucault, modern politics, including the seemingly benign constitutionalism, is a unique form of the *biopolitical.*

Because biopolitics takes Life as its object but obscures the fact that it is indeed taking particular *lives* as objects, this form of politics disperses the state of the exception through the social field and thus deploys myriad dividing strategies and models of representation throughout the social in order to fabricate the People—to create the unity our ontology commits us to. As I have suggested already and shall argue further in the next chapter, this is a function of the disembodiment of sovereignty, a division between the supposed locus of power and the institutions of formal authority.

Conclusion

In a series of lectures delivered in 1975–76, Foucault (2003/1997) announced, "The manufacture of subjects rather than the genesis of the sovereign: that is our general theme" (p. 46) Foucault consistently resisted viewing his work through the lens of sovereignty insofar as such a lens itself insisted on viewing power as repressive. Concomitant to this was a refusal to attribute the conventional "excessive value" (1991/1979, p. 103) to the problem of the state. "To pose the problem in terms of the state means to continue posing it in terms of sovereign and sovereignty, that is to say, in terms of law. If one describes all these phenomena of power as dependent on the state apparatus, this means grasping them as essentially repressive: the army as a power of death, police and justice as punitive instances, and so on" (2003c/1977, p. 122).

In lieu of the state and sovereignty, Foucault considered "government," which, he argued, is "a question not of imposing law on men, but of disposing things: that is to say, of employing tactics rather than laws on men, and even of using laws themselves as tactics—to arrange things in such a way that, through a certain number of means, such and such ends may be achieved" (1991/1979, p. 95). Govern*ment* is perhaps still too narrow to describe these activities, and deprives us of a useful term to differentiate domains of authority and knowledge. However, govern*ing* as the "conduct of conduct" (Foucault, 2000a/1983) captures the general activity of governing yet allows us to still differentiate among modalities and locations within which the conduct is conducted.

Foucault's shift from state to the conduct of conduct, though, invites us to view law in an essentially technical, tactical manner. Rereading the classical liberal conception of law—here expressed through Locke and Hobbes—via Foucault, law is decoupled from embodying the common good (see Dean, 1999, pp. 118–123). A *technical* capacity is identified in the law that thereby links it with various other techniques deployed to "legitimately" augment calculability and the directionality of social practice under the auspices of some *teleology*—that is, a common good, public interest, objectivity, way of life, and so on. It can be linked, in other words, with the model and copy logic of representation. Technique—two are considered in the next two chapters, on law and administration—is the mode of producing and assessing copies rooted in models. A political relation that is fundamentally technical is also fundamentally restorative: restorative, that is, in the sense of bringing the model into reality, the production or realization of the "actually existing" model of biopolitics.

The drive to fulfill the model generates the related commitment to control, manage, and often extirpate elements that disrupt the stabilization of reality and the integrity of the One. Representation, then, has less to do with stasis, with a literal fixed model, than regularity, stability, equilibrium, or *calculability* that in itself is ontologically constituted by the moment of exception and by the breakdown of an impossible calculation. Government, conceived in the broad Foucauldian sense, is concerned with the exception, which can be identified and determined in the first place only if there is a standard or model of calculability. Otherwise, how can we discern the good copies from the bad? The friend from the enemy? On the terrain of modern biopolitics, these models must be conceived of as representing immutable fullness, regularities of the order of things.

To return to a conventional political idiom, if representation were to be an answer to the inconveniences of the state of nature or, more portentously, the Hobbesian "warre of all against all," representation in fact would produce precisely that total war in this project of fabrication. Representation diffuses and generalizes combat under the naturalized auspices of the model's homogeneity and distribution. That is, the struggles for the position of the truth, to occupy and represent the gap that cannot be represented, are propagated through the social field. The exception becomes generalized. It is this multiform combat, the material working out of the political ontology of representation, that produces the effect of the popular sovereign, the very stability of the notion that there is the "People's Thing" which conventional politics can represent, a P/politics of Truth. To qualify Foucault's efforts, the problem of modern biopolitics is born at the moment in which "the manufacture of subjects" and "the genesis of the sovereign" are one and the same.

4
Law

I concluded the previous chapter with a decision to analyze the local deployments of representation insofar as these are the sites at which models of representation are operative and through which the People is fabricated or "made up" (Hacking, 1999/1986). That is, I will be considering the sovereign decisions on the exception that, in fact, work to fabricate the "object" of political representation itself, the popular sovereign, and arrest transformation at the level of the processes of subject-constitution in various states of the situation. Thus, here and in the next chapter, we will be concerned with questions of political technologies: the modes by which the logic of representation concretely is deployed throughout the social field to fabricate the People. The model-copy relation is put to work in different ways in different historical periods. Yet in spite of these differences, these technologies remain oriented toward the project of fabrication—of bringing into reality the unity that the political ontology of representation presupposes.

The rule of law or, more precisely, the *rule by law* was the primary technology for the fabrication of the People during the American nineteenth century. Asserting that law is a technique challenges an important premise of U.S. civic theology, namely, that the law is a source of legitimacy.[1] Indeed, this assumption is abundantly evident in the core projects of what McSwite (1998) call the "new normativism" of theorists such as John Rohr. In spirit if not content, this move is nothing new. Law has figured centrally in the intellectual history and practice of American public administration since the field's "official" conception in the Progressive Era. The very rationale for the development of a sophisticated, centralized administrative apparatus was held to be the carrying out or *execution* of the law in a more efficacious manner—or, in the words of Frank Goodnow (1900), "bringing about harmony between the making and the execution of the law" where law was thought to be "the expressed will of the state" (pp. 76–77). Was it not the case that the relation between the making and the executing was widely perceived to have broken down, thereby precipitating the deleterious infusion of (small-p) *politics* into the executive function? Was there not a perceived inadequacy of the rule by law? This was the essence of Wilson's (1887) now timeworn observation that it was "getting harder to *run* a constitution than to frame one." Administrative questions needed to be brought to the fore if a constitution were to *run,* if law were to be carried out, and if the popular will were to be executed. Law required a supplement.

It is ironic, then, that public administration was viewed as a *solution* to problems associated with the breakdown in the rule of law, since law, or rather administration's perceived deviation from and/or contest with law, has come to present such a problem for administration. To appreciate the conundrum law presents for administration—or, more precisely, how law presents administration as a conundrum—we need to ask, What is it that public administrationists *refer* to when they speak about the importance of the rule of law? What is in question and at stake in attempts to reestablish the supremacy—and, presumably, by extension the efficacy—of the law? The primary issue presented in law is not law per se, but rather whatever purports to *stand behind* it. Law is thought to embody something "higher" but nonetheless to be socially immanent since the actual sovereign People create the law even if they only represent a higher order. There is a Politics above politics, a popular will above any individual's, a public above self-interest, and a vantage from which to make these determinations. Law is a category no one is above and, as such, stands above everyone. As Ostrom (1989/1973) suggests, there is not or ought not to be a sovereign exception to the law.

Thus when public administration talks about "law" it both *is and is not* talking about positive law, the products of legislatures and judiciaries. There is a distinction between the higher Law embodied in the Constitution and the specific laws made by legislatures, reviewed by courts, and carried out and complied with by administration (Corwin, 1928). As there are two modes of P/politics, there is *l*aw, and then there is the *L*aw. Another double. More precisely, there are particular laws and then there is the Constitution, which is presumed always already to represent the life of the American People without exception. What positive law aspires to do is to represent this "higher" referent—the constitutional kingdom of Law and Life. But, as Locke and Hobbes suggest, positive law is quite often not adequately specific, as is evident in the gaps of administrative or judicial discretion, or it is specified but in apparent contradiction with higher Law or other pieces of positive law. To pose the division in everyday language, in the former cases, government is always to govern in accordance with the letter of the law (when the law correctly represents the Law), *except* when it must govern in accordance with the spirit or the *sense* of the Law, that is, when technical law is incorrect or under- or overspecified. Government is instructed to act according to the spirit or sense of Law; it must know when laws can be broken.

This split has not gone unnoticed in public administration. In *Public Administration and Law,* Rosenbloom and O'Leary (1997) write: "Today's public administrators must know the law as it affects their activities, and they must act in accordance with it. . . . But it is only a beginning. The law is ever changing and often ambiguous. The public administrator should assess its spirit as well as its narrower precedents" (p. 319). The notion of "sense" is essential to Rohr's (1986) conception of the Law. He writes, " 'sense' is emphasized because it captures the movement towards the particular and the concrete and away from the universal and the abstract. . . . Administrators who are steeped in constitutional traditions of this sort will have a profound sense of professional propriety. They will have a principled basis and, above all, a 'sense' for when to bend and when to hold firm" (pp. 193–194). Taking a less flexible attitude toward law and its sense, Chandler and Plano (1982) write the following of about Law/law: "The rule of law is embodied in the United States Constitution where it buttresses the doctrine of limited government. . . . Administrators at all levels of government are guided in a general sense and governed in a specific way by the concept of the rule of law. If they attempt to substitute their own judgment for the law, the courts will overturn their actions" (p. 379).

The task of this chapter is to demonstrate the construction of the Law and its sense through exclusion and the affectivity of the instrumentality of technical law. I will proceed in two parts, corresponding to these two dimensions of the Law, its sense and its technicity. The first part examines the general structure of the Law, which, I will argue, is essentially an empty space, a gap or void. The conflation, however, of the Law and the People generates the need for the determination or positivization of the empty space. I then turn to the question of how the "content" of the People is generated, both in terms of how the structure for the provision of content is invented and how this content is altered through biopolitical contest. Using the psychoanalytic concept of *fantasy* I then examine how the object of the instrumentality of the technical law is materialized and consider the relationship between the technical and higher laws. Then, in the second part, I shift to examine the regime of law in nineteenth-century America and how it worked to fabricate the sense of the Law, to manage the emptiness that is the very heart of the objectivity of the Law, and finally, how its failing efficacy produced the necessity for a new regime of biopolitical (re)production—administration.

Law: Constituting the People

It is the structure of *L*aw that permits the initial articulation or generation of the People. It is in this way that *l*aw emerges as technology productive of a specific ordering and social production and as an instrument of rule, rather than as a source of legitimacy. I wish here to show that the objectivity of Law is a rupture of indeterminacy where the People is "located." It is this location that constitutes the possibility for models of representation and the authority to command a way of life. Law becomes the Life of the People. In the terms of chapter 1, constitutions conflate a particular, qualified form of life, bios, with the whole of biological life itself, zoë.

I will call this particular collapse of zoë and bios, the historical nexus of popular sovereignty and the rule by law, *constitutionalism.* (I am confining my analysis to constitutionalism in the United States in which the identity of "We the People" and the document of the Constitution are acute and explicit, and so must accept the charge of parochialism [Farmer, 1995].) How does this collapse occur? Constitutionalism produces a position of objectivity precisely by conflating the Constitution with the Life of the sovereign People. The Constitution-as-Law becomes the horizon, as Rohr (1978) notes, for the historical being of a People and the objective reference for authoritative discourse and judgment. The popular, constituent power that fought the revolutionary struggle is deposited into the Constitution, a document crafted in accordance with the habits and life of the People. Antonio Negri (1999/1992) writes, "The constitutional political then becomes a sort of transcendentalism of reason, a free place on which collective freedom can be constituted. It frees us from any subjection to the social, and from all the passions that prevent us from dominating the social.

. . . Outside this political space, the social has a voice only as violence or anarchy: the consequences are known. . . . Through the political, society is returned to freedom, to an organized freedom" (pp. 167–168).

The objective empty space in the Law from which one might authoritatively judge among competing representations is, however, generated by bringing the determination of the People's way of life into the political realm; Life (zoë) becomes the object and terrain of constitutional politics. The objectivity of rational judgment hinges on a determination of the Life of the People, the particular element embodied in and brought into history by the Constitution and unexceptionally shared by the inclusive immanence of the nation. Political struggle within constitutionalism, fundamentally, becomes a struggle over Life and the determination of the natural, objective position that *authorizes the force of Law.* Victory in these political struggles, what can be called a biopolitical struggle, similarly authorizes the command for *representation,* for replication, of the model and the hierarchical array and distribution of copies.

It is important to keep in view that all this takes place *within* the Constitution; no sovereign "outside" is permitted in this construction. "Without the constitution, outside the constitution, outside the constitutional machine and the organism of government, there's no constituent power" (Negri, 1999/1992, p. 161). In other words, there is no element or position outside the Constitution that might speak for "the People." The Constitution defines an *all-inclusive* immanence; there are no exceptions to the Law. It is rather only by capturing or occupying zoë, the objectivity of the Law, or what the political theorist Claude Lefort (1986/1980) exactingly has called the "empty throne" of the popular sovereign, that one's judgment might be called authoritative. It is the opening of this position of the Law that mobilizes the logic of representation. In representing the life of the People, the Law organizes a multiplicity according to relations of the Same. There *becomes* only *one* People, whose life, habits, values, and so on are represented in the Constitution. There *becomes* only a *whole* People, a People that without exception lives under the rule of its own Law. Everyone is subject and sovereign, both legislator and object of the Law. It is the Law, the Life of We the People, that appears as the model of representation posited initially in the Constitution and, subsequently, in positive, technical law.

The schema of constitutionalism, this manifestation of the political ontology of representation, presents two practical problems. The first problem is, by what mechanism will the position of Law be given positive content? This problem may not be immediately evident since constitutionalism presupposes the positivity of the People. That is, it presupposes the actual existence of the People. We saw in chapter 3 why this cannot be so. This move conceals at least two decisions. First, there is the decision concerning the One itself, that is, the positing of the unity behind appearance and difference that generates the constitutive exclusion. Second, there is the sovereign decision that selects the specific terms and predicates of the model that allows for judgment and the fabrication of the People in specific states of the situation, and which subsequently compels ordering and distribution based on a copy's capacity to represent the predicates deposited in the model. The second problem follows from this—by what mechanism or process will the accuracy of competing representations be judged? There are two dimensions to this question. First, by what criteria will we know that the representations of the People as government are *really* accurate representations? When We look in the mirror of representation, how will we know it is Us? This is the problem of what I will call the *domain of sense.* Second, perhaps more fundamentally, how will constitutionalism be justified in light of the natural order of the People and, then, how can it sustain itself as a system of representation? How will it contain deviations and monsters that contest the terms of the model or do not accept being represented as such? How will it confront the fact of exclusion in the face of its universality? Difference in the face of a presumptive unity? Here, the constitutive exclusion comes into play as the materialized state of nature and another mode of the legal, the technical law, emerges as the technology of sustaining constitutionalism and fabricating the People.

Embodied and Disembodied Sovereignties

While a constitution might be said to embody the way of life of the People, the popular sovereign itself does *not* embody the Law as the medieval or absolutist monarch embodied sovereign power since it has no physical body. The event of sovereign embodiment is dramatized in Ernst Kantorowicz's (1957) classic text *The King's Two Bodies: A Study in Medieval Political Theology,* which details how the double image of the king's body, underpinned by the body of Christ, incarnated the feudal community. Kantorwicz quotes Edmund Plowden, a seventeenth-century thinker:

> the King has in him two Bodies, *viz.*, a Body natural, and a Body politic. His Body natural (if it be considered in itself) is a Body mortal, subject to all Infirmities that come by Nature or Accident, to the Imbecility of Infancy or old Age, and to the like Defects that happen to the natural Bodies of other People. But his Body politic is a Body that cannot be seen or handled, consisting of Policy and Government, and constituted for the Direction of The People, and the Management of the public weal, and this Body is utterly void of Infancy, and old Age, and other natural Defects and Imbecilities, which the Body natural is subject to, and for this Cause, what the King does in his Body politic, cannot be invalidated or frustrated by any Disability in his natural Body. (p. 7)

The king's body was double—both mortal and immortal, individual and collective. But the sovereignty of the "king's" body and the community transcended the death of the actual person of the king. The sovereign was eternal and perpetual, and thus the king's body could not be given to God, and neither could it have been killed (Agamben, 1998/1995). The royal body entered a relation with death that was not, strictly speaking, one of being deceased. Some immaterial surplus of life survived physical death and was unleashed into the world. This surplus was quickly enclosed within the domain of another royal body. The king's body "contained," both in the sense of possession and confinement, this surplus of life, the excessive element. With the People, however, it is different. There is no container, and this immaterial surplus is let loose into society.

Lefort (1986/1980) provides an elegant description of the popular sovereign's difference apropos of embodiment. It is worth quoting this passage at length:

> The modern democratic revolution is best recognized in this mutation: there is no power linked to a body. Power appears as an empty place and those who exercise it as mere mortals who occupy it only temporarily or who could install themselves in it only by force or cunning. There is no law that can be fixed, whose articles cannot be contested, whose foundations are not susceptible of being called into question. Lastly, there is no representation of a centre and of the con-

> tours of society: unity cannot now efface social division. Democracy inaugurates the experience of an ungraspable, uncontrollable society in which The People will said to be sovereign, of course, but whose identity will constantly be open to question, whose identity will remain latent. . . .
>
> The attempt to sacralize institutions through discourse is directly related to the loss of the substance of society, to the disintegration of the body. The bourgeois cult of order which is sustained by the affirmation of authority, in its many forms, by the declaration of rules and the proper distances between those who occupy the position of master, owner, cultivated man, normal man, adult and those who are placed in the position of the *other,* this whole cult testified to a certain vertigo in the face of the void created by an indeterminate society. . . .
>
> It is the image of society which is homogeneous in principle, capable of being subsumed to the overview of knowledge and power, arising through the dissolution of the monarchical focus of legitimacy. . . . what emerges is the image of The People, which, as I observed, remains indeterminate, but which nevertheless is susceptible of being determined, of being actualized on the level of phantasy as an image of The People-as-One. (pp. 303–304)

While the association of the sovereign People and the territorial integrity of the nation-state and the famous image of the Hobbesian Leviathan suggest otherwise, the People as a body politic in fact lacks a physical body. It is not a pregiven and therefore prepolitical material referent; rather, the coherence of the People is constructed through the processes of representation and animated by the experience of unsettledness and anxiety caused by "a certain vertigo in the face of the void" and the indeterminate quality of being.

Combining elements of Lefort, Jacques Derrida, Jacques Lacan, and Antonio Gramsci, Ernesto Laclau and Chantal Mouffe (1985) have described the way in which the People is *articulated* through a process of *hegemony.* To briefly summarize a complex and sophisticated theory, hegemony effectively entails the coming of a particular element or constellation of the social into the empty, open space of the People's throne. Laclau writes

(2000), "*The universal is an empty place, a void which can be filled only by the particular, but which through its very emptiness, produces a series of crucial effects in the structuration/destructuration of social relations*" (p. 58; emphasis in original). For Laclau and Mouffe, the battle for this empty position (in the present theoretical chain, throne, Law, zoë) is a *hegemonic* struggle. Within the context of what I have called constitutionalism, hegemonic struggle is also more basically a *biopolitical* struggle because what is at stake is not merely the determination of the identity of the universal but also the determination of the very Life, the existential condition of what it means to be as a "We." This is the way in which the empty position at the heart of constitutionalism is given content and establishes the terms of the model.

The gap between the disarticulated social field and the particularly articulated People generates a not insignificant institutional problem. Lefort captures something essential in the difference between the popular sovereign and, let us call it, the *embodied sovereign.* Again, the popular sovereign is *not* as such in the same way that the monarch is visibly sovereign and *the* sovereign. Rather, the People is a position, an "empty throne," through which successive representations of the One move. In popular sovereignty, there is a split between the institutions of government and the popular sovereign, which is *not* and can only be represented. Unlike the embodied sovereign, the institutions of government do not embody the excessive element, which is diffused through the social field and simply on loan to them. Though not in direct possession of sovereignty (it is delegated to them through representation), institutions possess coercive authority to act in the name of the People-as-One. The positivity of the People (not as object per se, but as articulated values, sense, Life, etc.) remains posited as the ultimate ground of this authority, yet this ground is paradoxically without substance.

The People is a "split sovereign" in which power has been dislocated from the sovereign body (indeed, representation is the presupposed decoupling of position and power) yet has not been invested in the apparatuses of government directly.[2] Power remains disarticulated and unrepresented. The basic contradiction here is: while the People-as-One is articulated from the field of power, thus constituting an authoritative representation and content for the empty throne, the assumption of that empty throne itself is nevertheless not justified as contingent articulation temporarily occupying the People's empty throne but rather through the presupposed ability of the articulation to represent and speak for the People-as-One. Representatives of the People are not ironists.

Fantasy and Split Sovereignty

The movement in the creation of the split sovereign of the People can be illuminated through Slavoj Zizek's (1989, 1992, 1993, 1996, 1998) remarkable discussions of *fantasy* and ideology. Consider constitutionalism and its split sovereign directly. In the first move, the People conceives of and willingly submits itself to its Law in order, as I will consider later, to escape the inconveniences and caprices of the state of nature. Yet this, too, is a forced choice of sorts since the Constitution created an entity ready for action in history, and in establishing limitations on government it wards off both tyranny and the inconveniences of the state of nature. Indeed, a space is cleared in the Law, zoë, that is the empty throne of the People, and the multitudes submit to the representation of the sovereign People.

However, we are confronted immediately with the failure of the Law and the fact that the constitutional "machine that would go by itself" is constantly breaking down, a paradox that will receive particular attention in chapter 6. The thing that is critical to appreciate here is that attempts to fix the machine occur on two levels: the struggles to produce for the state "pretenders" to the People's throne and the deployment of microlevel, situational models of representation. First, hegemonic articulations and biopolitical confrontations are produced to occupy the throne and categorically determine the predicates of zoë, the People. Here, I consider the affectivity of fantasy. Zizek (1998) identifies seven dimensions of the fantasy. First, fantasy is not merely the dream of a secret desire but a Kantian "transcendental schematism" that makes it possible to desire; it "teaches us to want to desire." Second, fantasy has two dimensions: fantasy$_1$, a beatific, stabilizing dimension of the society without disturbance or breakdown, and a destabilizing fantasy$_2$, "whose elementary form is envy" (p. 192). The affectivity of fantasy$_2$ accounts for and explains the failure of the utopianism of fantasy$_1$. Fantasy$_1$ may be viewed as the *very idea* of a People, and in American history there are any number of formulations of fantasy$_2$ (slavery, corporate concentration, and, I will argue later, government itself), going back to the very rationale for revolution. I will rely heavily on these two dimensions of fantasy in the sections and chapters that follow.

Third, fantasy creates a variety of different positions and identifications for the individual subject to occupy. One may shift among subject identifications within the fantasy but must accept identification as such. Fourth, as suggested above, fantasy collectively organizes individual desire from these subject positions. Fantasy answers the ontological question for the subject, what Lacan writes as *Che vuoi?* What do you, the Other, want from me? (2006/1960, p. 690; see Zizek, 1989, pp. 110–129). "Fantasy provides an answer to this enigma; at its most fundamental level, fantasy tells me what I am for my others" (Zizek, 1998, p. 195). In representation, this is answered politically as "I am an American. I am part of the People." More generically, though, fantasy answers the question "What does it mean to be?" It provides the answer or content to this ontological question: to be is to be as a People. Fifth, fantasy has a narrative function that arranges temporal sequences in order to resolve an inherent antagonism. The issue confronted with narratives, however, is that they always presuppose what they produce (p. 197). The best example of this in the ontology of constitutionalism is the liberal state of nature narrative. Here the antagonism that needs resolution is the presence of the governmental itself, which, in manner of speaking, is a symptom of the very failure of the Law (of Nature). This production of failure to maintain the success of the logic is integral to the political dimensions of representation.

The sixth element of fantasy "is that on account of this temporal loop, the narrative fantasy always involves an impossible gaze, by means of which the subject is already present at the act of his or her own conception" (Zizek, 1998, p. 200). Finally, seventh, "the fantasmatic narrative does not stage the suspension-transgression of the Law, but rather is the very act of its installation, of the intervention of the cut of symbolic castration" (p. 202). That is, a story stages the "moment it all went wrong" and embeds a diagnosis and remedy for social failure. The field of public administration itself is *precisely such a narrative,* and every reform movement embeds a diagnosis in a historical narrative of disjuncture. It answers the question "What exactly needs to be reformed?"

There is, however, a second "level" at or dimension in which the People is being produced. While the ontology of the One supports the plausibility of the People in fantasy, it is supplemented or complemented at the level of the production of reality, in the micro, material structuring and structured practices of everyday life. This is not merely to inject a kind of Foucauldian riff into this Lacanian melody. Zizek (1989) has called attention to the relation of the interface of structuring, nondiscursive practices of the everyday and their relation to fantasy. Fantasy works on the subject, but the subject also puts *fantasy to work;* and in putting the fantasy to work, social relations and practices are inscribed with the logic of fantasy. These logics are a kind of code inscribed in social practices that gives them a silent directionality; for this reason nothing is ever neutral. To this point, in *The Sublime Object of Ideology,* Zizek argues that belief in the fantasy "is always *materialized* in our social activity: belief supports the fantasy which regulates social reality" (p. 36). This is how a political ontology is reproduced, dispersed, and sustained. Its basic relation is taken up and put to work in various discourses and fields of practice. Developing Marx's notion of commodity fetishism through a Lacanian prism, Zizek demonstrates how belief is materialized in these "objective" practices of everyday life. So, even if I do not actively believe in the fantasy, the nondiscursive structures and practices of life "believe for us." For example, I might very well know that "the People" as such does not exist as an object for electoral representation, but I might nevertheless continue to go to the polls and accept the outcome as a legitimate expression of the "popular will." This is why the critical question of *doing* something other than representing the People is critical; a reflexive consciousness itself is insufficient since commonly accepted practices and institutions continue to believe for us. A definitive change in the mode of social reproduction, the conducting of conduct, is required.

As suggested in the final sections of chapter 3, it is at the level of material practices and states of the situation that fantasy$_2$ needs to be examined. Emerging from fantasy$_2$'s particular diagnosis of failure of the unified, undisrupted society, *political technologies* are deployed to manage the People's ontologically constitutive failure. That is, fantasy$_2$ is not merely the diagnosis of failure. The particular construction of the fantasy simultaneously entails the prescription of techniques for effacing and controlling the exclusion. In this way, the biopolitical ambitions of representation and constitutionalism impose a heavy and dangerous price since, first, hegemony "speaks" as the People-as-One or from the place of Life (zoë) and second, ontologically, there *can never be a harmony since the very ontology of the constitutional political demands the constitutive exclusion.* Paradoxically, with political technologies the constitutional pretension is, in fact, reversed. We think we get a government to represent the interests, habits, and life of the

People. But government through technology is, in fact, producing, creating, and sustaining the particularity standing at the place of Life. We think we get a limited government but, in fact, we mobilize the whole of the social for political ends. Here is where fantasy$_2$ comes into play in a manner analogous to the structure of the decision described previously. It is true, as Zizek (1996) suggests, that fantasy$_2$ can be conceived of in rather dark, catastrophic terms, as, for example, "the foreclosed obverse of the Nazi harmonious *Volksgemeinschaft* returned in the guise of [the] paranoiac obsession with 'the Jewish plot'" (p. 116). But, like the earlier discussion of Schmitt and the exception, it need not always be so dark, ominous, or obvious. More generally, fantasy$_2$ prescribes the course of action for the particularity occupying the position of the People by formulating a *narrative of failure* or breakdown asserted as a "positive" program. But the program is positive only in that it attempts to *positively* define the exclusion and create a target of and space for governing. A People-as-One fantasy$_1$ is articulated, and it is maintained through its recourse to its depiction of the failure in fantasy$_2$. But fantasy$_2$ is also the location from which the "political program" is conceived in this failure—what (or who) needs fixing and how.

The Domain of Sense

The dilemma of the gap between the disarticulated, disembodied "locus" of political power and its articulated, instituted particularity conditions the necessity for producing, stabilizing, and managing a *common sense.* This sense must account for both the necessity of representation and the operative hegemonic representation. What is required is a strategy for managing the nonrepresentable, constitutively excluded element in both these matters. How does constitutionalism accomplish this? Constitutionalism grounds its fantasy$_2$ in the state of nature. By positing this fictional point of departure, two of the central issues are want of a common judge and the problem of "calculability." I have already considered in the discussion of the split sovereign and hegemony how the process of providing particular criteria for the "common" occurs. Here, I will focus on the production of calculability, that is, the authoritative institution and implementation of modes of material ordering that are (re)productive of a common sense.

As our story goes, in the state of nature there are certain "inconveniences." While men and women once lived under natural law, they were also self-loving and partial to "themselves and their friends" and so might go too far in the punishment of others (Locke, 1988/1689, §13). Thus, a *political* or *civil* society (§89) appeared by people "agreeing with other Men to joyn and unite into a Community, for their comfortable, safe and peaceful living amongst one another, in a secure Enjoyment of their Properties, and a greater Security against any that are not of it" (§96). Government as the common judge emerges from this presuppositional commitment to serve an essentially technical function, that of a neutral arbiter of disputes and general executor of, and punisher under, the laws of political society, or civil (positive) law. I will call this kind of law "technical law" to distinguish it from the Law of the Constitution. Government executed functions through law designated to it with the *consent of the People,* who themselves had constituted a *single* political or *civil* society (§§87–95, §104). "*Supream power*" remained on the side of the People, who merely delegated authority to government: "there remains still *in The People a Supream Power* to remove or *altar the Legislative*" (§150). It must be stressed that, despite appearance, it was not law qua law that underwrote political legitimacy but rather the efficacy of law in fulfilling its designated technical functions—namely, to make more *calculable* the affairs of the state of nature through a "Standard of Right and Wrong" (§§123–124) in constituted civil or political society. In other words, law worked as a technique that presupposed the Law and worked to realize a harmony, one lost in the state of nature, now to be regained in political society. Government through law, in this way, was a strategy for rendering the natural Law of society embodied in the Constitution more certain, more regular. Technical law was a *political technology* for achieving this.

A *domain of sense* establishes a symbolic, discursive space in which law can operate legitimately. Technical law generates a division of signification that determined what was within and what was beyond the Law. Even when zoë, the all-inclusive immanence of life, became the topography of the political, an exclusion is still required by the logic of the Law. Technical law, I emphasize, did not accomplish this in terms of a simple distinction between the legal and illegal. Rather, the division was expressed in terms of a specific domain of sense within which law could operate, one within which the "illegal" is also selectively and purposefully organized and administered. The illegal is not beyond the Law any more than it is necessarily a function of the literal text of the law. The illegal along with the legal is constituted *within* the domain of sense of the Law. The Lockean formulation gave Law the ability to embody an implicit standard of judgment, a *positive and specific* domain of sense. Resting upon a popular will, this domain could be called the "common" or the "neutral," which marks it as legitimate. However, the designation of "common" again obscures the constitutive judgment that has already been made which constitutes the common; some element has been excluded in order that the common might be defined and given content; this is an exclusion that proceeds according to the representational logic outlined in the previous chapter. The force of the designation of the "common" permits a particularity to legitimate itself as the natural and neutral position of the People through hegemonic articulation, as that which is presupposed to be universally shared (or *ought* to be shared) by all the actual people. Correct judgment, then, becomes merely a function of representing, or of replicating, the naturalized judgment of the People. Indeed, judgment should not seem to be judgment at all, but merely the exercise of common sense.

How are these decisions and exclusions made? Given representation's originary decision to an ontology of the One, constitutionalism, first, defines the People with regard to an exclusion in the legal terms of citizenship. However, even within the category of citizen a domain of sense must be defined from which, secondarily, specific categories of the People are hierarchically distributed, excluded by virtue of degrees of distance from the predicative content of the model. There is a division in kind, and then an array of differences that is contingent upon the terms established in the model. This is where the particularity installed in the throne mobilizes its authority to govern on and through the processes of life immanent to the social field. That is, the particularity represented in the model articulates a vision of the People-as-One called fantasy_1. Fantasy_2 provides a diagnosis of breakdown and failure and embeds within it the specifications of a reforming project that operates directly on social relations and produces a reorganization of the social in an attempt to produce the sense appropriate to the operative fantasy.

Technical Law: Regulating the People

The Idea of Technical Law

I want to shift and focus specifically on how technical law was put to work in fabricating the People in nineteenth-century America since the technicity of law—i.e., law as an instrument of social reproduction—is difficult to see from behind the veneer of the idyllic "stateless" American nineteenth century. Public administration has stubbornly failed to identify generative, "purposive" functions because it has continued to search for "administration." Conceptualizing administration as a political technology for fabricating the People turns attention to techniques and modes of social reproduction and away from legal formalities. Thus the analogue to administration in the nineteenth century is found not in the professionalized national administrative state but in state and municipal law operative in the nexus of the national court-party governance regime. Technical law is actively and persistently deployed in the nineteenth century to produce a "well-regulated society."

The *technicity* of the law means that law was used to instrumentally bring about a determined conception of the Good. Technical law worked to realize a conception of the Law. The promotion, therefore, of a defined conception of the Law relied upon it being articulated from an authoritative social position that was recognized as representation of the Law itself. This understanding of law is deeply informed by Foucault's (1991/1979) studies of the governmentalities of modern societies in which "law is approached not as a source of legitimacy . . . but as an instrument of rule" (Dean, 1999, p. 130, n.1).[3] Here, I both accept and qualify the claims of Foucauldians such as Mitchell Dean, who would argue that in liberal societies, law as an instrument of sovereignty is displaced by the "postmetaphysical" norm, which "depends on values that are relative to the group and are revisable rather than absolutes . . . [and] no longer emanates from the sovereign's will but from the collectivity without being willed by anyone in particular" (pp. 119–120). Michael Hardt and Antonio Negri (2000) have made a similar point about the notion of sovereignty expressed in the U.S. Constitution. "Against the modern European conceptions of sovereignty, which consigned political power to a transcendent realm and thus estranged and alienated the sources of power from society, here the concept of sovereignty refers to a power entirely within society" (p. 164). To a point, I think that this is all accurate.

However, law derives its force because of its purported representation of the popular sovereign's (objective) "higher" (though socially immanent) Law, which itself refers back to a higher natural law and a clear ontological commitment. Again, it need not represent an objectivity in the naive sense of the object, but it must bear the mark of the common, a kind of normative neutrality, to ground its authoritative, hierarchical imposition. Rather, it is precisely the nexus of the immanentization of the law and the retention of a transcendent and positive *position* of Law that give form to biopolitical struggle, the apparent neutralization/naturalization of the rule of law and the drive to instrumentally realize the model. Thus, Hardt and Negri (2000) are correct when they qualify their enthusiasm for constitutionalism and identify in it an "imperial" (not imperialist) logic which begins with an *internal* (or domestic) empire that takes representation as its weapon—the dominating command, often by violence and force, to replicate and normalize (which often takes the apparent "democratic" form of the rule of law.)

Judicial Decision and the Reconstitution of the "Common"

In the history of U.S. law, there was an important rift between the common law tradition inherited from England and the democracy of the new Republic, perhaps a movement from *discovering* natural legal rules through precedent or custom to *making* legal rules that characterized the displacement and qualification of some of the new Republic's English legal inheritance (Horwitz, 1977, p. 2).[4] While varying considerably from state to state, transformations in the common law during the course of the nineteenth century also saw the drive to codify case law into statute.[5] (The exception to the colonial reception of common law is Louisiana.) Here, the common law was, in part, folded into the larger revolutionary rejection of the perceived arbitrary, secretive, and undemocratic nature of sovereign authority and judicial prerogative. This was, for example, particularly evident in the growing unacceptability of common law crimes that "boiled down to the assertion that if the federal judiciary possessed jurisdiction to impose criminal sanctions without a statute it would be able to obliterate all constitutional limitations on the federal government" (p. 10). How could citizens know how to act and behave if the law itself was unwritten and unpublicized? This was to be a "government of law and not men."

Two points warrant comment. First, it is possible to view the "withering" of the common law as itself indicating a breakdown in the conception and identification of the "common" in both its institutional form and content. That is, in terms of form, the erosion of the judicial action as bearing the mark of the common qua application/discovery of a natural legal rule is consistent with the general republican sense of the supremacy of the legislative assembly as the primary instrument through which the voice of the People could speak. It is indicative of the immanentization of the Law and the "disembodiment" of sovereignty described above. However, as seen in chapter 3 and as was suggested earlier, immanentization did not displace the notion of Law, which simply was buried in the mute, organic processes of Life. In terms of content, the breakdown in the common law signals a breakdown in precisely that common sense that the common law carried. That is, the common law operated in and was sustained by a symbolic network that allowed for the closing of the "gap" of the Law, and thus grounded authoritative judicial decision and was recognized to be a representation of natural law.

Second, immanentization does not resolve the problem of the gap. The passage from common to statutory law and its coincidence with the "growing perception that judges no longer merely discovered law; they also made it" (Horwitz, 1977, p. 15) displaced the locus for the determination of the common from the court to the legislature and a naive positivist view of language. But embracing the literality and specificity of statutory law (and not men) *does not* resolve the problem of sense. To paraphrase Fredric Jameson (1981), even if we agree on what a text says, there remains the question of what it *means.* In other words, there is the implicit question, left to the courts, of the inevitable interpretation of legal statute. But what form would this interpretation assume? How would the act of interpretation be conceived? How could the common be conceived? Here, in the moment of the inconclusiveness of the technical positive law (more fundamentally, of language itself), it was to be *common law* that would fill in the gap. But what was the common law now?

As Morton Horwitz (1977) suggests, the years following the revolution witnessed the search for "a unitary foundation for both statute and common law" (p. 18). In our terms, the resolution to this dilemma was the coincidence of bios and zoë and the creation of a biopolitical state. John Milton Goodenow wrote in his influential 1819 *Sketches of the Principles and Maxims of American Jurisprudence,* "The judge . . . of a criminal tribunal is *governed* himself by *positive* law, and executes and inforces the will of the supreme power, which is THE WILL OF THE PEOPLE" (cited in Horwitz, 1977, p. 16; emphasis in original). The People and its will grounded the establishment of constitutions and positive law made by legislatures duly created by those constitutions. Thus, while the locus of the model and its representation shifted to reflect the splitting of sovereignty, this shift can hardly be labeled "postmetaphysical." The "norm" represented in *both* statute and common law would ultimately be reducible to the posited but unlocatable unity of the People. This, in turn, would justify the legalization of "Our" customs and ground a conception of judicial decision as an instrument of popular will, while the products of legislative deliberation were already justified by virtue of their creation by representatives of the sovereign People.[6]

In summary, the former distinction between a positive law enacted by a legislature in furtherance of the will of the sovereign (or state) and common law application and adjudication in specific incidents of dispute broke down and collapsed into one another. Common law application increasingly could be seen as the "supplement" to statutory written law since both were conceived of as emanating from the same source, the People. This movement, however, inaugurated two fundamental changes in the way in which individual cases were considered by the judiciary. First, individual cases began to be viewed as "matters of law" (Horwitz, 1977, p. 28) or moments in the Law. That is, individual cases became instances to be viewed through the prism of a general Law. What *question of Law* was being addressed in a given case? The second change followed from this. Location of the grounds for decision "outside" the situation necessitated conceiving the situation itself in light of some higher or ultimate end represented in the Law. This, in turn, required the determination of that end; the model must be given positive content. The "empty universality" of the People's Law must be provided with particular elements to be represented in the positive law itself.

Producing Order by Technical Law

The previous section sketched the way in which the common law took on a "positive" instrumental function in judicial decision making. The contentiousness of judicial discretion and the sovereign decision, however, did not go away. Briefly, this is visible in three ways. First, beginning in the last quarter of the eighteenth century, at the state and municipal level, there are the beginnings of a movement to elect judges. Although "there was no simple way to compare elected and appointed judges . . . it was felt, if judges were not elected, how could the public be sure that judges would respond to the public will?" (Friedman, 1973, p. 111). Second, state legislatures frequently turned to constitutional amendment as a means for arresting undesirable judicial decisions by specifying constitutional provision. This was part of a trend that continues through today—the proliferation of specific provisions in state constitutions. Over the course of the nineteenth century, state constitutions exploded: in part because political conflicts were settled through amendments that incorporated the wish of some particular faction or interest, and in part because of a growing sense that "the constitution would control the problem of bad laws through its own, overriding superlaws, which took the form of anti-laws; that is, (constitutional) laws against (legislative) law" (p. 303). The upshot of this was, paradoxically, *increased* judicial review of state statutes in light of the often contradictory "thickening" of constitutional prescription (p. 312). Finally, third, it could be argued that the lingering anxieties caused by the hole of the Law were certainly part of what gave impetus to the movement of legal formalism (anticipating administrative neutrality), which would propose to base legal hermeneutics on the deductive reasoning of the natural sciences (pp. 334–335; Scheweber, 1999) and subsequently formed the target of the twentieth-century pragmatist legal rebellion, legal realism (e.g., Fisher, Horwitz, & Reed, 1993).

I will set the issue of the courts and judicial action aside and turn attention toward the other axis of the court-party regime of nineteenth-century American government (Skowronek, 1982). As suggested in the second point above, courts were not the only "instruments" producing the common good. State legislatures and municipal authorities were also aggressive in their pursuit of realizing a positive social order through law. First, however, I need to say something about the function of parties in this regime. Then I will consider the high level of social regulation during the nineteenth century and examine particular means for handling the exclusion.

As is well known in the folklore of public administration, with the exception of the Civil War years, national governmental institutions in the United States during the nineteenth century were skeletal. Postal and custom offices and, episodically, the military (itself highly decentralized) constituted the bulk of federal employees. In the national government itself,

> the most pressing operational problems were how to integrate the support services of national government with these widely scattered regional centers of action and how to maintain an overall coherence

> within this broad dispersion of governing power. An ingenious solution was found in the cohesive procedures of parties and courts. . . .
>
> The success of the early American state came to depend on the working rules of behavior provided by courts and parties. These two nationally integrated institutional systems tied together the state's peculiar organizational determinants and established its effective mode of operations. They coordinated state action from the bottom to the top of this radically decentrated governmental scheme. (Skowronek, 1982, pp. 23–24)

Party organization, patronage, and internal discipline linked local sites to the national government and "brought a measure of cohesion to national politics and a measure of standardization to governmental forms and processes throughout the federal system" (p. 25). Here, parties fulfilled a regularizing and integrative function and less a national programmatic one. Summarizing this view, Richard Bensel (1990) observes, "The nineteenth century patronage-based party system was characterized by issueless competition" (p. 5). Similar to Fox and Miller's (1995) argument about contemporary postmodern, symbolic politics, the system was a political "factory," in the metaphor of historian Ronald Formisano, that churned out a steady diet of campaign and Election Day spectacle. Certainly this reflected the general absence of any effective national structure as well, making any national policy more style than substance (Wiebe, 1967, p. 32). Courts supplemented the parties' "all-consuming electoral machines" (Skowronek, 1982, p. 27) by determining the meaning of the law and using the law instrumentally to define and intervene within the parameters of governmental action in the economy and society.

But while national policies were arrested by the absence of a robust administrative apparatus, state and municipal authorities acted widely and deeply to regulate behavior and to conduct conduct. This regulation has been demonstrated comprehensively in William J. Novak's (1996) exceptional study of law and regulation in nineteenth-century America, *The People's Welfare.*[7] By his own account, Novak is out to dispel the "myth of American liberty. For this book argues that the storied history of liberty in the United States, with its vaunted rhetoric of unprecedented rights of property, contract, mobility, privacy, and bodily integrity was built directly upon a strong and consistent willingness to employ the full, coercive, and regulatory powers of law and government" (p. 17). Novak recounts how municipalities in nineteenth-century America extensively deployed government's police power to regulate the large and small of American social life through law. Naturally, none of this is visible if regulation is viewed as an exclusively federal or national phenomenon. Using Novak, I will note two of the ways a positive social order was fabricated: economic regulation and the common law of nuisance.

Nineteenth-century American society was highly regulated and conducted. In the economic sphere, local governments passed extensive "product laws" that were designed to constrain cheating and fraud in commerce. These statutes detailed the way vast arrays of products were to be manufactured and sold, including "strict controls on packaging, weights and measures, and quality and merchantability; branding; inspection and certification; restrictions on exportation; oaths; and, of course, penalties (fines and seizures)" (Novak, 1996, pp. 88–89). States took a strong role in the granting of professional licenses, which, in the nineteenth century, concerned far more than "routine public registration" but were special privileges given by the state "granting permission to do that which was otherwise illegal or against public policy" (p. 90). In some states, this could be something as seemingly straightforward as selling a ware for profit. The liquor license is the one of the most obvious remnants of this practice of licensure; however, nineteenth-century governments exerted the right to license a wide range of goods and services, including timber, jewelry, and printed books.

Morality and manners were similarly dictated by state regulation, which often took the form of "moral suasion" via criminal law and the more contemporary association of police power with authoritarianism (Novak, 1996, p. 153). Much of the force of public morality law was trained on constraining dangerous behavior in the home and policing and controlling the exceptional "dangerous classes" in public under the broad authority of the *common law of nuisance* (pp. 60–62). In the nineteenth century, nuisance law embodied the maxim *sic utere tuo,* "use your own so as not to injure another." In this way, nuisance was neither a "trifling inconvenience" nor cover for "capital-friendly" judges to relax liability standards. Rather, it referred a powerful "public ordering principle" that vested government with wide authority to regulate public and private behavior, dispose of private property, and radically circumscribe individual liberty in the interests of social order. Novak writes, "Declaring an activity or establishment a nuisance in the nineteenth century unleashed the full power and authority of the state" (p. 62). "Full authority" was conceived in terms of restraining another's injurious behavior; it was viewed as the protection of one's liberty against the infringements of another. Nuisance did not recognize rights (including that of property) in any absolute sense but only rights relative to an unspecified community standard. Here, nuisance appeared to serve the same function as the common law supplement and, in turn, opened it up to precisely the problem of judicial decision, namely, the ability to maintain and recognize a good *in common.* In this operation, the positive and constraining action of government in protecting the Law was complemented by the structuring delimitations and exclusions of law.

Exclusion and the Bounds of the Law

Exclusion through law fundamentally turns on the status afforded various claims on the content of the Law. This is a quite practical and straightforward problem. It is easier to define, delimit, and maintain the bounded domain of legal sense if the claims on the content of that domain are themselves restricted or *bounded out* by the law. More directly, it is a lot easier to have a common sense or sense of the community when who "counts" as Us is categorically and legally restricted. This section specifies some of the ways in which technical law operated to bound out and constrain legitimate claims on and determination of the content the Law.

There are at least three ways of managing the exclusion through law, depending on the form the exclusion takes. First, there is keeping out those who are not here, the *kept-out.* Second, there is excluding those already present but categorically excluded, the *written-out.* Third, there is excluding those who are not only physically present but partially "included," those "poor copies" described in chapter 3. We can call them the *included-out.* It is impossible to be exhaustive here; rather, I want to simply touch on the various ways in which the integrity (again, in the double sense of the perceived moral and structural integrity) of the People was maintained through exclusion by providing several historical examples of how such an operation could work. Like the "dangerous" behaviors that became the object of nuisance actions, these are all materializations of the liberal state of nature, the constitutive exclusion, those unruly elements that one way or the other threaten the calculability of the social order.[8] Again, calculability can be understood in an absolutely practical way: legal exclusion restricts the positions that must be accommodated in the Law. Exclusions allow for the production and sustenance of a common sense *and* the production of the recognition of the mark of the common when it appears.

The Written-Out. The U.S. Constitution, soon after it declares itself in the name of We the People, quickly exercises a division between those who shall and those who shall not be counted-as-Us for purposes of congressional representation. In article 1, section 2, counted are "the whole Number of free Persons," which included free women and children and indentured servants. Excluded are "Indians not taxed" and slaves, who are to be considered three-fifths of a person. As Hardt and Negri (2000, p. 171) observe, African American slaves were both partially written in and written out. They are three-fifths in and counted as a *person* (in fact, as considered below, included out) and two-fifths out, counted as property; human and nonhuman hybrids that lucidly illustrate the mechanism of excluding the included.

Perhaps more radical is the exclusion of the Native American, who was a "negative foundation" for the constitutional order (Hardt & Negri, 2000, p. 170). This is true in a double sense. First, in the profound arrogance of this anthropological age, Native Americans were conceived as being in an "authentic" state of nature. In other words, Native Americans were viewed to be not simply materializations of the irrational and wild dimensions of Nature; they were the materialization of a *natural* and *past* time of white constitutionalists themselves. They materialized an actual past and thus were not even permitted to be present in the new time of the revolution (see Fabian, 1983). But Native Americans did not mark merely a temporal frontier or boundary; they also marked a spatial one. Analogous to their status as past-in-the-present, the visibility/invisibility of the native made the constitutional frontier possible. That is, Native Americans were "invisible" because "if they had been recognized, there would have been no real frontier on the continent and no open spaces to fill" (Hardt & Negri, 2000, p. 170); yet they were "visible" in that their line of withdrawal and extermination marked the "progress" of the march of constitutional Law across the continent and the bloody erasure of the materialized past.[9]

The Kept-Out. Though the first federal immigration statute was not passed until 1875, Gerald L. Neuman (1993) challenges the mythology of America's open and unrestricted boundaries and demonstrates that restrictions on who might be admitted were prevalent and extensive throughout the nineteenth century. Again, these were often not federal statutes. The categories will not surprise us. Particular states barred convicted felons, those with contagious diseases, and the disabled, though the success of *physically* barring those people was limited. Less obvious were the extensive limitations that "sovereign states" imposed on the internal immigration (i.e., state to state) of free blacks. In the antebellum period, slave states generally barred the entry of free blacks who were not already residents, and some "often required that emancipated slaves leave the state forever, on pain of reenslavement" (Neuman, 1993, p. 1868). Testifying to the nebulous category of "citizen," even some sovereign free states, such as Illinois, constitutionally forbade the entrance of free blacks into the state; others, like Iowa, statutorily restricted entrance (p. 1867, n.220 and n.221). With the end of the Civil War and the adoption of the Reconstruction amendments and Civil Rights Act of 1866 (which, in part, declared that all persons born in the United States were now citizens, without regard to race, color, or previous condition), black Americans shifted into the ambiguous category of the included-out, described next.

The Included-Out. Here, I will focus on the status of women and paupers. While it is well known that property qualifications were attached to the franchise in the early years of the Republic, it is less appreciated that by the 1850s states had essentially eliminated these requirements, replacing them with taxpaying or manhood suffrage provisions. Thus, in focusing on the removal of property qualifications, the subtle techniques that restricted penetration into the domain of the political commons remain out of sight. Critically, the political and legal exclusion of women and the dependent poor or paupers coalesced around the category of "independence," which turned on the ability to freely dispose of one's labor power (Cott, 1998; Steinfeld, 1989). And at the heart of this notion of independence was the presupposition that the *dependent* lacked sufficient will for *self*-governing and so were unfit for political life.[10] These were qualities that, unlike the instrumental and dynamic potentials of the People's Law/law, were posited as *inherent and natural* incapacities.

With the fading of property requirements, a new division among the propertyless emerged—the wage earner and the dependent pauper—to accommodate what Robert Steinfeld (1989) identifies as a tension between, on one hand, the republican conception that property ownership conveyed independence and testified to a commitment to the community and, on the other, the revolutionary universalism of "all men being created equal" (p. 338). In defending the rights of what was effectively the *commercial* class, it was argued that "in a commercial society one would have to look to something other than property ownership to determine whether people were truly dependent. Rather, one would have to examine their balance sheets" (p. 359). The central question was whether men had the legal right over their persons. On this score, the poor did not meet the mark. Until the 1880s many of the non-wage-earning poor entered into a dependent labor relation with the towns from which they received relief—they were under the direction of others (often even when they worked for their alms) and were not the autonomous arbiters of their own fate; they were "unfree" insofar as they no longer had control over their own labor power. Paupers were broadly disenfranchised directly or indirectly through poll taxes.[11]

Women, though, were the foundation of this included-out mode of constitutional exclusion. As Nancy Cott (1998) argues, "The model for the pauper's dependence lay in domestic relations. If the essence of the pauper's lack of self-governance was his inability to dispose of his own labor, the same was true of the wife's position" (p. 1453). Here the form of dependence of state and pauper mirrored the household relationship of husband and family.[12] Though the nineteenth century saw significant improvement in the civil status of women (e.g., the Married Women's Property Acts of the 1850s [see Gignesi, 2004]), political and legal participation came more slowly. Indeed, even after the passage of the Nineteenth Amendment, many states refused to allow women to serve on juries. The issue, again, was female dependency, at the center of which was marriage.

The many and "innovative" ways in which white men acrobatically contrived to legally restrict and oppress women cannot be recounted here. The single point I wish to emphasize, following Cott (1998) and Stivers (2000), is how the realm of male political independence was constituted through female dependence. Cott notes how "independence . . . for the male household head existed in counterpoint to the dependence of others. Having and supporting dependence was *evidence* of independence" (p. 1452). The primary technology for reproducing and sustaining this relationship was, of course, marriage. Marriage carried a woman into a relationship of dependence that rendered her "incapable" of disposing of her own labor, at the same time as it took from her what was still the most visible symbol of political independence, property. In marrying, men were elevated to a state of independence and rendered qualified for the public realm. Even after the passage of the Married Women's Property Acts, courts continued to refuse to grant women control over the value of their own domestic labor, justification for which was grounded in the "natural" and naturally bounded capacities of women (pp. 1453–1454).

Representing the People and the Biopolitical Fracture

In concluding, I wish to return to my general theoretical argument and explore why the peculiarity of this construction through law of the constitutional order makes it dependent upon general mechanisms of *representation.* The domain of sense, by positing itself as the natural and the common, posits a model of thought and action that demands to be replicated, or represented, and which, in exceptional instances, may assert a right to compel representation precisely because it expresses its actual partiality as the *natural* order of things. I must emphasize that this is *not* to merely say that the law or politics is *biased.* Bias remains embedded in a representational order that retains the possibility of *neutrality.* It harbors the hope that a better, less biased legal interpretation might be found, that the "real" law might be distinguished from its "distorted" execution or interpretation. The notion of bias merely declares that this copy is inaccurate, while retaining the grounding idea of the neutrality or naturalness of the model. Rather, my point here is that the world of constitutionalism is constituted by an elemental exclusion. It thrives on and demands the element that cannot be calculated, though it proposes a politics driven to calculability. The charge of bias, so to speak, merely declares a deviation from bios, the assertion of a single, qualified form as *the* natural and correct form; it is a moment in a biopolitical struggle. It is symptomatic of the inherent failure of the attempt to positively (or normatively) define an empty universality.

Social relations (even oppositional or critical ones) within the domain of sense function in terms of degrees of *Sameness.* There is a requirement of, to paraphrase Adrienne Rich (1986/1980), compulsory homogeneity. I do not mean strict adherence to an absolute ideal but rather consent to a domain of sense and the distributions of value and differences it establishes. The People is a partiality commanding the fabrication of a totality through the (re)production of representational categories that restrict and exclude. The People purports to express not simply *an* order, but *the* order, the natural order (though restricted as a member of the system of nation-states and Peoples), and on this basis justifies the command to reproduce and represent, and to decide on the state of the exception. The empty place of the throne is given authority, content, and programmatic direction through biopolitical struggle and the articulation of the two sides of fantasy. Technical law is the initial technology that seeks to produce a distinctive kind of social order, a distinctive mode of social collectivity, the People, which is conceived essentially as calculability or regularity.

In constitutionalism, politics itself is technical; this does not mean, though, that constitutionalism *de*politicizes or neutralizes politics. Rather, politics now takes the form of technology, and the scope of governing expands to the end of calculability and the fabrication of the People. Acting through law (initially), government exists to make more calculable the order presupposed in the hegemonic articulation. It is in this way that constitutionalism establishes the *necessity* for hegemonic struggles in order to institutionalize a vision of social order; though we ought not be distracted from the general logic of representation at work as successive articulations pass through the People's empty throne. In an ontology in which a natural way (model) of Life is presupposed and in which government appears in a functionally restorative mode, politics becomes a struggle for the definition over the terms of the model, a definition over what shall be calculated and rendered calculable. Hegemonic struggle over the calculative law becomes the technology for defining the empty place in Law, what shall be calculated, and in turn *the fabrication of the People.*

What is most critical to emphasize here is that it is *not* simply a vision of the People that is being produced. The production of the People, insofar as it is relying on this ontology, is an intervention in the processes of biological life and subject constitution. It is an intervention into the material practices and discourses that structure, delimit, and produce the coherence of those very same processes. This is done, initially, through technical law, rule by law. But, because there is necessarily indeterminacy inscribed into the heart of the Law, because the People as such *does not exist,* the technical law will *always fail.* This leaves the definition of the model eternally open to contest, especially in light of the presumptive universality of the People. Here, I agree with Lefort (1986/1980) and Laclau (2000), who argue that the popular sovereign inaugurates an open terrain of contestable politics. It is the ability to contest the terms of the universal in political hegemony that distinguishes and makes great the institutions and practices of constitutions. On the other hand, biopolitical struggle means that there is considerably more at stake than the mere articulation of a representation of the People. Modern politics concerns the determination of Life and the processes that "make us up." Yet it takes up these matters in a *specific* manner—that is, representationally.

The terms of constitutions prepare the conditions for injecting hegemonic struggles into the fabrication of the body politic itself and, more particularly, at the level of the individual subject of the Law. The gap between the technical (represented) law and the model Law establishes the grounds for repetitions as reforms that aim to render things more calculable in the face of the void. This process is met simultaneously by one that exacerbates the effects of the gap. As Fox and Miller (1995) note in their diagnosis and as I discussed in the section on state constitutional amendment, successive models are deposited or sedimented within the corpus of the law, laid down in institutionalized practices, procedures, and subjects. The problem is obvious. As successive "objectivities" produced by hegemonic political struggle in an effort to fully determine the People are deposited in the technical law, the law itself comes to contain competing, proliferating objectivities that are all premised upon the objectivity of the Law.

The capacity for law to generate and sustain a *common sense* is rendered highly problematic by the texture of the sedimented objectivities of technical law. That is, the effort to produce a successively more objective articulation of the Law through law, in fact, produces a corpus of technical law that is conflicted, disjunctured, and polyvalent even at the superficial level of syntax. Moreover, since law is a political technology *productive* of the People—the People as a collectivity and as individual subjects inscribed—the collectivity, its institutions, and its subjectivities become rife with conflicting representations of the model insofar as they are constituted by these antagonistic discourses and practices. Yet the notion of the model is retained, and it is for this reason that *integration* emerges as the central technical task for the government (i.e., public administration) of the twentieth century, displacing the primacy of the technical law.

What the representational logic of the People *proposes* to do is to incorporate successive regimes of law in the immanent, dialectical movement toward Law itself. With each hegemonic battle over the articulation of the People, the People is said to become increasingly more robust, the law more equitable and more discriminating, closer to the Law. More people get included into the People. The category becomes more encompassing, less divisive, and the gap between representative and referent narrows. But this is not at all what occurs; indeed, the effect is precisely the opposite. In the first place, the Law cannot be *realized* as a unity since the logic of representation requires an exclusionary moment. Incorporation into the corpus of law requires accommodation to the model-copy relationship of representation. This process indeed may be additive, but it is not cumulative or teleological. Second, the representational logic of Law/law in fact undermines the plausibility of the former and the efficacy of the later, all the while intensifying the *necessity* for the former. As successive models are deposited into the law and its internal objectivities multiply, plausibly "objective" readings and interpretations of the law correspondingly multiply. This increases the necessity for a reference that is outside (yet still posited as internal) to the Law in order to stabilize judgment and behavior and select from competing, contradictory laws. At the same moment, the destabilization of the law through the very contestation of its objectivity and, thus, the authority of binding judgment, raises and brings into doubt the possibility of the reference to Law. Simultaneously legitimate subject positions multiply through the law's own inventiveness, thereby multiplying the positions that must be represented in the law.[13]

There is a second fundamental problem with the law as a mode of biopolitical reproduction, and it concerns its generality. Certainly, law can penetrate into the life of individuals, reproducing social regularities, routinized calculabilities, practices of exclusion, and common judgment. In short, law can work to produce representations of the People. But whatever its ability to codify, enumerate, and specify, law remains a blunt instrument. It remains an instrument for the *general* both in terms of a categorical (e.g., citizen) and a "topography" supplemented by physical violence in lieu of "regulation" (Althusser, 1971/1970) and blatant violation of its own pretensions to universality. This problem of the general is wonderfully exemplified in an 1845 text on marriage law and women's nuptial legal rights. Antebellum legal writer Edward Mansfield lamented that the nuptial code was "too narrow in jurisdiction and too imperfect in its knowledge, to determine, regulate, or constrain those internal affections upon which, at last, the whole harmony of and efficacy of the marriage relation depends. Too many expect from law more than law can give" (cited in Grossberg, 1985, p. 30). Technical law could not penetrate to the level of the "affections." In its very generality, law gradually ceased to be able to fabricate the People.

Conclusion

From Law to Administration

Constitutions *constitute* (McSwite, 1997b). They are generative events that define the scope within which it is possible to live with one another and recognize certain objects and relationships; they embody ontological commitments. When the People's Constitution (bios) becomes conflated with Life itself (zoë), the question of transforming the constitution of the body politic (in the sense of how it is made up) is itself bracketed, and the future becomes simply the project of unfolding the logic of the promise of the People. It is in the context of popular sovereignty that politics is representation; it is a hegemonic struggle over the terms of the model. Left (un)defined as monstrous are *not* deviant representations per se but concepts or events of the Political that do not define politics in terms of representation, subjects who refuse representation and concede to the designated models. It is in this *double* sense that every notion of the People is partial. First, certainly, every vision of the People fails to articulate the whole. It is partial. But this is not the key point. The People is *partial in the way in which it insists on the very idea of defining or identifying a whole,* the way in which it insists on *a* (acting as *the*) model that defines the "naturalness" of the totality of social process. The People is partial in the limiting way in which it insists on representation as the machine of social (re)production and the model-copy relation of being-together. It presents a conception of the whole that not only is not whole (it is always "biased" or partial) but furthermore is a fully "cooked" conception of the final form of the human world itself. To be is to be as the People.

Second, the coincidence of zoë and a qualified bios produces not only a misrecognized theory of limited government but also a limitation on that which *can be lived.* This is the subtle invidiousness of popular sovereignty; the delimitation of what is deemed "livable" is justified in terms of a model of the natural, which is represented in terms of law. Yet there is no "higher" authority to which law can refer. The Law exists only as a structural possibility within the logic of representation. Neither it nor the People represent a priori normative content. Rather, the domain of the "common" is created by the instrumentality of law itself. It is when the efficacy of technical law fails that public administration emerges, a more intense and at once both more specific and more general technology to fabricate the People.

5
Administration

I turn now to examine the administrative mode of the biopolitical production of the People. Administration as a self-conscious enterprise emerges amid the breakdown in the regulatory efficacy of law and institutes a novel strategy in the movement of representation that I will call the *internalization of the exclusion.* Here, we will need to differentiate between the internalization of the exclusion and conventional techniques of inclusion because, certainly, brutal *ex*clusionary social practices persist in the administrative world. The internalization of the exclusion, then, does not name a particular political effort but an orientation toward the constitutive exclusion at the level of the abstract model-copy relationship that aims to maintain and reproduce the ontology of representation.

Consistent with the sedimentary, discontinuous-continuous logic we saw in law and representation more broadly, administration will be seen not to displace the technology of law but to supplement it in a specific fashion to the end of fabricating the People. Administrative practices begin in the traditional terrain of the local yet use these local reforms to suggest a means for national integration or fabrication. Further, public administration makes use of two seemingly contradictory integrative modes of fabrication which, following Camilla Stivers (2000), I will call *bureaus* and *settlements.* Stivers argues that the Progressive reform movement out of which a self-conscious public administration emerged was divided substantively between the work of the men of the municipal bureaus and the women of the settlement houses. These two sides of the movement represented rather different approaches to confronting the shame of the cities (p. 16). The bureau men saw the city as a business and emphasized a scientific approach to reform with a focus on efficiency, professional expertise, and structural change. Government was a corporation; citizens were stockholders who could call government to account for its actions but did not participate directly in governing (p. 69). In turn, they proposed reforms that focused on centralizing executive control, neutralizing the administrative apparatus in the face of the corrupt boss system, and systemizing the budget function. Settlements, by contrast, saw the city as a home and the citizen as neighbor. This sharp difference of metaphor led to reform initiatives that focused more on "improving living conditions" (p. 16) and enriching the relationships among science, politics, administration, and the citizenry. Rather than seeing administrative inefficiency as the source of urban disorder, settlements saw "city government in a new way, as a vehicle for ministering to its population's basic needs and for enabling people to take part in the process of deciding what to do" (p. 98) in order that larger public purposes could be advanced.

In opposing itself to the rough-and-tumble world of politics by attempting to clean up politics morally and otherwise, the reform movement as a whole became "tainted" with femininity. Stivers (2000) writes, "nineteenth-century electoral politics was a masculine realm. The paradigmatic citizen was the free, white, self-supporting man who joined with his fellows in open-air rallies and saloon gatherings (p. 8). Reform was coded as "women's work." But by summoning the rhetoric of science and its deeply rooted associations with masculinity in Western thought, bureau men "were able to counter and deflect the castigations of machine politics about their deficient masculinity" (p. 125). As McSwite (1997b) also suggest, the bureau men won out because of a particular "fit" between the sociohistorical context and the ideology of managerial science.

Despite these profound differences, I want to argue here that these two faces of reform, in fact, are not per se contradictory if understood within the biopolitical project of the People and the political ontology of representation. Rather than standing in tension with one another, they tend to resonate with one another, amplifying rather than contesting one another, as they emerge against the shared backdrop of the People and its presumption of harmony and Oneness. To advance this point, I will locate public administration amid a series of other administrative or *disciplinary* discourses and practices to reframe the conventional understanding of the unique functionality of the administrative state and the object of administrative action. Aside from declarations of public service and the public good, what ends does public administration serve? What is the proper object of the administrative state? How does its logic of internalization interface with other disciplinary, administrative sites and practices? We want to consider, in other words, the long-standing question of the "proper" boundaries and domain of public administration and the role of the governmental proper in society. Yet the question is here approached neither from the consideration of the content of the discipline, profession, or area of study nor by working backward from the imaginary divide between politics and society to the role of the governmental. Rather, public administration needs to be set in relation to a wide variety of other locations and discourses of governing the conduct of conduct across a disaggregated social field and differentiated by virtue of its unique disciplinary object.

Internalization

Charles Hyneman (1950) wrote in his study *Bureaucracy in a Democracy* that "the things that government does today cannot be accomplished by the enactment of laws alone" (p. 3). Hyneman's statement may serve as a hinge of sorts for the transition from the regime of law to the regimen of administration. In the first place, he intimates that law had become insufficient as an instrument of governing. There are things the law could not do. Second, he continued to recognize the use of law as an instrument. This is an important point to keep in mind for, as suggested above, what I am going to consider is *not* the displacement of law as an instrument of rule, but rather the ways in which it is *supplemented* by the technologies of administration. Richard Hofstadter (1955) captures this when he describes the Progressive attitude toward legality thus: "if the laws are the right laws, and if they can be enforced by the right men . . . everything would be better" (p. 203). Certainly, this was how Frank Goodnow conceived of administration: the right *men* to execute the law from specific locations and using specific instruments.

There is a shift, however, in the concept of law and the mode of the execution at the end of the nineteenth century. There seems to have been a shift from viewing law explicitly in terms of an instrument for rendering a social order calculable and as deriving from natural law to conceiving of law as being embedded in social process, from conceiving of law as embodying the life of the People to viewing the life of the People as being governed by social laws. There is a shift from a normative discourse of the People to an objective, scientific one, from the (particularly) common law to the neutral law. This simultaneously marks a shift of attitude and technique toward the exclusion, from bounding action through law to conceiving society more as a "planet" temporarily out of its orbit—a status to be remedied by administrative and scientific rigor and realignment. It is a movement that homogenizes beneath the routine of administrative and bureaucratic technique and generality, yet also particularizes and individualizes at the level of the given body or case. These bodies and cases become the focused target of representational techniques; the individual is now acted on by a variety of instruments and discourses that entail both a concentration and diffusion of authority. The loci of governmental authority shifts to municipal and, more slowly, national institutions, decentering the instrumental authority of state legislatures and courts. Local centers and spaces of expertise focus disciplinary authority but also consciously fragment and disperse biopolitical reproduction throughout various enclosures of expertise and legitimate authority.

The general process I shall describe in this chapter is the "internalization of the exclusion" (see Hardt & Negri, 2000, pp. 225–229). From the outset I want to be clear about the dimensions of this internalization because I do not mean to imply that, for instance, the three modes of exclusion outlined in the previous chapter were "brought in" under a happy Progressive big tent. Without question, brutalities of racism, sexism, and ethnic discrimination would persist and be eagerly and pervasively deployed during this period—certainly through to the contemporary moment. By "internalization" I do not mean to imply that group and/or categorical and coercive exclusion ceased to be a violent reality, producing a reality that depended on violence. But something did change. A different process was initiated that transformed the broader context of this violence.

By internalization I mean that at the level of reproducing the political ontology of the People, there was a shift in attitude and technique toward the constitutive exclusion. The exclusion ceased to be viewed as categorically *external* to the order of the People. Additionally, while the chronology and compression of these chapters might suggest otherwise, it is also important to keep in mind that internalization unfolds over the course of the twentieth century, as more of the "outside" is brought in and the predicates that define the People expand through confrontation with the term's pretenses to universality. This process of internalization is understood in two connected ways. First, consider it explicitly in terms of law and a transformation of the sociopolitical topography. In an earlier regime associated with the technique of law, Giorgio Agamben (1998/1995) argues that the state of nature and the state of law were conceived as distinct and separate. A constituted order brought the People in from the state of nature, though certain "natural states" persisted in the forms of categorical exclusions that were hedged out by law at the same moment law "guided" and produced the state of law. The People was produced and sustained by insisting on the externality of the exclusion. In the next movement (i.e., internalization), however, this exclusion—the state of nature—is conceived of as being *internal* to the state of law and therefore capable of being objectified and incorporated in various states of the situation. In a literal sense, nature is conceived as being internal to society and thus capable of becoming an object of control and rationalization.

How does the breakdown in Law unfold? In the realm of conventionally defined politics, as states of nature or *irrationalities* are recognized by and incorporated into the Law, the Law is "revealed" as an actual partiality working for particular elements of the People; the (normative) specificity of the Law is confronted with its own pretension to universality. This entails a destabilization of the model and the legitimacy of the compulsion to replicate and consent to the domain of sense. Common sense is no longer accepted as being in common. This is manifested, for example, in the call for the retreat of governmental action itself; indeed, like today, at the end of the nineteenth century "the only popular mandate that politicians in the nineteenth century received demanded an even further curtailment of their powers as the one cure for the government's failure" (Wiebe, 1967, p. 37). Nevertheless, the ontological presupposition of the People-as-One is retained, and a process of reconstituting, rebinding, in fact *fabricating,* the People—i.e., of bringing into reality the unity presupposed—began. The enterprise of public administration plays a central role in this project. Second, internalization entails a shifting relation of the rational to the irrational, or, more particularly, of the necessity of objectifying and neutralizing the latter in order to generate the place of administrative mediation and integration. Within internalization, the "irrational" shifts and becomes a subcategory of the rational and, by extension, an object for instrumental integration or *reform.* Paradoxically, this reduction generates an augmented terror of the irrational itself (Adorno & Horkheimer, 1976). In contrast to the Law/law's mode of exclusion, which defined *natural* (in)capacities of the exclusion to justify its location beyond the independent domain of the political, the exclusion comes to be coded in terms of an internal deviation or disturbance, which now will assume apparent "micro" and "macro" effects and produce corresponding forms of authoritative determination. Rather than being conceived as some sort of absolute limit separating the natural and political or dependent and independent, the exclusion is conceived increasingly, to take a term from Deleuze and Guattari (1987/1983) out of its context, as a *displaced internal limit.* Two examples will serve here that will illustrate the two related dimensions of rationalizing the irrational: scientific and political integration.

Scientific and Political Integration

A familiar example of the displaced internal limit of scientific rationality is Herbert Simon's (1997/1945) well-known model of the "Satisficing Man." Unlike the impossibly omniscient Economic Man, Simon's more modest Satisficing Man recognizes his inherent limitations (or, sadly, has "not the wits to maximize") and the uncertainty inhering in the decision, and so operates in a realm of bounded rationality. However, the recognition of limit, of course, applies only to the pathetic Satisficing Man and not to the formal organization, which becomes a complex system for rationalizing the "irrational," subjective element of the individual decision. Rational systems and decision processes are fundamentally "hedges" against subjective limitation (pathology). Subjective limitation, in turn, is itself rationalized through a subject-model of psychology that represents individual motivation for participating in an organization and, then, motivation and compliance once in an organization. Thus, organizational processes of rationalization represent this model of satisficing and, in essence, serve the expert function of identifying organizational, macrolevel irrationalities and, subsequently, advising systemic change that is concerned with individual, microlevel correction to the ends of macrolevel stability and rationally derived outcomes. Bounded rationality does not, therefore, recognize an *inherent* boundary to the rational but rather posits the irrational as a displaced *internal* limit to rationalization. In this sense, Harmon's (1989a) characterization of Simon's concession as an "artful caveat" is quite apt. While seeming to be a sensible accommodation to the critique of rationality, Simon really gives nothing away to anything. The formula of fantasy is on vivid display here. A model of the human is posited, replete with a diagnosis of its "failure," which prescribes a sophisticated battery of technical, managerial remedies. Significantly, on one hand, the mode of the subject homogenizes while, on the other, it recognizes (internalizes) the "subjective" element as beyond the boundary. *It is this element, then, that is subjected to rationalization by the organization.*

Next, consider political integration. Though, again, we cannot lose sight of the continuation of visible modes and methods of exclusion, neither can we afford to miss recognizing and understanding the less obvious discontinuities, exclusions, and transformations inaugurated by the pervasive and powerful discourse of the pluralism of interest group liberalism and integration. The shifts of the early twentieth century initiated within the logic of representation would unfold into the 1960s and ultimately stage a fundamental crisis of the regimen of administration. Internalization postponed confrontation with the emptiness of the People and the necessity of the hegemonic articulation of content, informed by the programmatic dimensions of fantasy$_2$. Internalization marks an attempt to take the presupposed universality and oneness of the People and the Law seriously and to view government as the neutral instrument or location (Wamsley, 1990; White & McSwain, 1990) for the simultaneous recognition of heterogeneity and its integration into the higher unity of the People. Again, though, the construction of the content of neutrality, the elevation of predicates, and the reduction of difference are required.

In a way, it must be appreciated that the advent of the pluralistic, integrative administrative state signals a genuine accommodation and recognition of categorical differences. Differences were to be celebrated but not, as the saying goes, differences that made a difference. Rather the administrative representational domain remains determined by the notion of what Brian Massumi (1992) names *the general in general,* a logic considered in the discussion of representational models in chapter 3. The entrance of categorical exclusions into the space of the People is contingent upon agreement to the terms of representation, on relations of essential sameness within their category or model of inclusion, and, by extension, degrees of resemblance vis-à-vis the operative model. These are genuine standards of deviation. This has a contradictory dimension since the assertion of a collective identity mobilizes resistance to exclusion yet this replicates the form of representational domination. To this point, Hardt and Negri (2000) write, "Precisely the structures that play a defensive role with respect to the outside—in the interests of furthering the power, autonomy and unity of the community—are the same that play an oppressive role internally, negating the multiplicity of the community itself" (p. 108).

Massumi (1992) frames the problem with greater precision: "a body can join with others deemed to be of its kind in carving out a customized social space for itself. It need not accept an identity category as is—but it must accept identification. It need not accept a particular general idea—but it must accept the idea of the general in general" (p. 124). That is, individual cases or copies of the model must accept one of the categorical subject positions opened for it by the articulated fantasy. As is well known, the administrative "agency" is posited as the neutral site for the integration of (macro) social interests regardless of what categories they are integrating into the "higher" order of the People or public interest. In this way, Wamsley's (1990) "agency perspective" is another "view from nowhere" (Nagel, 1986). This integrative functionality certainly also underlies John Rohr's (1986) charge to public administrators to "choose among their constitutional masters" (pp. 184–185) in furtherance of constitutional principle. Neutrality, constitutional principle, the agential perspective—these all require the elevation of predicates and the reduction to the proposition in the construction of the neutral *and* the simultaneous proliferation of technologies oriented toward first, producing precisely what is presupposed and second, stabilizing recognition of the neutral as such.

Thus the question is: What is the *relationship* between these "macro"-level issues of politics and the apparently more mundane but nevertheless weighty matters of administrative integration? Further, what is the relationship between public administration (narrowly conceived as governmental administration; running the Constitution) and other social processes? In displacing Law, the complex, governing processes of internalization would indeed transform the role of government proper. Yet for a set of institutions and structures already besieged by accusations of bias and colonization by particular interests that impeded the People's will, this transformation would occur strategically, purposively, and with considerable consequence. For specific reasons, government would need to be, in the felicitous phrase of Hofstadter (1955, p. 234), "severely neutral" in its expanded and active role in society and economy. It would act through and in conjunction with a host of scientific discourses and practices to control behavior in the present and predict it into the future from a depoliticized neutral zone. This neutralization, however, does not mean that politics is ending or that it marks a movement into a postpolitical world. The ontology of representation continues through the *p*olitical technologies of administration.

Bear in mind, too, that this is precisely the position occupied by Law under the rule by law. Neutrality substitutes for the commonality of the Law in the wake of the reproductive failure of technical law.[1] Professional competence substitutes for common sense (which was, again, never common in the sense either of being shared or being widely available). The particularistic universality of Law is displaced by an equally false neutrality. Amid these changes, the new profession or academic discipline (or enterprise or area) of public administration would emerge. Itself symptomatic of the failure of the constitutional machine that would go no longer by itself, public administration would retain the restorative vision of government, a regularizing and rendering-calculable political technology for fabricating the People. I turn now to sketch out the historical contours of the breakdown of law and the rise of administration in the biopolitical state.

Integration

The Contours of the Progressive Diagnosis

The Political problem of the People and its presupposed unity persisted in America through the nineteenth century. Ironically, it became increasingly acute not long after the end of the Civil War seemed to clear the way for the expression of a nation unified at long last. By the late 1870s, soon-to-be Progressives found themselves in a situation similar to that of the Federalists. As they surveyed the social landscape, they saw factionalism, the triumph of special group and individual interests, eroding the Republic. Class, in particular, was a cause of deep concern. Frank Goodnow (1889), for instance, in the first of two exhaustive articles on Prussian local government, commended Bismarck for developing an administrative system that "shall make it difficult for any one class of society to employ its powers of government for purely selfish ends" (p. 648). In Goodnow's view, Bismarck had succeeded in "neutralizing the effects of class prejudice and the conflict of social interests" (p. 666). In the second piece (1890), he concluded that "Prussia deserved the credit of recognizing that the administrative system is one of the factors to be taken into consideration in solution to this great problem—the conquest of human selfishness in the form of class tyranny" (p. 157). Where factions had plagued Madison, class appeared to be the cause of Goodnow's troubled sleep.

Class cut two ways for Progressives like Goodnow. Denouncing it meant positioning oneself in an apparent middle ground between the runaway capitalism of the robber barons and the "divisive" collectivism of bossism and the labor movement. Capitalism could not be left to the capitalists; community could not be left to the communists. Progressivism strategically posited itself as the reasonable and popular in-between. Many Progressive ideas, in turn, emerged to stand against, or rather *above,* the class, that is, factional, menace—the People, Society, the Public Interest, State, Nation, and so on. Each of these terms, however, speaks to the same biopolitical problem of the People. Each names a unity within which these destructive particulars could be subsumed; they are instances of Wamsley's (1990) "required transcendence." It was only by thinking through these purifying, harmonizing categories that the Progressives, a group disinclined to trust the capacities of the people, learned to stop worrying and love the People. While the symptoms of the crisis diagnosed by the Progressives remain objects of considerable historical dispute—so much so that some historians have wondered if anything usefully called "Progressivism" existed (Filene, 1970; Rodgers, 1982)—it is worthwhile nonetheless to try to sketch the general, if necessarily stylized, contours of the crisis as it appeared in the Progressive diagnosis.

American society had been mired in a cycle of economic depression for much of the last three decades of the nineteenth century (Licht, 1995) and, since the great railroad strikes of 1877, had been shaken by successive waves of violent labor disputes. The memories of the 1871 Paris Commune smoldered and remained for many an awful symbol of labor's power and possibilities (Painter, 1987, p. 24). But the economic explosions of the period rocked not only the rapidly developing American industrial sector; they also spurred the substantial uprisings and dislocations among American farmers that would inspire Populism and inflame sectional tensions over the future of the American political economy. Questions would be raised (and conflated), both domestically and abroad, about the civilizing necessity of empire building in tandem with the demand to open markets for U.S. products (Williams, 1969).

The upheavals in the economy brought concomitant upheaval in community and social life. Internal migration during the period, in particular among blacks, was massive. The insatiable desire of industry for labor also meant significant immigration. Lured by higher wages, nearly 15 million immigrants arrived between 1890 and 1914, and most stayed (Dinar, 1998, pp. 77–80, 150–154). Their origins shook the constitutional order as soundly as did their numbers. While immigrants continued to arrive from the traditional sources like Germany, Ireland, and England, most were "new" immigrants from southern and eastern Europe and Russia. Their arrival ignited a firestorm concerning the criteria of "fitness" for the People's democracy that left no corner of American society unsinged. The evaluation of the intellectual, moral and, by extension, political capacities of the new immigrants was integral to the Progressive discourse (Jacobson, 2000), and its interface with the perceived loss of community self-determination in the face of economic corporatization (see Galambos & Pratt, 1988; Roy, 1997) was critical in configuring the dimensions of the "crisis in the communities" (Wiebe, 1967, pp. 55–110). In this way, questions of bossism, corporate power, and eugenics constituted a common topography.

No less significant was the rupture of another domestic boundary—the one that unleashed a deluge of women into public life. As suggested earlier, Stivers's (2000) *Bureau Men, Settlement Women* lucidly recounts the prominent roles that women emerged to play, not simply as active reformers but also as actors influencing and shaping the agenda and consciousness of reform as *women,* and, further, by redrawing the boundary of what constituted and was recognized as belonging to the domain of politics. In their language of "municipal housekeeping," women redrew that boundary by explicitly *politicizing* areas of social life that had been naturalized under the regime of law. This is a lucid example of how exclusions could be internalized. As Amy Kaplan (1998) writes, the emergence of women into public life effectively extended the scope of the "domestic" sphere and constructed a "national domain" within which (largely white) men and women could unite in opposition to the "foreign" and alien in a defense of an imagined collective home. Stivers also details how these gender-infused tensions permeated the whole of the reform movement as women struggled to construct "another side of reform," perhaps not unlike the other side of politics that the new immigrants were slowly constructing in the boss system.

In sum, constitutional society had broken down. The definitional categories of the domestic and foreign, the inside and the outside, the People and its exclusion, were confused and in flux. Robert Wiebe's (1967) famous characterization of a "distended society" is quite to the point. "To distend" is "to stretch asunder, stretch out, extend; to spread out at full length or breadth" or "to stretch or extend beyond measure; to strain; to draw out of joint, to rack" (*OED*). The elements of exclusion—naturalized questions of labor, race, sex—had both seeped and been forced unpleasantly into the main channels of society, contaminating and corroding the People's order and its stable dominions. Progressivism, thus, was indeed a "healing tendency," as McSwite (1997b, p. 113) suggest; however, it was, more important, an effort to *re*constitute or extend the boundary, to restore or heal, not simply *order,* but *an* order. The *dis*tended society did not appear out of nowhere. It emerged against the historical backdrop of a well-"tended" society, a society well fitted with legal boundaries. Political institutions began to fail in their capacity to represent the totality of life, the People's life and the normative objectivity embodied therein. It is in the context of this biopolitical crisis, the strident claims of the exclusion on the order of the People and its prescribed form of life, that I propose to understand the emergence of public administration. Goodnow was right—administration would be the mechanism for restoring the People's national dominion, of fabricating a natural unity presupposed.

Municipalities and the Production of "the New State"

Construction of the People would occur along what have often been taken to be contradictory axes—national/local, rational/pragmatic (McSwite, 1997b) or, as Stivers (2000) argues, bureau men and settlement women. It is, however, too simple to divide or rigidly dichotomize these strategies, marking one as the lost possibility, the other as an end to a robust American nineteenth century and kickoff of the bureaucratization of American life and the corruption of democracy and the rule of law. Rather than viewing the two as separate, competing elements in tension with one another, we should consider how they worked together within the resurgent pluralist, integrative ethos of the Progressive Era. I say "resurgent" because it must be conceded that the Constitution itself, with all its elaborate machinery for checking, balancing, hedging of factions and producing the People's will is, of course, from one perspective a pluralist, integrative document. And pluralism, according to Theodore Lowi (1969), "begins with recognition that there are many sources of power and control other than the state. In our differentiated society, there will be many basic interests represented by organizations able and willing to use power. . . . Since there are so many well-organized interests, there is, in pluralist theory, no possibility that a unitary society, stratified in two or three simple, homogeneous classes, could persist. The result, however, is not the Marxist revolution where the big class devours the small, but an evolution in which the unitary society becomes a pluralistic one" (p. 42). In theory, the competition of various interests produces a state of equilibrium that is "really the public interest" (p. 47).

The matter to keep in view is that the project begun during the last decades of the nineteenth century was the fabrication of the People-as-One, the reconstitution of a popular sovereign without exception. This was indeed a search for order, but a specific kind of order with a specific mode of ordering. Again, this is a biopolitical order operating according to a representational logic. I must do better here than simply restating the commonplace notion that the administrative state becomes the zone for the attempted production of social equilibrium, the arena for interest group integration, just as more sophistication is required in approaching the establishment and development of the field of public administration. Locating both within the framework of biopolitical production is an attempt to do this, to understand how different practices and discourses resonate to produce the effect of social cohesion. I argue that they resonate because they are reproducing a particular logic—namely, representation.

Pluralism and the administrative state did not break with the unitary conception of the People but, as suggested in the first part of this chapter, they did quite radically change the inventory of techniques deployed to manage the exception and the topography upon which they operated. Specifically, the empty throne of democracy shifts from one being primarily focused on Law to one of neutrality as the ground for justifying authoritative and binding judgment. This is a double movement that simultaneously both *abstracts* to the level of macrostatistical aggregates and *concretizes* to the level of individual bodies. Again, do not mistake this as a total rupture from the rule by technical law. Technical law was productive of an order under the auspices of the People's Life. However, it was precisely the inadequacy of law in maintaining the reproduction of Life that necessitated the invention of a new regime of reproduction that would attempt not only to integrate the various excluded elements of society into a higher public interest but also more intensely operate on and through the processes of Life to regularize and discipline representational copies.

The process of integration recognized differences, however, not differences in themselves but rather differences between categories and as deviations from the model, and insofar as they could be integrated into a higher unity or subsumed by a more fundamental logic or process. We saw this at work in the discussion both of representative bureaucracy and the general-in-general. Here fantasy$_1$, the beatific, stabilizing dimension of the society without disturbance or breakdown, continues to operate. Fantasy$_2$, I have argued, not only provides for the account of the failure to realize the unity but also, by virtue of the manner in which it accounts for the failure, provides technologies for producing positive content of the model of the People and a set of techniques for reproducing and stabilizing the terms of the structure of the fantasy.

As suggested above, the process of internalization turns on the generating of a neutral arena. The constitution of a neutral position in the institutionalized political system began with the advent of civil service reform. While there is a lengthy history of reform efforts during the nineteenth century, the gradual "neutralization" of governmental administration famously begins with the 1883 passage of the Pendleton Civil Service Act, which brought approximately 10 percent of the modest federal workforce under the purview of a national personnel system. Aimed at creating "the conditions of good administration," the Pendleton Act, among other things, established a system of competitive examination that mandated the testing of skills ostensibly relevant to the position in question, explicitly forbade usage of public office for political purposes or coercion, and banned receipt of gifts or financial inducements. Competence, not party loyalty, became the common currency for service. Merit-bearing "neutral zones" were slowly reproduced throughout the United States at the state and local levels of government during the next sixty years.

By 1925, only nine states had adopted the merit system (Conover, 1925, n.1), but provisions of the 1935 Social Security Act accelerated adoption by mandating the creation of some merit system for employees in programs partially or fully funded by federal dollars, though many states adopted *de minimus* requirements (Cayer, 1975, p. 37). At the municipal level, reform accelerated after 1895, and by 1930, perhaps as much as 60 percent of larger

U.S. cities (i.e., more than fifty thousand in population) had adopted some form of the merit system (Tolbert & Zucker, 1983). At the federal level, coverage was episodically extended to encompass nearly 90 percent of the federal government's civilian employees by the 1970s (Cayer, 1975, pp. 24–26). But the self-evidence of competence is no more simply given than is the common good. The terms *knowledge* and *neutral competence* are as empty as the rule of law until given content and context; neutrality and competence must be identifiable as such, useable to some desired, desirable end.

The instrumentality of law—and its eroding efficacy—are evidenced by these early civil service reform measures. In other words, certainly laws were passed and an arena ostensibly beyond politics was created, but the technologies for reproducing, *recognizing,* and dispersing neutrality had not yet been devised; like the common, neutrality must be recognized and accepted as such. In assessing the results of the Pendleton Act five years after its passage, one political scientist, Fredrick Perry Powers (1888), concluded, "The Civil Service law failed to justify the hopes and the claims of its advocates. It has failed, not for lack of a fair trial, for it has been honestly enforced by two successive administrations, but because the means which it provides are wholly inadequate to accomplish the end sought. It has done something toward lessening the evils of the spoils system, but the boundaries of that system are far wider than the limits of the law" (p. 247). Powers thought expanding civil service coverage a good idea, but that "the only remedy entirely adequate to deal with the disease [of the spoils system] is the education of public sentiment to the point where the use of public offices for private and party purposes will provoke a revolt at the polls" (p. 280). (Powers went on to support a second remedy—term limits for the chief executive.) In speaking about the tasks of the National Municipal League, the prominent reformer Clinton Rogers Woodruff (1908) said, "To [use an] ecclesiastical simile the League labors as an evangel to convict the American people of their municipal sins and shortcomings and to bring about a change or conversion in their municipal conduct" (p. 132). The second wave of reform would colonize and structure this space of neutrality within a larger discursive, symbolic space and, moreover, profoundly appreciate the importance of external, popular recognition both for the cause of "good government" and for defining "good" as efficient and scientific.

Much of reform would assume the fever pitch of a moral crusade, striking a chord of moral superiority, not to say condescension. Writing of the pioneering men of the municipal bureaus, Waldo (1948) wrote that the reformers were "fired with the moral fervor of humanitarianism and secularized Christianity." But it was not *just* this, as Waldo quickly added. Like the constitutional framers, whose encomium for the People extended only as far as a detached, skeptical republicanism, theirs was paradoxical moralism since reformers *themselves* were tired of the "simple moralism" of nineteenth-century civic republicanism. "They detested politicians and were firm in the belief that citizens by and large were fundamentally pure at heart, desirous of efficient and economic government, and potentially rational enough to 'reach up' to and support a vigorous government wide in its scope, complex in its problems, and utilizing a multitude of professional and scientific skills" (p. 32). Hence, specialized expert knowledge and education, its vehicle for transmission, emerged as critical components in the reconstitution of the People's new state. The People was deemed smart enough to do as it was told. In this diagnosis and suggested prevention lay a new capacity to think the citizen as a *social* phenomenon, as reformable as society was.

The creation of this new state was not a monolithic process, but one of seemingly contradictory movements. Certainly reformers (but not only reformers) thought in terms of unitary entities like "Society." At the same moment, however, they thought in terms of individuals and the capacity to change and reform specific particularities. They thought in terms of elite expert knowledge but also, more generally, in terms of the capacities for civic education. "Progressive education aimed at relevant education which would awaken children to human values and capabilities and instill good moral habits which would serve both them and a changing society. [In the burgeoning universities,] educators sought to inculcate the traditions and values of a liberal democratic culture" (Chambers, 1980, p. 88). Access to education expanded, and those who "merited" access also expanded.

We should not gloss over the pervasive racism of the period since even the "truly" Progressive elements that were open to difference were themselves characterized by an unsubtle racism. While "assimilation" programs and Progressive education did not explicitly proclaim an insurmountable racial or moral hierarchy, neither did they really embrace the differences, for instance, of newly arriving immigrants brought to the nation. Settlement workers, for example, were ambivalent at best about the cultural and ethnic differences of those they worked with. They were often contemptuous of the political decisions of immigrants to follow the local "good men" of the machines and leery of the opaque, informal networks of social and economic support that they oversaw. Indeed, settlements themselves were organizations for integrating and fabricating a cosmopolitan America; they served as mechanisms for replicating a model of behavior and judgment whose predicates were embodied in the normatively neutral position of the white upper- and middle-class reformers who led them.

As Rivka Shpak-Lissak (1989) argues, "the settlement workers' claim for leadership depended on the argument that in maintaining ethnic identity the lower-middle-class leaders did not represent the real wishes of their constituency" (p. 67). Settlement leadership colonized the position of the People; it became the content for the empty throne. Settlements were well meaning in their recognition of the capacity of, in the words of Jane Addams, these "primitive people" to be reformed and to become reliable citizens (cited in Jacobson, 2000, p. 188) and in their belief that the normalizing of "irrational" decision making through education would create an "efficient citizenry."[2] Yet the dynamic of the social side of reform set in motion the contestation of the very terms of civic education itself, as what demanded representation became increasingly unclear. Here, the efforts of the settlement women and the bureau men joined since much of the impetus to rationalize municipal government was simultaneously a drive to loosen the grip of local bosses. On the bureau side, reformers thought in terms of abstract rational "principles" of management and administration, but abstraction that was self-consciously practical, relevant, and useful to the lives of cities, in addition to more straightforwardly concrete concerns exemplified by the settlement movement.

Transformative processes indeed bureaucratized and homogenized at the same moment they individualized and particularized. This is, perhaps strangely, evident in Taylorism. Though admired by his apparent antithesis, Mary Parker Follett, Frederick Taylor is the universal whipping boy for all "scientific" attempts to standardize and regularize the labor process; the tyranny of scientific management has been decried to no end. But Taylor also brings the individual worker and its body into view—and, moreover, the different elements of the body—for integration into the labor process. Recall that Taylor began with an assessment of the "laziness" of management, which had sent workers into factories without the skills needed to effectively and efficiently execute the task. Management needed to methodically collect and analyze each task and use it to educate workers. Thus Taylor (1997/1912) wrote of his second principle:

> It becomes the duty of those on the management's side to deliberately study the character, the nature, and the performance of each workman with a view to finding out his limitations on the one hand, but even more important, his possibilities for the development on the other hand; and then, as deliberately and as systematically to train and help and teach this workman, giving him, wherever it is possible, those opportunities for advancement which will finally enable him to do the highest and most interesting and most profitable class of work for which his natural abilities fit him, and which are open to him in the particular company in which he is employed. (p. 31)

Management needed to become more efficient before it could expect the same of its workers. This dual efficiency would enable work to be dichotomously shared among management and workers.

Processes centralized but also decentralized as the orthodoxy of nineteenth-century dual federalism (i.e., federal and state government) were eroded by movements for municipal home rule (Fox, 1977). Reformers assailed the authority of state legislatures to govern localities, giving birth to the municipal "home rule" movement. Here, the argument was quite contemporary. Frank Goodow (1997/1895) in his other seminal text, *Municipal Home Rule: A Study in Administration,* set out the basic theoretical and legal argument for local autonomy and called for "the grant to municipalities of such a degree of local autonomy or home rule as will cause all municipal citizens to feel a healthy sense of responsibility for the evils from which they suffer, as well as an ensured conviction that they have it in their power to work a sensible improvement in their condition" (p. 9). Citizens did not feel responsible, Goodnow suggested, because state legislatures controlled municipalities, themselves creations of the states, and so the unique powers and authority of municipal government needed to be carved out to specify the domain of unencumbered local action.

What is significant is why and how municipal home rule—local government—was considered primarily an *administrative* problem. Goodnow explained that municipalities were considered to be corporations chartered by *constitutionally contracted sovereign* entities. As such, municipalities had a dual function—they were agents of the state government and, by extension, the sovereign People, but they were also "organizations for the satisfaction of local needs" (1997/1895, p. 18). He would make the same point in *Politics and Administration* (1900): cities and towns are "at the same time local communities and state administrative districts" (p. 47). Municipalities, in other words, have both political (expressive) and administrative (executive) functions. They carry out the "will of the state" as expressed through the legislature, but also express local needs and desires. The American constitutional system, however, had ignored the political dimension of *local* governmental behavior and that "sphere of local action in which they should move freely and largely uncontrolled" (1997/1895, p. 19). Indeed, over the course of the nineteenth century, state legislatures had continually assumed responsibility for local authority, "causing not only a great lack of local interest in the management of local affairs, but also an ignorant and inefficient management of these affairs" (p. 24). This encroachment on local authority "has been productive of greater evil than its attempted encroachments on the domain of the rights of private individuals. For, while the courts could protect individual private rights, they have been unable to protect the rights of local government of [*sic*] municipal corporations" (pp. 54–55). The flip side to this was that localities would or could be virtually free from any effective state control, making the execution and enforcement of state law inconsistent and arbitrary. Local popular will found expression largely through the refusal to enforce legislative acts or acts enforced with local, informal modification.

For this reason, Goodnow (1900) advocated administrative centralization and legislative decentralization, which, theoretically, would ensure enforcement of the state will (i.e., the will of the whole People) and open up a space for the expression of local needs. This double movement would also, so Goodnow argued, relieve localities of the "tyranny of the national parties" (p. 68) by making localities the object of *administrative,* that is, *neutrally competent,* control rather than (party) political control. Party attention would shift to higher levels of government and the articulation of an "authentically" popular will of the whole. In turn, localities would be recognized for their political as well as administrative functions, which would decouple the two as they had been fused in the boss system. A neutral civil service would constitute the space of administration here as well. This would tend less to destroy the boss system as an institution than make the boss "amenable to the public will" (p. 196). Making parties and their leaders more responsible and representative of the popular will formed the natural complement to Progressive "good government" reform. Government was split into two sovereign domains.

The sophisticated theoretical and historical work of Progressive activist-intellectuals of the bureaus and settlements, coupled as it was with the vast regime of practical and institutional innovation, was a stunningly brilliant achievement that transformed American society. In its theoretical and institutional originality, it certainly qualifies as a "Second Founding." Analogous to the position of civil service, municipal home rule meant to create a neutral zone for action *within* the political system that was subordinate to national and state politics yet autonomous from it. This was why Goodnow's *functional* split between politics and administration was so essential. In essence, what reformers sought to create was a network of neutral zones across the nation by clearing the space of and within local government, centralizing and decentralizing, neutralizing and repoliticizing. Indeed, mirroring concern for individuals, organizations such as the National Municipal League viewed municipal good government to be more than merely a program of national scope—since *any* city could benefit—it was a technique for weaving a *nation* back together again, and for forging what Mary Follett (1998/1920) called *the new state.* Here, even someone as heterodox as Follett was basically in concurrence. "I speak of the new state as resting upon integrated neighborhood groups. . . . The movement for neighborhood organization is a deliberate effort to get people to identify themselves actually, not sentimentally, with a larger and larger collective unity than the neighborhood." In the same passage, she also captured the central problem of the People and its fantasy, writing that while "for convenience I speak of each group as a whole . . . from a philosophical point of view there is no whole, only an infinite striving for wholeness, only the *principle* of wholeness forever leading us on" (p. 249).

This weaving, integration, and identification, as I have repeatedly suggested, were not characterized by a simple bureaucratization of Life or some other pejorative. Neither was it quite the salvation of democracy Progressives have taken it to be. So eager has the field of public administration been to declare winners and losers, so reluctant have we been to examine the relationship between the idyllic nineteenth century and brutal and categorical exclusions that produced the People that we have not stopped to examine the structural homology between our dichotomies. And no wonder—for at that point the entire edifice of our democracy is exposed as something radically other than its self-presentation.

The advent of a "civic efficiency" (Campbell, 1995, p. 62) was characterized by a *double movement* in this new zone of administrative neutrality, of technical knowledge to replace the common sense of the Law, which we can understand as an attempt to reconstitute the People by reconfiguring the topography through which the logic of representation would work and be put to work. We would work differently, but it would still be the "*principle* of wholeness forever leading us on." It is obvious in the case of the scientific principles of management and their claims to value neutrality. Equally *normatively* neutral, however, in their claims for knowledge was the other element of reform that took a certain model of citizenship and hitched it to a bounded domain of useful and relevant knowledge. The call for civic education presupposed the model of the engaged citizen and the knowledge, sense, and understanding one would need to have to effectively *and* efficiently carry out one's civil responsibilities.

Without needlessly downplaying the difference between these two elements, it is clear the two worked together, resonated, insofar as the logic of representation was at work in both via the modes of qualitative resemblance and quantitative equivalence. Fiscal controls, reporting requirements, the criteria of economic efficiency, standardized administrative procedures, and the like established the techniques and products of neutral competence that would work to produce the People and bring discipline, regularization, and homogenization to the organismically rooted machinery of administration. On the "outside," education and professionalization were reconstituting and ossifying the boundaries of the People, producing a more efficient citizenry through education reform and a whole host of other disciplinary technologies that fabricated the People through the reproduction of the logic of representation. Indeed, as I shall suggest in the next section, these two movements in the administrative domain of biopolitical production were by no means solely responsible for fabricating the People. Rather, they must be understood within the context of a whole complex diffusion of *disciplinary technologies* that linked truth and knowledge to modes of social control, normalization, and reproduction.

Public administration emerged as a technology that presupposed the People; it presupposed some underlying unity to which all "empirical" differences could be integrated or at least oriented, and according to which differences and copies could be arrayed and distributed. Yet the breakdown and diagnosis out of which it emerged also conditioned the attitude that it assumed toward the exclusion, *internalization.* The excluded element of representation was conceptualized fundamentally in terms of an internal *irrational* element that could be restored to the terms of the model, or the rational norm. The irrational *can* be rationalized and social equilibrium re-achieved. Both at the level of the particular individual and macrosocial processes, life came into view as an object in such a way that appeared to displace the bias and normativism of legal technique. Public administration constructed a normatively neutral space for operation and subsequently developed a variety of sophisticated rationalizing techniques, programs, and campaigns to fabricate the social order its ontology said was there. In its operation, public administration would require and utilize the regularities being produced at the microsocial level to inform macrolevel policy formulation and execution.

Techniques of Internalization

Internalizing the Exclusions: Discipline and Administration

Above I outlined the general orientation (internalization) that began in the Progressive Era toward the exclusion. Next I described a diagnosis of disintegration, a bursting of boundaries, and the way in which public administration emerged as an integrative, reconstituting strategy. In this section, I want to locate public administration among a broader proliferation of administrative or *disciplinary* techniques that work to fabricate the People and operate on the exclusion and specify more clearly the functionality of public administration.

If the Progressive Era brought the exclusion "inside," something needed to be done with it to make it less unruly. It needed to be *disciplined.* Discipline is Michel Foucault's (1995/1975) term for a "means of correct training" that initially appeared in the eighteenth century. "Discipline 'makes' individuals; it is a specific technique of a power that regards individuals both as objects and subjects of its exercise" (p. 170). This suggests a confrontation between the modes of the law's categorical exclusion (and subsequent political inclusion) and the mode of disciplinary individualizing. Discipline is a "political anatomy of detail" (p. 139) that ranks and hierarchizes individuals with regard to a model, mold, or rule, the *correct.* Individuals are distributed and arranged in a network of relations. They are individualized, but at the same instant subsumed within a general category of the mold that makes them countable as objects and representable as cases.

Discipline operates on the bodies of individuals within specific *enclosures,* for example, the factory, the school, the hospital. It involves a material reorganization of space within which bodies can be subjected to the rules and constraints of the operative disciplinary technologies. Analogous to the neutral zones of merit and neutrality, discipline creates "useful spaces" of enclosure that can be geometrized, homogenized, and easily overseen (Foucault, 1995/1975, p. 141). These spaces become necessary for containing the irrational—or, perhaps, a-rational—state of nature. Discipline, subsequently, partitions and differentiates space by task; the division of labor is a spatial division in which subjects are largely interchangeable. One is as good as another because a body is a body is any body. In this reconstruction of space, discipline can therefore make specific assumptions about the ontological status of bodies. They can be viewed as essentially *docile,* as inert Cartesian objects,[3] which can assume the form of the disciplinary model without influencing the model or modeler itself. "The body is docile that may be subjected, used, transformed and improved" (p. 136). The body may then be subdivided into manageable elements and subjected to focused, calculable training. Thus the states of nature enter as fragments. Identity is broken down into representational political categories and identities of discrete disciplinary enclosure (home, workplace, etc.); bodies are dispersed across various zones of disciplinary expertise to be objects of regimentation and normalization. Yet this fragmentation occurs, ultimately, toward the ends of integration and fabrication.

The nexus of correctness and movement across an ordered, if fragmented, distribution facilitates the ease of oversight and judgment. The combination of these factors allows for the judgment of efficiency. The relation of segmentation of the act and control of the elements of a body according to a rule of technical judgment is to rephrase the well-known idea of "the one best way." As suggested by the phrase "civic efficiency," efficiency expresses a particular dimension of disciplinary *normalization* in much the same way that teaching is normalizing and productive of civic efficiency. Teaching is a pedagogical directive concerning knowledge of what *is.* Success is measured according to conformity to the general rule, the accuracy with which one represents the norm, and is evaluated through examination. Deviation from this norm can be quantified and ultimately punished (Foucault, 1995/1975, pp. 183–184). Efficiency names a mode of correct behavior in the workplace, whose normalizing effects are monitored and incorporated into a code of conduct and punishment. *Efficiency (including civic efficiency) thus names less a particular technique of economic production than a general mode of social reproduction within representation.* However, discipline is nonetheless different than law. With discipline, the mode of correct behavior becomes more specified, more focused on the control of each individual body and the specific and differentiated enclosures in which it lives.

Administering Disciplinary Society

Disciplinary technologies penetrate deep into the practices of everyday life, and Hardt and Negri (2000) write of the emergence of a *disciplinary society* at the end of the nineteenth century. A disciplinary society suggests that the techniques of discipline have been dispersed across the entire social field; rather than being subject to strict exclusion, social antagonisms are internalized and subjected to disciplinary control. Discipline is enforced across the professions and social sciences, for instance, through certification, examination, peer review, tenure review, and other self-regulatory mechanisms. The household itself becomes standardized and disciplined through the nascent advertising industry and the impact of Fordist mass production and consumption (Banta, 1993). Health, both physical and mental, becomes subjected to professionalization and normalization (Foucault, 1978/1976). Higher education enforces discipline among students through examination, grading, and the presumption that there is something canonically correct that *ought* to be taught (Thayer, 1975) and, by extension, bodies of knowledge that may not demand inclusion into the regimen of civic efficiency. As the Constitution homogenized persons under the categories of citizenship, discipline, too, homogenizes through its rule-based, standardizing, representational techniques. It also differentiates bodies and spaces by creating discrete disciplines and areas of specialization and expertise that posit, measure, and distribute general standards of deviation. Discipline fragments and breaks apart in order to manage the exclusion and to integrate it—and, finally, to fabricate the People.

Note how the techniques of discipline impact the notion of law. Law as a regulatory device of biopolitical production is exposed as clearly insufficient in the Progressive Era. With a more robust understanding of efficiency, we can see that Goodnow (1905) was correct when he said, "We have passed through an age of constitutional private rights and are approaching one of social control. What needs emphasis is no longer the inherent natural rights of the individual, but the importance, indeed the necessity, of administrative efficiency. For upon administrative efficiency depends the effectiveness of social control without which healthy development in existing conditions is impossible" (p. 43). In its broad generality and simple exclusion, law cannot penetrate to the level of the individual body and its "affections" to mold, manage, and reassemble them. While it is possible to speak of a regime of law, there is no *regimen* of law, in the sense of either the rigor or routinization of disciplinarity. The regimentation of the factory, the school, the barracks, the hospital, the consumer marketplace is intensely focused, particularized, and individualizing, even as it homogenizes, normalizes. Through its fragmentary logic, discipline can internalize; it can enclose and operate on the fragments of individual bodies in specialized ways.

As a disciplinary institution, public administration embodies a comparable concern with rule-based biopolitical reproduction. In the Progressive Era, government became concerned with the activities of men and women in their ordinary everyday lives, rather than merely as subjects with rights and duties (Dreyfus & Rabinow, 1983). This is, in part, a legacy of the settlement movement, which deftly sought political inclusion through the politicization of their naturalized domain. It is logical, therefore, that those "intimate" and "natural" realms would become spaces for disciplinary normalization since the exclusion had succeeded in redefining the symbolic space of politics. The microregulation of Life now became the explicit concern of government. A generalized form of life became the mechanism for realizing the presupposed harmony of Life itself as the physical welfare of society became the target of *administrative* action. The specificity of the activities in question, their particularity and enclosure, created the space and demand for administrative action and, by extension, the demand for professionalization, the *disciplines,* and expertise in these emergent zones and bodies of action. Moreover, it is only within disciplinary society's reproduction of representation's political ontology—of the geometrization and routinization of social space, the presupposed docility of bodies, the ability to monitor through behavior, the presupposition of a natural harmony of interests expressed in the form of the People—that modern public administration even became *thinkable.*

Dimensions of Biopolitical Production: Discipline and Biopower

The critical question thus far unanswered is, What is the particular function of public administration in the disciplinary society and its new state? It is possible to say, for instance, that psychiatry professionalized and disciplined sexuality; sociology inquired into the general laws of society to understand how to harness and control them; management science emerged to study and facilitate the disciplining of the workplace and the shattering of the worker's body; mass public education socialized and standardized students; advertising and popular culture began to discipline demand, desire, and consumption in private life. And while the administrative state was itself internally disciplined (Foucault, 1991/1979; Howe, 2001) and regularized, what object does *government* itself discipline? What kind of disciplinary institution is it? What does it neutralize, rationalize, and normalize?

Before answering this directly, let me take inventory of the various dimensions of the argument to this point. I identified, first, a general shift toward the exclusion called *internalization.* Internalization entailed the recognition of exclusions fundamentally in terms of irrationalities, disequilibriums, or deviances. These are internalizations of states of nature within disciplinary enclosures. The next section outlined the emergence of the field of public administration and how the logic of representation was replicated in two seemingly contradictory movements, bureau and settlement. This double movement of public administration was then located amid a more general transformation of constitutional society into disciplinary society in order to understand the broad contours of the biopolitical project of the People. In a manner of speaking, there is a kind of partial recognition of the disembodied nonexistence of the People as its body politic is conceived as dwelling in a "pluralist universe" of group interests in need of integration into a higher unity; so too, is the individual body fragmented into a series of disciplinary objects that ultimately can be subsumed by a higher, national identity.

Normalization and, simultaneously, individualization and homogenization are productive of individual judgment and behavior and, in doing so, are generative of the collective capacity for macropolitical recognition. It is worthwhile here to recall Zizek's (1989) point that processes themselves are not neutral; process and organization *believe.* The concrete is theoretical. The organization of social life is embedded with specific theories and beliefs, themselves resting on fundamental tenets about reality that guided their invention. Yet these processes and organizations themselves, in the final instance, are conditioned by fantasy$_1$, which posits the plausibility of oneness and authorizes hegemonic articulation, the production of discourses and practices in the name of this One, the People. The particular dimensions of the Progressive diagnosis informed the production and deployment of a battery of political technologies, including public administration, which operated in conjunction with the other disciplinary enclosures.

We can draw an important conclusion: microlevel discipline is productive of "the Thing," or the object that the political process ostensibly represents. The People is being produced throughout the social field; sovereign decisions on the exception are being made over and over in discrete states of the situation, thereby producing the capacity for authoritative governmental decision on the People's outside and local recognition of neutrality. The coherence of macropolitical judgments and recognition of hegemonic representations are maintained and sustained through the specificities of *models of efficiency,* the name given to the form of representation produced when the immanentist commonality of law is displaced by the immanentist objectivism of neutrality and competence. As I suggested earlier, models of efficiency are not merely models or rules of economic performance. Rather, social efficiencies are achieved through the generalized replication of the model's "one best way" regardless of whether it is expressed as a ratio of inputs to outputs or behavioral norms such that judgments and expectations become standardized and regularized, and macrocalculability might be produced.

I will now turn attention toward the action that began to take place on these fabricated regularities. That is, as social process became more highly regularized, harmonized, and rationalized, the processes themselves grew more calculable and probabilistic. Microlevel regularities began to reestablish macrolevel statistical aggregates across the *population* or across a *nation,* where a population is a "mass of living and coexisting beings who present particular biological and pathological traits and who thus come under specific knowledge and technologies" (Foucault, 1994b, p. 71).

It subsequently became possible for action to be taken on the basis of these normalized macro societal processes—both to identify when some element appeared to have become irrational and to propose reformative corrective action. Foucault (2003/1997) has identified this macrocomplement to discipline:

> Now I think we see something new emerging in the second half of the eighteenth century: a new technology of power, but this time not disciplinary. This technology of power does not exclude the former, does not exclude disciplinary technology, but it does dovetail into it, integrate it, modify it to some extent, and above all, use it by sort of infiltrating it, embedding itself in existing disciplinary techniques. This technique does not simply do away with the disciplinary technique, because it exists at a different level, on a different scale, and because it has a different bearing area, and makes use of very different instruments.
>
> Unlike discipline, which is addressed to bodies, the new nondisciplinary power is applied not to man-as-body but to the living man, to man-as-living being; ultimately, if you like, to man-as-species. . . . So after a first seizure of power over the body in the individualizing mode, we have a second seizure of power that is not individualizing but, if you like, massifying, that is directed not at man-as-body but at man-as-species. . . . we have, at the end of the eighteenth century, the emergence of something that is no longer an anatomo-politics of the human body, but what I would call a "biopolitics" of the human race. (pp. 242–243)

This new mode of massifying power is "biopower" and the new mode of politics "biopolitics." I have made one important amendment to Foucault. I have contended that the discourse of popular sovereignty takes life itself, the determination of the People's Life, as the object of politics; thus I cannot agree entirely with Foucault's chronological account of the emergence of biopolitics, at least as it pertains to the development of the United States. However, his identification of a second mode of power also based upon knowledge, biopower, that operates through and by massifications is quite useful for understanding the emergence of powerful, centralizing administrative apparatuses and their relationships with local disciplinary applications.

Foucault states that there are two axes of modern biopolitics. First, biopower deals with the "population, with the population as a political problem, as problem that is at once scientific and political, as a biological problem and as power's problem" (Foucault, 2003/1997, p. 245). Second, it deals with phenomena that become visible only at the mass or macrolevel and that are created over a period of time. The appearance of these objects "will introduce mechanisms with a certain number of functions that are very different from the functions of disciplinary mechanisms. [They include] forecasts, statistical estimates, and overall measures" (p. 246). Where normalization is the objective of discipline, regulating social equilibrium and managing a population are the object of biopower. Foucault states that these two modes of power operate in concert with one another. And, as we have seen, they must. For in order for there to be regularities at the macrolevel, microlevel discipline and efficiency must be produced. Given the ontologically constitutive exclusionary moment in representation, these stabilities themselves will always be temporary and always be breaking down. The dimensions of the breakdown are visible, however, *not* from the subjective irrationalities on the factory floor, but from the administrative crow's nest. Biopolitical regulation was precipitated and occurred at the rupture of the disciplinary enclosure, at the moment where an exception became visible and actionable.

The regime of the disciplinary society in its dual modalities of discipline and biopower was dependent upon a certain resonance of these two modes. That is, the individualizing and homogenizing tendencies of discipline produced regularities in behavior and judgment that enabled the recognition of a macrolevel deviation from the normal. In turn, that very recognition and determination of deviation was given credibility by the formalism of neutral competence and associated techniques working within the apparatuses of administrative state and its neutral zones.

These are important points because they begin to destabilize a series of taken-for-granted assumptions in public administration about the divisions of the social field. In the first place, we see that public administrators are being produced by those disciplinary practices operative within traditionally conceived governmental institutions but are also continuously being worked on by disciplinary discourses and practices (educational, medical, consumerist, etc.) "external" to government. At each moment, though, the logic of representation is at work, positing a model and requiring replication. In this sense, the "public" sector is produced beyond itself and in fact comes to establish the internal limit of the "private." This is critical because, as I will argue in the next chapter, the public sector, government, by shifting into this limit position of regulatory stabilization, will shift again and move into a perceived position of limitation as the internal dynamics of integrative strategies collapse under their own presuppositions. Second, it is clear that the governing and production of the popular sovereign, the People, are occurring in the "private" realm—in factories, offices, homes and recreation: those alleged domains of the individual, the natural, and the "idiosyncratic," in liberal mythology. Indeed, what is pushed into the "public" is precisely the irrational or pathological element since the realm of the administrative public sector and its sphere of action are defined by failure in disciplinary production made visible in aggregation and the assessment of deviation.

But there are some strange consequences of this. First, while at the level of biopower, rationalization of the irrational, or *internalization of the exclusion,* is delegated to the government, macrostabilization in fact can be achieved only through local, contextual microdisciplinary adjustments. Macroregulation must be actualized again and again at the level of the individual body. The second consequence is that, while remedy of deviation is ostensibly carried out by public administrators in biopolitical regulation, the required microdisciplinary adjustments are, in fact, *carried out* by the subjects of discipline in various sectors of the "private." For example, if a regulation is adopted requiring an alteration in the handling of some toxin produced as a by-product of an industrial process, the "public" administrator, that person tasked with carrying out or executing the regulation, could be the private firm or its manager. Paradoxically, then, the "private" sector is productive of the public sector, and the executives of public directives, the "frontline" public administrators, are often located in the private domain and, indeed, they penetrate quite deeply into "private" life and interpersonal relationships insofar as those spaces are disciplined by the spatial and categorical representations of civic efficiency. The People is everywhere being fabricated, and the stability of divisions between the conventionally governmental and nongovernmental, the public and private, even the individual and the community is by no means clear. Indeed, the private-public division is simply implausible as a matter of practice since much of "public" administration is occurring in the domain of the "private," and furthermore, the *popular sovereign itself* is being fabricated through contextual disciplinary regulation. This makes identifying the function of public administration quite difficult. Nevertheless, there may still be something distinctive about public administration, and perhaps we can use something of the foregoing analysis to forge an intelligible definition that might subsequently assist in the analysis of the legitimacy problem.

Conclusion

What Does the Administrative State Administer?

So, then, what does public administration itself, defined narrowly as governmental administration, take up as an object of discipline for itself? What does the administrative state *administer?*

When I juxtapose definitions of public administration with the foregoing discussion of discipline and biopower, we see how little help most are. Let us consider here a handful of contemporary efforts to get a definitional handle on public administration. David Rosenbloom (1999) provides a widely cited definition of public administration as "the use of managerial, political and legal theories and processes to fulfill legislative, executive, and judicial governmental mandates for the provision of regulatory and services functions for the society as a whole or for some segments of it" (p. 6). Though this definition is seemingly quite encompassing, its kernel is conventional: public administration is the carrying out of political directives. In their textbook *Introducing Public Administration,* Shafritz and Russell (2003, pp. 5–35) expand Rosenbloom's triad of public administrative functions to a quartet and provide an impressively thorough, encompassing definition of public administration. Public administration can be defined from political, legal, managerial, and *occupational* perspectives. Political definitions of the field concern "what government does," its processes and procedures, its role in the policy-making process, and its responsibility for implementing the public interest. This last element suggests that public administration is "doing collectively that which cannot be so well done individually" (p. 11) Legal perspectives view public administration as an instrument of law or as "law in action." This perspective also encompasses the domain of the quasi-legal and illegal, such as largess and receipt of bribes. The managerial perspective concerns the function of the executive in government and the internal operation, structure, and management of the executive function. Related to this is public administration as an occupation or a profession. This most basically concerns the status and nature of a *field of labor* concerned with "public service," in terms of both the concrete work of professional public administrators and the academic (inter)disciplinary inquiry into the various and complex dimensions and histories of that service and the training and preparation of those who enter public service. To this Shafritz and Russell (2003) add that public administration in the United States is bound up with "putting into practice legislative acts that represent the will of the people" (p. 18). This is the dimension of public administration that concerns theorists of a unified sovereignty. Finally, to take one further example, in his widely used textbook, *Public Administration: An Action Orientation,* Denhardt (1999) writes that "all actions of public administrators take place within an important political context: commitment to democratic ideals and practices [i.e., individualism, equality, and liberty]" (p. 4). Rohr (1986) and Frederickson (1997) (see chapter 2) might concur insofar as public administration is primarily concerned with "running the Constitution," the compact of the American People, and carrying out the business of the state and its related agents.

These definitions illuminate the methods and goals, the means and ends, of public administration, but in a conventional sense that presupposes the stability of the domains of the public, a sectoral and chronological division between the political and the social, its interests and values, and the sovereign People—no matter how complex, they still serve as regulative principles or ideas, as did Follett's commitment to wholeness. Based on the foregoing analysis we see, though, that conducting our conduct according to these basic commitments carries with it significant consequences. But, more precisely, what of public administration's *object,* the thing or space it operates on or through? I belabor this point because, as Louis Althusser (Althusser & Balibar, 1997/1970) wrote apropos of Marx's critique of political economy, to criticize public administration is "to *confront* it with a new problematic and a new object": that is, to question the very *object* of public administration. Furthermore, public administration's "pretensions to existence are a function of the nature and hence of the *definition of its object*" (p. 158; emphasis in original). It is difficult to consider, as I will in the next chapter, the question of the legitimacy of the administrative state—its pretensions to existence—much less formulate an alternative if it is not clear what the nature of the particular processes under examination are and what the objective function of public administration is. "Serves the public!" "Democracy in action!" "Carries out the public interest!" "Runs the Constitution!" These tired normative battle cries do not advance our understanding any more than pseudo-scientific theories of decision and management.

Let me then restate some key elements from the argument to this point that can be used in formulating an understanding of the functionality of public administration:

- Representation operates in the gaps and deposits there a fundamental relationship among the objects of the model and its copies. Representation denies difference in two ways. First, it conceives the social relations in terms of sameness, as representations of the model. Second, it denies the elementary heterogeneity of series and the empty set. That is, it seeks to reduce one series to a representation of the other and create a positive, content-laden foundation for being. The model derives its authority not from a position or imposition per se but from its association with the natural or correct.
- Public administration works at the level of *both* discipline and biopower. It operates at the level of macrorecognition of irrationalities and microdisciplinary correction and reform.
- Discipline illustrates public administration's double movement of models of efficiency, which establishes formally neutral modes of analysis and decision in conjunction with substantively rational modes that create civic efficiency. These two must resonate since neutrality and the one best way *must be recognized* as such.
- With the administrative state, there is a "macro" *biopolitical* model of efficiency—which, to a greater or lesser degree of explicitness, defines *the body politic of the People*—in the presupposition of the homogeneity of social processes themselves. In this model, there is also an exception to be decided upon in the diagnosis of macrodeviation and consequent prescription of regulatory remediation or remaking. There is a *nationalizing* element to biopolitics in disciplinary society but also a decentralizing movement toward municipalities and specific sites of disciplinary reproduction.
- Regulatory remediation of the administrative state impacts disciplinary enclosures insofar as macrodeviations are a function of aggregate microdisciplinary irrationalities. Thus, ultimately, visible macro-

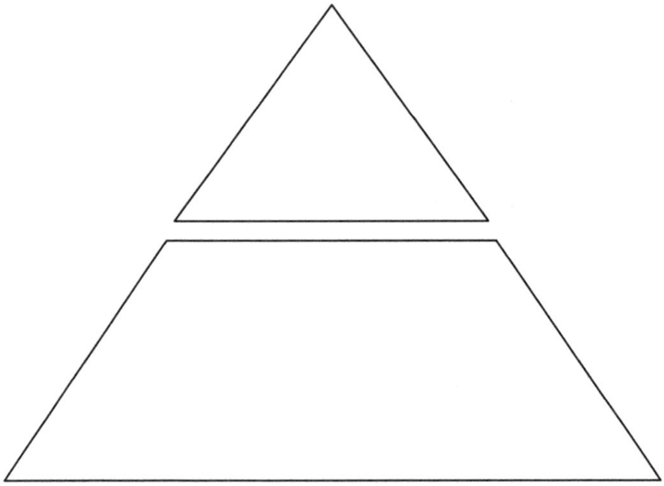

Fig. 4. Vertical or "Altitude" Conception of Administration

irrationalities are *acted upon* in microdisciplinary adjustment and materialized targets of reform.

- The nexus of public administration as discipline and the administrative state as biopower I would call *the biopolitical state,* where "state" denotes not the (relatively) autonomous functioning of the political but this dynamic matrix of discourses and practices that fabricate the People through sovereign decisions in states of the situation that fix representational models in disciplinary enclosures irrespective of whether subjects ostensibly act in or with regard to the micro or macro domains; all reproduction of specific representations occurs within given states of the situation, a designation that allows us to displace the apparent "level" of micro and macro. I will pick this final point up next.

In reviewing these key points, a problem emerges. In using the terms *macro* and *micro* to describe the distinction between discipline and biopower, I have blocked the approach to the object of public administration. These terms are misleading insofar as they connote a difference of "altitude," not only in terms of perspective on the social but also potentially in light of the normative association such a "higher" perspective might be

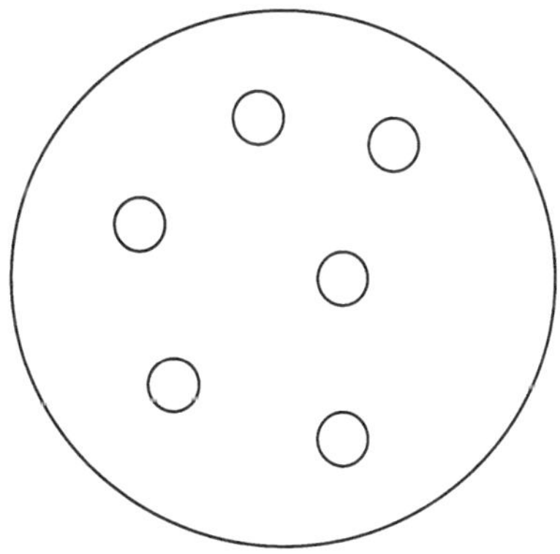

Fig. 5. Flat or Horizontal Conception of Administration

marked by. These are *not* differences in altitude but distinct topographical positions on the immanent surface of a social field. The following diagrams will assist in illustrating this distinction.[4]

Figure 4 is a crude vertical "base-superstructure" diagram of the state-society, government-People distinction upon which modern politics rests and upon which the democratic feedback loop described by Fox and Miller (1995) depends. For reasons described above, this understanding simply cannot be sustained. Figure 5 diagrams the flat topography of the bio-political state. The small circles mark disciplinary enclosures and the space in between the arena of biopower, itself deployed from disciplinary spaces. Yet it is biopower that in fact sets limits on the enclosures through regulation and other legal techniques. It is true that the diagram itself could be contested insofar as it intimates an actual outside in two-dimensional space to the biopolitical state. In the biopolitical state, the unspecified realm beyond could be read as the presumed chaos beyond the geographical border of the nation-state. This is the interstice of the international system, and much of the foregoing analysis might be extended to consideration of bio-political production along this "foreign-domestic" frontier (see Bartelson, 1995).

With this topographical distinction, I offer the following definition of public administration: *Public administration brings discipline to the interstices of disciplinary enclosures.* Public administration deals with that which cannot or ceases to be disciplined, that which cannot be contained. *It is fundamentally a boundary or rebounding practice generated by the political ontology of representation.* It is in light of this understanding of public administration and the administrative state that we can now approach the contemporary problem of legitimacy and the undoing of this disciplinary world of which it is a symptom.

6
Legitimacy and Control

We have seen that administration is not illegitimate vis-à-vis law insofar as law itself was shown not to be a source of legitimacy per se but an instrument of rule. Furthermore, administration's contemporary legitimacy problem cannot, therefore, be a function of professional competency or the production of the "right" kind of "useful" knowledge (be it normative or technical) precisely because the very idea of professional competence emerged as a technology for ameliorating the breakdown of the efficacy of law and fostering the production of a common sense; administration and professional neutrality emerged as supplements to the failure of law as an instrument of rule and "management" of the exclusion. The contemporary crisis of governmental and administrative legitimacy needs to be viewed within the movement of this logic of exclusion and the biopolitical project of the People.

As we will see more clearly later, both normative and scientific approaches to public administration misrecognize the origin of the legitimacy problem. The legitimacy question in public administration is an *effect* of the political ontology of representation and the relationships it establishes and the divisions it posits between domains of human interaction. This is not to say that legitimacy is not a "real" problem. Rather, it is a problem without a *real solution* insofar as it is produced by specific underlying conditions and assumptions that sustain its problematic status. The only "solution" to the problem is to displace these conditions and assumptions. As we will see, contemporary conditions may be making such a displacement plausible.[1] However, the desirability of displacing these conditions lies not in legitimizing the administrative state but in changing the underlying relation of representation.

I will approach the dimensions of the contemporary legitimacy problem of the administrative state in three steps. The first step will be to argue that the political ontology of the People in fact makes the legitimacy question irresolvable because the presuppositions of the People render any government always already suspect on account of the particular divisions and relations it establishes among its posited objects. Second, even though leeriness toward government is a necessary consequence of the structure of the People, it is essential to understand more precisely our contemporary conditions and the apparent escalation of antigovernmental sentiment. To this point, I will consider the particular dimensions of contemporary antigovernmentalism in order to clarify the thesis that it is the efficacy of representation and not simply one particular political technology that is now failing. I will consider the biopolitical breakdown of the disciplinary regime of reproduction that precipitated the contemporary legitimacy crisis of the administrative state and outline the broad changes in social relations and social space that characterize the current period. Following Gilles Deleuze (1995/1990), we can call this postdisciplinary order the *society of control*. The general attitude toward the exclusion in the society of control creates a general *state of exception* (Agamben, 1998/1995) that abandons the project of fabrication and inaugurates a new mode of social regulation through *dis*order and *dis*integration against the lingering commitment to the One.

In the third section I consider the general problem of government in this order of disintegration. I will contend that government itself has shifted into the position of the constitutive exclusion. While fantasy$_1$ is still operative, the diagnosis of fantasy$_2$ has shifted government itself into the position of the pathogen and the cause of social disorder. In many ways the current period resembles the constitutional order of the nineteenth century and so rightly earns the designation "neoliberal." The uniqueness of the contemporary moment, however, is that, as a result of the dimensions of the biopolitical breakdown, fantasy$_1$, the notion of a People-as-One, is becoming increasingly untenable, as evidenced by the fact that conducting of conduct now occurs through disintegration and separation. Integrated differences are recognized but set against one another. In this shift, politics effectively loses its referent. Neither a stable object of political representation nor the capacity to recognize a representation as Ours is being fabricated. It is as if we now look into the mirror and rather than seeing an integrated image of Ourselves, we see undirected flows of fragments, parts, and intensities. The consequence of the fragmentation of this image is the perception of a governmental apparatus that appears captured, incompetent, biased, and authoritarian in the exercise of authority. With government as the materialized exclusion, government turns on itself, reducing to its "core" security functions and returning governmental functions to the "natural" dominions of the social; this, in turn, exacerbates social dislocation and disintegration, which serve simply to reinforce the self-reductive impulse.

At the same time that government appears to be turning on itself, the naturalizing mode within which this takes place paradoxically generates conditions for the limitless expansion of government and augments the temptation to displace the failure of $fantasy_1$ onto "invisible" enemies. That is, since the capacity for politics to represent the People erodes, so does the capacity to identify stable friends and enemies. The world ceases to appear sensible and orderly, and the disciplinary institutions of sense making and identity stabilization lose their legitimacy. The exception becomes the rule and an ambiguous, ubiquitous, invisible, and boundless threat emerges to cover the void. We now live in a state of the exception (Agamben, 1998/1995; Diken & Laustsen, 2005), a permanent state of emergency (Gross, 2006; Hardt & Negri, 2000).

Legitimacy and Representation

We saw in the three "sovereignty in question" theories (McSwite, 1997b; Harmon, 1995; Hummel and Stivers, 1998) that while these accounts demonstrated the centrality of the constitutive exclusion (the element beyond the boundary in McSwite, the constitutive paradox in Harmon, and the unrepresentable aspect of the human experience in Hummel and Stivers) in the domain of the sovereignty of the facts, each nevertheless left administration as problematic for itself. Hummel and Stivers come closest in linking the problem with the political form of representation, and elsewhere McSwite (1996) call into question the very possibility of representation. Here, I will return to this problem to show why administrative legitimacy is not a problem internal to the discourse of public administration. Rather, public administration's legitimacy question is symptomatic of the very presuppositions that make its enterprise possible: the People.

The Social and the Political: Differences in Kind

Public administration became thinkable only upon a certain ontological foundation, and it emerged to supplement the technical law. Left unaddressed, however, was the generic question of why legitimacy has proven to be such a dogged problem for public administration. Certainly, much of the issue centers on the disembodiment or depersonalization of the source of authority into the domain of the invisible, mute structures of Life. A gap opens up between subject and object, between the representative and the object of representation. Narrowing this gap becomes the concern of a diverse range of philosophical and political projects. For government, the initial conditions of the problem are identical. The disembodying of sovereignty produces a gap between government and the People which, in turn, initiates efforts to narrow the gap and produce more accurate and inclusive representations of the People. Underlying this is the assumption that the oneness of the People can, in fact, be reproduced in a representation.

The invention of liberal government on this terrain adds another set of wrinkles to the open, contestable gap between instituted representations and their displaced origins. Tom Paine provides a useful way of getting into the broad problem of governmental legitimacy created by the People. Recalling Harmon's argument about the problem of "lost innocence" (1995, p. 77) in *Common Sense*, Paine (1976/1776) begins his famous text this way:

> Some writers have so confounded society with government, as to leave little or no distinction between them; whereas as they are not only different, but have different origins. Society is produced by our wants, and government by our wickedness; the former promotes our happiness *positively* by uniting our affections, the latter *negatively* by restraining our vices. The one encourages intercourse, the other creates distinctions. The first is a patron, the last a punisher.
>
> Society in every state is a blessing, but government even in its best state is but a necessary evil. . . . Government, like dress, is the badge of lost innocence; the palaces of kings are built on the ruins of the bowers of paradise. For were the impulses of conscience clear, uniform and irresistibly obeyed, man would need no other lawgiver; but that not being the case, he finds it necessary to surrender a part of his property to furnish means for the protection of the rest. . . . *Wherefore*, security being the true design and end of government, it unanswerably follows that whatever *form* thereof appears most likely to ensure

it to us, with the least expense and greatest benefit, is preferable to all others. (pp. 65–66; emphasis in original)

For Paine, government is from its inception a foreign element in society and a sign of lost innocence; it is a marker of failure. It is interesting, though, that Paine suggests that the appearance of government is not merely a sign of society's fall from grace. He trains his lament on the failure of individual conscience and "the inability of moral virtue to govern the world" (1976/1776, p. 68). Critically, Paine also suggests a basic division, a *substantive* difference in *kind*, between government and society.

In perhaps the earliest formalization of this conception of the social/political relationship (Mayhew, 1968, p. 578), the same core formula appears in Locke. In the *Second Treatise*, Locke (1988/1689) writes, "He that will with any clearness speak of the *Dissolution of Government*, ought, in the first place to distinguish between the *Dissolution of Society*, and the *Dissolution of the Government*" (§211). Society was essentially *prepolitical*. This prepolitical society itself might dissolve, but only through a foreign act of aggression (§211). In this *prepolitical* society, each individual was a free executor of the Law of Nature, or Reason (Barnes, 1917; Locke, 1988/1689, §6). This law could function because all people were products of the One: "the Workmanship of one Omnipotent, and infinitely wise Maker; All the Servants of one Sovereign Master," "sharing all in one Community of Nature" (Locke, 1988/1689, §6). Yet people were also self-loving and "partial to themselves and their Friends" and so might go too far in the punishment of others (§13). Thus, a civil society appeared contractually, "by agreeing with other Men to joyn and unite into a Community, for their comfortable, safe and peaceful living amongst another, in a secure Enjoyment of their Properties, and greater Security against any that are not of it. . . . When any number of Men have so consented to make one Community, or Government, they are thereby presently incorporated, and make *one Body Politick,* whereby the *Majority* have a Right to act and conclude the rest" (§96).

Lockean government emerged to serve an essentially technical function, that of a neutral arbiter of disputes and general executor of and punisher under the laws of civil or political society, or civil law. Law became the political representation of the natural will of this prepolitical society. Government executed functions through law designated to it with the *consent of the People*, who themselves had constituted a *single* political or civil society (Locke, 1988/1689, §§87–95, §104). And it was the People who remained supreme in deciding the extent to which government remained legitimate in the execution of the functions assigned to it. Indeed, this was the formula that Locke used to justify political revolution. However, to return to an earlier point, it must be stressed again that it was not law qua law that underwrote political legitimacy, but rather the efficacy of law in fulfilling its designated technical functions, namely, to make more *calculable* the affairs of property through a legal "Standard of Right and Wrong" (§§123–124). Government, in this way, was a *strategy* for rendering the business of society and the security of property more certain and regular.

Subjectivity as the Object of Modern Government

The innovation I wish to concentrate on is the inventive institutionalization of a specific distinction *in kind* between society and government. The positing of the separation of the social and the political is advanced, in part, to impose a limitation on governmental prerogative. The essential dimension of this is the disembodiment of power. As argued in chapters 3 and 4, in this disembodiment, natural law itself became embedded in the social field and its individual parts in a society. As in the move of epistemological representation, this creates two problems for the maintenance of social order. We already have considered the first problem. Because this representational logic displaces the ground for authority into the mute, all-inclusive immanence of the social field, instituted authority becomes disembodied (Catlaw, 2006c) and can only represent its empowering source. In conventional political terms, this manifests itself in the "split sovereignty" of the People, a division between the disarticulated foundation of political power and institutionalized, formal authority. This produces, again, the impossible project of closing the gap between representation and referent, the People's power and authority, the People as object of representation and the People as sovereign (if represented) ruler.

The second problem is this: if there is an essentially prepolitical entity in possession of a potentially self-regulating natural law, the question arises, "Why have governments at all?" As Paine and Locke suggest, it is here that some variant on the fictional state of nature and its attendant fall from grace narrative appear, injecting elements of threatening *insecurity* and moral deficiency. The Hobbesian war of all against all, of course, is the most extreme, threatening example of the state of nature; it is milder in Locke's account of its "inconveniences" and in Paine's criticism of the capricious obeisance of conscience. Regardless, government arises because there is some dangerous or incalculable element (namely, one another) circulating in nature from which "society must be defended" (Foucault, 2003/1997). Ultimately, as Locke and Paine suggest, that element is the irrational, incalculable dimension of human subjectivity that does not conform to the law of nature.

Returning to the sovereignty in question theories, this effort to control and render calculable *subjectivity* comes into sharper relief. First, through McSwite (1997b), we see the intrinsically problematic dialectic of boundary and absorption that they demonstrate is endemic to the Reasoned point of view. The tendency of Reason is to attempt to infinitely extend the boundary, be it of category or consciousness itself. Drawing from Hummel and Stivers (1998), the bounding work of representation in politics can be viewed as an effort to confine and restrict the undefined, empty set of the human subject to the defined, explicit domain of interest. Yet interest itself is insufficient for (literally) capturing the human subject and its desires; something is left over on the other side of interest. All the interests in the world never add up to One.

This leftover is the primary object of control and, as Harmon (1995) shows, of administrative ethics. In Harmon's critique, we see in the rationalist discourse on government effort to quarantine subjectivity through series of moral and procedural constraints and, in doing so, recapture that harmony of "lost innocence." Harmon argues persuasively that for rationalist (mainstream, conventional) ethics "responsible action is synonymous with morally or legally *correct* action, and that the purpose of moral discourse on government and of laws and other guidelines regulating administrative action is to preserve or restore a state of moral innocence." Note that this recovery is now undertaken *within* society since the problems and inconveniences of the state of nature have necessitated the creation of political society. For Harmon, paradox "describes the condition of innocence lost irretrievably with the dawning of consciousness" (p. 4). Rationalist ethical discourse, however, denies that this is lost irretrievably and participates in the project to restore in society what was lost in the state of nature by controlling through moral injunction and administrative rules any element that has escaped representational techniques of normalization or discipline. Representational governing, then, is charged with quarantining the irrational element of the human subject. It does so, however, by attempting to foreclose the subject itself from the domain of governing by regularizing thought and action and eliminating the moment of inconvenience from judgment. Government is the technical enterprise of making society calculable by regularizing self-legislation and conscience; and in managing this threat, it aims to remedy in actual society what could not be achieved in the fictional state of nature.

Government as Symptom of the People

This gap described above in the disarticulated, split sovereign, the People, is homologous to the division posited between the social and the political. An object of political representation is posited, and the correct representation must be discerned from among other competing representations of the social from the position of government. Differences are arrayed against a background of a taken-for-granted unity and are conceptualized as deviations from the oneness of the People's interest, an interest that requires, internally, the positing of specific content of the People's common good and externally, the production of recognition of that commonality. In rendering judgment, it becomes the responsibility of government to accurately represent society through its judgments, actions, laws, and policies and, in doing so, to act on society to make it more secure and calculable. This is essentially Fox and Miller's (1995) "feedback loop" model of democracy. This loop produces two anomalies, though. As suggested in chapter 3, the paradox of this construction, which aims to limit the actions of government, is that the potential reach of government now extends infinitely into the opaque recesses of society because government is charged with the making regular of society and the control of subjectivity. This is the essence of modern biopolitics. Society is posited as an originary self-functioning entity that creates an ostensibly limited government but, in actuality, it produces a government that takes the totality of society (expressed as social life itself) as its object. Second, under the reign of the People, the only explicit reason to have government is to render an order more secure and more calculable in the service of an originary wholeness and actually to *fabricate in political society* that lost innocence of society and the state of nature. Utopia lost in the state of nature is utopia refound in political society.

Constructed from the myth of lost innocence and so always already marking our moral failure, government exists, then, for this silently determined end in a double sense comparable to the double partiality of the People. Government is partial, first, in its content insofar as it articulates particular predicates that define the common and acts as common judge, excluding other predicates. This is a difficult trick to pull off when the discourse of limited government speaks the language of universality. The People's government is partial, more basically, as a particular political form and a way of being together and, more precisely, a form for which calculability and control of subjectivity are the end of government.

This construction rests on a foundational paradox. The prepolitical domain of the People is asserted as the origin of government, one, in effect, tasked with the fabrication of a presupposed harmonious, calculable order of the state of nature. *Yet the very presence of government marks the failure of that self-regulating unity.* Thus, we can say, "*The People does not exist and government is its symptom.*" In representation, *government* marks the impossible fullness of the People. It is the symptom of the *failure* of the People, but the presupposition of the People actually displaces this failure onto the state of nature and the incalculable quality of the human subject. Furthermore, prior to any specific hegemonic articulation (i.e., production of content), it is *government* itself that already stands for the second dimension of fantasy, the seamy underside of the beatific fantasy; government is *substantially different* than the People. At the core of the representational political ontology, government (conventionally defined) is the "*exterior representation of the limit*" (McSwite, 1997b, p. 249; emphasis in original).

Lateness and Partiality

There are, preliminarily, three reasons why the legitimacy of government, including its liberal iteration, is structurally always in question in the political ontology of representation. The first concerns the temporal and substantive disjuncture inaugurated by the positing of the division between the political and the social in the People's disembodied, split sovereignty. Government chronologically follows the People or society; it is the foreign element whose very existence must be accounted for. Government is always *late* to the scene, a lateness that marks a difference *in kind*. Second, the disembodied nature of popular sovereignty creates an irreducible gap between the government qua representation and the exclusion(s). Government can in fact *never* represent the *whole* People since the People does not exist except as a hegemonic *partiality* that inhabits a discourse of naturalistic universality.

The critical third reason that government's legitimacy is suspect concerns the general way in which representation reproduces a stable and coherent social order. As suggested in the paragraphs above, the People in the liberal context establishes a "limit-government." Governing is vast and pervasive, yet it is undertaken under the auspices of a self-regulating whole. But, in fact, government proper represents the very failure of the People. The interplay of the two dimensions of fantasy work to constitute and contain the People, primarily by targeting that inconvenient leftover of human subjectivity; indeed, this is precisely what spills over into the interstices of disciplinary enclosures. Government represents the impossibility of the People but also makes possible the articulation of the People through constitutive exclusion. At the same time, representational logic erects limits qua models throughout various sites in society, as discussed in chapter 5, in order to fabricate a harmonious unity. Thus there are three levels: (1) subjectivity is controlled through identification with the model; (2) social interactions are mediated through the terms of local models; and (3) small-p politics is the hegemonic struggle for the authority to define the model (People-as-One). The whole of the social field is combatively directed toward the future realization of a lost, impossible whole external to itself.

The rub of the situation is this: maintaining the world of representation demands failure, since failure is ontologically required for the logic of the People to "succeed." Government action, defined as this biopolitical project of realizing the coincidence of the people and the People, *must* in some sense fail, and this failure is in large part sealed by the impossible requirement that the heterogeneity of the social field be homogenized (represented) in the biopolitical conflation and the deferral of reality to the impossible grounds of the model. To borrow from Dreyfus and Rabinow's (1983, p. 195) comment about Foucault and the great incarceration, the question is not, *Why does government fail the People?* It is, rather, *What other ends are served through this failure, which is not a failure after all?*[2] The ends served are at least twofold. First, as suggested in chapter 3, there is the paradoxical consequence of the presupposition of a unified People as the war of all against all—the proliferation of combat throughout the social field and deep into the so-called apolitical domains of the economy and personal relationships. Second, again following Dreyfus and Rabinow, "[reformers] promised normalization and happiness through science and law. When they fail, this only justifies the need for more of the same." In this tautological hermeneutic, the ends served through the recurrent failure of law and science is the continued call for "More law! More science!" (p. 196). This "failure" is, ultimately, a function of representation's positivization of the void and the empty set at the heart of the human world and its subject. Its very logic drives to positivize and reduce the void to the proposition or terms of the model.

To rethink government today means to rethink fundamentally the relationship between instituted authority and its displaced nonorigin, to shift the biopolitical relationship such that the void remains open rather than materialized, targeted, and arrested. Contemporary conditions appear to both imperil and enable this kind of thinking. As the German poet Friedrich Holderlin (1980/1802) wrote, "But where the danger threatens/ that which saves from it also grows" (p. 463).

The Exception Becomes the Rule: Security, Control, and Indistinctions

I shift now from a general theoretical analysis of the liberal democratic discourse of popular sovereignty within the framework of representation to a more focused examination of the conditions of the contemporary legitimacy crisis of the administrative state. Recall that the two regimes of biopolitical production, law and administration, were distinguished by a particular orientation toward the exclusion and by a set of techniques and apparatuses for producing and maintaining the sovereign decision on the exception. In this section I will describe a third moment in the biopolitical state and later link this emergent topography and set of technologies to the contemporary legitimacy crisis. This is an account of the movement from internalization to contemporary "state of exception" and the biopolitical regime of "securitization" (Bigo, 2002; Feldman, 2004; Martin, 2004).

Breakdown of the Disciplinary Society: Space and Subject

There is an ample supply of theories, histories, and narratives of the complex period from roughly the late 1960s to the extending transitional period of the present (e.g., Albrow, 1996; Beck, 1992; Beck, Giddens, & Lash, 1994; Castells, 2000; Harvey, 1990; Jameson, 2000/1984; Putnam, 2000;

Rosenau, 1990). Though the dimensions of it are, of course, contested and contestable, there is a general consensus that there has been a fundamental change in sociopolitical and economic relations in the wake of the social revolutions of the 1960s and the end of capitalism's "golden age" and its robust post–World War II expansion. These changes ushered in a period that has been called, variously, postmodern, late capitalist, postindustrial, postaffluent and, more recently, globalization. What seems clear is that a central trigger of these changes was the rejection, in the phrase of Herbert Marcuse (1964), of certain elements of the one-dimensional world of disciplinary society and its public administration.

As we have seen, the integrative logic of internalization cut two ways. On the one hand, its pluralistic ethos (over the course of several decades) recognized differences, and the possible predicates of the People gradually expanded. Its attention to actual living conditions (albeit, as Stivers (2000) shows, its attention was perhaps compromised) and to maintaining social equilibrium points to a determined break with the exclusionary legalism of constitutionalism. On the other hand, however, disciplinary society retained the ontological commitments of representation and put them to work in new neutralizing, enclosing technologies that, in fact, crushed and homogenized differences, demonstrated an abstracted disregard for living conditions, and aimed to manage materialized exclusions in intense and invasive ways. It sought to narrow thought and behavior to one-dimensional efficiency in service of the project of fabricating the People-as-One. The upheavals of the 1960s signal a rebellion against the disciplinary order's one-dimensionality as well as the sedimented legal exclusions inherited from constitutionalism. They signal a rejection of the models and molds of representation. They signal a demand for the universalist pretensions of the People to make good as well as a demand that individuals become "sovereign" over the terms of their governing model. These demands profoundly destabilize the representational order and produce a radical reorientation in the biopolitical project of the People and the conduct of conduct. When the People ceases to be produced, the exception becomes the rule.

The Society of Control

With Deleuze (1995/1990), we can call *the society of control* a state of affairs in which disciplinary enclosures rupture and, in Agamben's (1998/1995) phrase, "the exception starts to become the rule" (p. 38). When the exception becomes the rule there is an increasing difficulty in authoritatively defining the terms of the model and materializing the exclusion, rendering the whole fantasy structure of the People unstable. Thus, from this view, what we have been experiencing over the last thirty years is a gradual breakdown in the technologies that produced the collective capacity to identify and materialize the exclusion, thereby generating the object of governmental activity in the public realm and, by extension, the People. The referent of political representation (that which politics purports to represent) fades; the administrative state's interstices blur. However, this breakdown also cuts in another direction. Rather than seeing a collapse in the biopolitical project of the People, we witness intensification and personalization of these efforts on a distinct social topography in which exceptions and threats proliferate, the position of government shifts radically, and biopolitical calculability assumes new technological and divisive forms.

I want to call attention to two important aspects of this passage from disciplinarity to control: spatiality and subjectivity. As Foucault (1995/1975) demonstrates and as discussed in chapter 5, disciplinary spaces are places of confinement. Extending Foucault's work and exemplifying the theory of representation as one of model and copy, Deleuze (1995/1990) writes, "Confinements are *molds*, different modelings, while controls are a *modulation*, like a self-transmuting molding continually changing from one moment to the next, or like a sieve whose mesh varies from one point to another" (pp. 178–179). Disciplinary society was characterized by enclosures and stoppages. One worked at the factory or office and stopped, and went home; one went to school and stopped, and came home (Hardt & Negri, 2000). At each stop one encountered relatively stable identities and expectations through acknowledged authoritative models of judgment and behavior. As Deleuze writes, one of the distinguishing characteristics of control societies is not *stopping*, but modulating. Work, for instance, never *stops*. One only works more or less at a given moment without regard to physical space or location. "In disciplinary societies, you were always starting all over again . . . while in control societies you never finish anything" (p. 179). Similarly, the explosion of temporary, outsourced, and contract labor dissolves the stability of the workplace as labor becomes scattered throughout various "client sites." New technology diffuses through contemporary life, carrying with it the expectations of being constantly available for work. This problematizes spatial demarcations between work and home, rendering as a *decision* those exceptional, non-work-related moments. The spatial reconfiguration is critical. Space becomes *smooth* and begins to lose its distinctions; boundaries between market and government, inside and outside, the criminal and the everyday, public and private begin to blur. As we will see below, the smoothness of space does not, however, mean the disappearance of borders and technologies of exclusion, as globalization enthusiasts suggest. Rather, their modalities and loci have changed.

Concomitant with the blurring of disciplinary enclosures, a destabilization of identity also occurs. Identification in the administrative state and disciplinary society was already fragmented by disciplinary technologies that were spatially differentiated. But the integrative project of the new state aims to reconstitute these fragments in the higher, national identity. The rupturing of enclosures, however, renders the discrete spaces of action uncertain but does not do away with the operative models. Thus, while we are still mothers and fathers, workers and students, we simply are no longer certain about when and where any given logic is operative and which identification is primary in any given space, a dilemma compounded by the growing expectation that we will bring more and more of ourselves to work (Hirshhorn, 1997; Pfeffer & Sutton, 2006). Individual identity is experienced as an unregulated, disintegrated flow of identifications or parts of a personality that never seem to add up to One. The upshot of this, as Zizek (2000c, p. 368) suggests, is a subject that is highly narcissistic and unstable. The subject is unstable because a coherent identity is sustained through the "balancing" of these fragments of personality, which is constantly under siege from perceived threats and competitors. It is narcissistic because, first, ubiquitous competition pushes the subject into a mode of "continuous self-improvement" and second, because this vulnerability is coupled with the injunction to become fully responsible for the management of one's life and all its complex contingencies. I will return to this point below.

Underlying many of these changes are shifts in authority. This has been described as a breakdown in the authoritative structure afforded by "tradition," a condition in which "what has been" no longer provides the moral and normative content for "what should be done" in any general way (Giddens, 1994). Of this posttraditional world, Zizek (2000c) writes, "there is no Nature or Tradition providing a firm foundation on which one can rely, [so] that even our innermost impetuses . . . are more and more experienced as something to be chosen. How to feed and educate a child, how to proceed in sexual seduction, how and what to eat, how to relax and amuse oneself—all spheres increasingly 'colonized' by reflexivity, that is, experienced as something to be learned and decided upon" (pp. 366–367). When the past provides little guidance for the future, more and more of daily life becomes *exceptional:* something nonroutine and nonprogrammed to be decided upon. When viewed in light of the erosion of the prescriptive designations of tradition, this state of exception also opens the individual subject to the manifold possibilities of constructing oneself. Decisions are not merely selections among alternatives (i.e., which is the better insurance plan) but in many cases hinge on the conscious, precarious undertaking of constructing personal identity. Certainly, for many living in industrialized nations, we now may choose our utility companies, our financial planners and retirement plans, and our health care providers (Schwartz, 2004). But, as Zizek suggests, we also can exercise fundamental choice in issues like how we want to look physically, what gender we prefer to be, and what sex we want our children to be. Bioengineering is the outer limits of this brave new world of choice, and in it we see vividly the breakdown of any notion of any given, unconstructed boundary between nature and society. However, this infinite possibility also produces feelings of insecurity and vulnerability about making the "right" choice.

Access and the Regulation of Mobility

The transformation of social space from the differentiated enclosures of discipline to the smooth spaces of control changes the work of fabrication fundamentally. Disciplinarity aimed at changing the individual by subjecting him or her to various "molds" of thought and behavior. However, as it happened, changing people proved to be difficult and expensive (Simon, 1988, p. 773). Control, though, *modulates* and operates on what can be called an *actuarial* basis (O'Malley, 2004, 1997), seeking to modify the effects of behavior and/or change circumstances through an assessment of potential risk rather than making people up through disciplinary normalization. Actuarialism incorporates failure into a program or policy, and in doing so radically constrains the scope of its intervention. Rather than attempting to regulate society to a new state of integration as disciplinary biopower did, control acts strategically and locally, and attempts to mitigate and calculate contingency. It polices borders and boundaries while appearing to recognize that instability or risk is not pathological, but simply the way the world is. The attitude appears hesitant, cautious and, seemingly, quite pragmatic. What is controlled in the society of control is less behavior and thought per se than *access* to discrete locations. Control is a boundary or frontier practice that aims to guide and regulate *mobility* (Shamir, 2005). With this actuarial focus on riskiness, the subject becomes further fragmented and dispersed into a series of abstract vectors, such as nationality, ethnicity, spending and consuming habits, credit worthiness, and so on, from which determinations of riskiness and access are made in lieu of the impositions of disciplinary molds.

The workings of this calculus can be seen vividly in the contemporary efforts to create a "virtual border" and arrest the movement of undocumented persons into the United States. True to its name, a virtual border does not refer to geographical boundaries between nation-states but rather extends invisibly through space, promising to screen out people (i.e., deny access) before they even reach the geographical boundaries of the United States. Its virtuality resides in a network of some twenty databases, the United States Visitor and Immigrant Status Indicator Technology, or "US VISIT" (Amoore, 2006). Louise Amoore writes that US VISIT "enacts a series of dividing practices in which the subject is broken up into calculable risk factors, both within herself (such as, for example, 'student' and 'muslim' and 'woman') and necessarily in relation to others (as, for example, 'alien,' 'immigrant' or 'illegal')" (p. 339). It is underwritten by "the guiding assumption . . . that encoded risk profiles can be used as a basis to predict and prevent future acts" and to draw a line "between those with legitimate claims to mobility and those whose claims are somehow dangerous" (pp. 340, 341). Patterns can be mined and discerned from the mounting caches of data in order to rank, array, and distribute representations of dangerousness. Like the war in Iraq and the "pre-crime" division in the blockbuster film *Minority Report* (Spielberg, 2002),[3] then, the regulatory control of mobilities and access is *preemptive* technology (Diken, 2004). It purports to exclude people or "weed out" (Amoore & De Goede, 2005) *in advance of a computationally anticipated undesirable* act.

In this context, we can appreciate the rise of the "sovereign individual" (Davidson & Rees-Mogg, 1999; Thorne, 2004) and the curious *re*assembling of the fragmented subject of risk as well as the pervasive, everyday quality of preemptive, weeding-out strategies. We saw above that the rupture of disciplinary enclosures has precipitated a destabilization of individual identity and integrative strategies. Consistent with the ethos of post-traditionalism, *self*-calculation of risk becomes the task of the supposedly autonomous subject. Rose (1997) writes, "Individuals are to become 'experts of themselves', to adopt an educated and knowledgeable relation of self-care in respect of their bodies, their minds, their forms of conduct and that of the members of their own families" (p. 59). We are expected, then, to surveil and police ourselves. As the story goes, those who do not manage their own personal risk or police themselves and their families cannot lament any denial of access or restriction on their mobility. We must all learn to act preemptively and be able to see into the future to anticipate and plan for all possible contingencies. Yet, as psychic technology remains the stuff of Hollywood, this is a hopeless task, though, here again, it discursively *succeeds* in locating fault and responsibility in the individual body and its owner's "poor" choices as well and in reinforcing the experience of fear and vulnerability that grounds contemporary narcissism and the desire for security.

The discomforting paradox of control is the simultaneous presence of open, reflexive choice and the risk-based essentialization of *fragments* of identity. Thus, while the world of individual choice seems to open us to a radically self-constructed future, that future in fact closes in the face of preemptive, bounding-out strategies that seem to foreclose that future. While the future opens up into an ocean of constructable possibilities, embracing that future seems more dangerous, less secure, more closed off than ever. The dominion of the sovereign individual is a lonely and fearful one.

Representation in the Society of Control and the "War on Terror"

Here we begin to see how representation is reworked in the smooth, "open" spaces of the society of control through preemptive strategies of risk-based exclusion. The so-called war on terror provides a good example of how this is occurring. It is critical, first, to appreciate that this "war" emerged in and capitalized on the contemporary construction and fragmentation of social space and identity; it takes hold of and redirects existing discourses of insecurity, risk, and mobility. It also is rooted deeply in the liberal constitution's teleology of calculation and security. Well before the events of September 11, 2001, Americans experienced "the world as a dangerous place" (Bush, 2002). At its core, liberalism organizes a political life predicated on the fear of states of nature and the need for rendering society calculable.

This new war, however, brings into sharp relief key dimensions of the current biopolitical regime and the crisis of representation. First, in this war, both the threat and the domain of battle are limitless. We can see this in several ways. In terms of territory, the homeland is itself virtual, extending indiscriminately across geographical or physical borders;[4] external and internal security concerns effectively collapse into one another (Salter, 2004, p. 81). Related to this, the business of rendering secure is, similarly, without any definable boundary or limit. Everything from electronic networks to food and water supplies to physical buildings and infrastructure become objects of securitization. Similarly, the distinction between the civilian and solider is blurred not only by the use of contractors and private military firms to provide security and to wage war (Singer, 2005; Suess Kennedy & Jensen, 2004; Traynor, 2003) but also by the declaration that after September 11, 2001, "every American is a solider" (Bumiller, 2001).[5] There are no exceptions, no spaces, and no subjects that are exempt from control and surveillance. Finally and more prosaically, as discussed above, the everyday space of control is marked by the growing indiscernibility of distinct, autonomous spaces, such as private and public, the home and the workplace, and by the proliferation of the exceptional, nonprogrammed decisions in everyday life. The breakdown of disciplinary boundaries, the generalized state of risk, and actuarial determination of dangerousness render us all potential objects of preemptive securitization (Diken & Laustsen, 2002; Gregory, 2004; Minca, 2005). The threshold of exclusion is now mobile and fluid.

In this state of exception, the ubiquity of threat and danger impede the general materialization of the exclusion in the social field, and the referent of representational politics is no longer produced. This occurs, again, because of the particular construction of the society of control, which breaks down the individual subject into divisible categories and vectors of risk and dangerousness. Models of representation become, in part, "virtualized" in electronic databases, and the *individual human body,* the carrier of these risk factors, becomes the fragmented terra firma for representation. Amoore (2006) writes, "the body, in effect, becomes the carrier of the border as it is inscribed with multiple encoded boundaries of access" (pp. 347–348). The body becomes "a password" (Lyon, 2001). Shifting from a concern with the regulation and molding of the processes of social life and the integration of fragments into the new state, representation now locates the "real" in the *individual* body rather than the *body politic*; securitizing biometrics replace integrative disciplinary models and enclosures.

Categories of difference are determined in terms of riskiness that allegedly permit the assessment of a given copy's accuracy as regards its dangerousness and riskiness and, by extension, legitimately allow exclusion from whatever domain is in question, be it a nation, an apartment, or credit in a manner that appears to overcome earlier forms of discriminatory social and political exclusion. Control "transgresses the duality of mass and individual" (Diken & Laustsen, 2002, p. 297); differences are managed or self-regulated rather than suppressed. Indeed, from a limited perspective, maintaining excluded, racialized Others works against the logic of the global market. As Hardt and Negri (2000) sardonically write, "Trade brings differences together and the more the merrier! . . . The world market establishes a real politics of difference. . . . Marketing itself is based on differences, and the more differences are given, the more marketing strategies can develop. . . . Every difference is an opportunity. . . . When one looks at U.S. corporate ideology (and to a lesser extent, at U.S. corporate practice), it is clear that corporations do not operate simply by excluding the gendered and/or racialized Other. In fact, the old modernist forms of racist and sexist theory are the explicit enemies of this new corporate culture" (pp. 150–153).

Suggestions, however, that the exclusion is no longer materialized may appear to be a conclusion driven simply by internal logic, and we need to consider an important objection. Certainly, we can recognize the generalized state of exception and risk and the extent to which various dimensions of our identity or behavior might suddenly be rendered risky. But must we not also recognize that not all bodies are the same and that not all vectors carry equal measures of perceived dangerousness? Indeed, this so-called war—as well as much of political discourse over the previous thirty years—seems to make extensive use of racialized, criminalized Others. Like the legal forms of exclusion of the nineteenth century, political discourse appears to rely on clear categories of exclusion—the Immigrant, the Terrorist, the Muslim—in order to sustain the fearful spectacle of popular sovereignty. As Randall Kennedy (1997) suggests, in today's society of control, color may serve as a *visible* preemptive carrier of dangerousness irrespective of the "objective" risk vectors projected by the domain of the virtual. By collapsing dangerousness into coloredness, color appears to work as a kind of everyday shorthand for identifying the risky in the state of exception and its distorted embrace of difference. It, moreover, serves to reinforce sedimented disparities that, in turn, justify contemporary classification of danger and risk.

Yet even in these codings we can see the break between former strategies of managing the exclusion and those deployed in the society of control. In control, neither integrative-disciplinary technologies nor legal strategies that assert qualitative, hierarchical differences between those inside and those outside the People are at work, even though control technologies draw from and bear resemblance to both. Rather, as suggested above, control technologies basically manage access and mobility, and so exercise contextual forms of segregation. Consistent with the logic of representation, these segregations take place as deviations from the model; these are distributions made *internal* to the originary, constitutive exclusion. Thus this theory of representation challenges the notion that color in general names the exclusion or a general Other; it questions whether color or race can be elevated always and in general over other terms of rank and distance such as class, gender, sexuality, able-bodiedness, and so on, and as such seeks to track hegemonic models both within and among these categories of identity and against the background of the presumptive ontology of the One. Indeed, one of the practical problems in this state of exception is not merely contesting the terms of the model but naming the dominant term that structures and overcodes all other relations of dominance and, by extension, locating a privileged point of resistance or opposition to the model. With the fading of the People, the face of the enemy, too, becomes less clear. As I will argue later in the chapter, the materialization of the exclusion assumes an unexpected and dangerous form, and the segregation of control takes two general, spatial forms in a new biopolitical configuration.

The Camp and a New Biopolitical Relation

In this state of exception, amid the collapse of the traditional limits that sustained the order of the People (e.g., public-private, social-political, nature-culture), a distinctive biopolitical relationship is emerging. Recall that the project of fabricating the People was characterized by efforts to impose a single qualified form of life, bios, on life itself, zoë. This can be written as:

$$\text{Bios}_1 \rightarrow \text{Zoë}$$

The biopolitical project of the People attempted to fabricate an order, to bring into reality the unity that was presupposed. It presumed a unity behind all difference and appearance and drove to fabricate that oneness through a differentiating logic of exclusion, division, and distribution; its political technologies were deployed according to the second dimension of fantasy. Securitization in the society of control, however, is less concerned with fabricating a social order or making up a body politic than with regulating access to discrete spaces and with guiding *dis*order (Agamben, 2002, p. 2); control thrives explicitly on the success-in-failure logic of representation. It accepts the universalist discourse of inclusion and humanity yet "realistically" abandons the integrative, calculative project of the new state to focus on the core task of securitization and decentralizing decision making to the sovereign individual. The relationship between bios and zoë assumes a new form:

$$\text{Bios}_1 \leftrightarrow \text{Zoë}$$

The political form of life and biological existence enter into a *relationship of nonrelation* (Agamben, 1998/1995). It is not simply a matter of being a poor copy of the model but of being in nonrelation to the model itself. That is, the political retreats from its imposition, rendering zoë as bare, insecure, stripped naked of any political or symbolic designations or predicates.

As discipline inaugurated the enclosure, this contemporary biopolitical relation also institutes a new general spatial logic. The generic name Giorgio Agamben (1998/1995) gives to this space that creates the relation of nonrelation between life and politics is "the Camp," a site where, Agamben writes, "everything is possible" (p. 170) and its "inhabitants [are] stripped of every political status and wholly reduced to bare life" (p. 171). In the Camp, a political subject becomes *homo sacer*, the Roman legal name for the life that can be extinguished without either homicide or sacrifice. No longer does the Camp name an anomalous, exceptional part of our social order—if it ever did (Bauman, 1989; Agamben, 1998/1995). Today the exceptional space of the Camp is now the rule; and in a time in which the extraordinary logic of the Camp dominates, we are all potential *hominis sacres*.

If the Camp is so prevalent, where can we see it? We see the proliferation of the Camp's relation of nonrelation since the advent of the war on terror in literal camps and detention facilities like Guantánamo Bay, Abu Ghraib, Australia's notorious and now closed Woomera refugee camp, and the secret prisons (Priest, 2005) that have (dis)appeared around the world to interrogate those suspected of terrorism (Thorne and Kouzmin, 2004). The language used to describe these politically denuded bodies speaks to this nonrelation, for example, "ghost detainees" (Human Rights Watch, 2004). Though these new spaces may shock, we must appreciate that the United States slowly has been constructing these kinds of spaces in the U.S. prison system for more than thirty years. "Lane McCotter" might name this intersection. McCotter, a former Utah state prison official and head of the departments of corrections in New Mexico and Texas, is an executive for the innocuously named Management & Training Corporation, a Utah-based company that is the third-largest owner and operator of private prisons (Butterfield, 2004). McCotter oversaw the reopening of Abu Ghraib in Iraq, and his name marks a line of continuity that erases the inside/outside distinction that psychologically comforts and distances us from the exceptional locations "over there."

There has been in the United States a gradual reduction of prisoners to the status of bare life. Loic Wacquant (2002b) describes the explosive growth of incarceration in America (nearly 7 million people are now under the control of the corrections system [Vogel, 2003]), particularly of African Americans, as *warehousing*, which marks a radical departure from the normalizing logic of the disciplinary society. Wacquant (2002b) writes, "What makes the racial intercession of the carceral system different today is that, unlike slavery, Jim Crow and the ghetto of the mid-century, it does not carry out a positive economic mission of recruitment and disciplining of the workforce: it serves only to warehouse the precarious and deproletarianized fractions of the black working class" (p. 53). As the term *warehousing* suggests, prisons cease to be zones of normalization and become places for human storage, places to exclude bodies for specified or indefinite periods of time. As stored bodies, prisoners are denuded of minimal "privileges" or "amenities" like "educational programs, sports, entertainment, and activities aimed at rehabilitation such as job development and counseling" (Wacquant, 2002a, p. 21). This unfolds in tandem with civic and political denuding which excludes convicts from participation at the polls and from the receipt of government services, such as public housing and welfare benefits, often forever and irrespective of the offense (Wacquant, 2002b). Prisons become warehouses for bare life; prisoners become bodies in relations of nonrelation.[6]

Camps for "the Winners"

The denuding practices of the Camp and the proliferation of the relation of nonrelation are visible throughout U.S. society and, as the prominent criminologist Nils Christie (2000) has shown, across the globe. So expansive is the increase of incarcerated bodies and so loud the booming of the crime-control industry that has that grown up with it that Christie writes of the development of "gulags, Western style" (see also Thorne and Kouzmin, 2004). Following Agamben, Bulent Diken and Cartsen Bagge Laustsen (2005) have provided a provocative sociological account of the Camp that illustrates the proliferation of its spatial logic beyond, but inclusive of, the confines of this gulag archipelago. They argue compellingly that the profound mistake we make is to view the Camp as an anomaly rather than *as the rule.* This once-exceptional space is the now dominant spatial logic in the society of control. Thus, while we "see" the detention centers and refugee camps and, with some effort, can surface the U.S. carceral archipelago, we fail to see that many of us already live in camps, albeit "benevolent" ones for "the winners" in the contemporary world.

Diken and Laustsen (2005) identify two kinds of modes of access for these winner and loser camps (p. 9): two forms of segregation, one voluntary, the other involuntary (p. 95). For the winners, entry is blocked but exit is free; for the losers, entry is free but exit is blocked. The winner camps, or what elsewhere Blakely and Snyder (1997) identify as "luxury laagers," include gated communities, theme parks, shopping malls,[7] and tourist resorts. Having considered above camps whose exits are blocked, let us consider the examples of the gated community and the tourist resort, camps whose entries are blocked. These gated communities are meticulously planned and designed to create an imagined fantasy of community that never existed, one undisturbed by antagonism or political conflict. Indeed, they are materializations of the very fantasy of the People: sanctuaries—insulated, protected zones amid a dangerous, insecure world, the gate demarcating the secure inside from the insecure outside. Yet gates themselves may not be necessary. As Barbara McCabe's (2005) work suggests, perhaps the more profound proliferation of this kind of community is concealed by the gates—namely, the explosion of invisible private governments in the form of home owners associations (HOAs). HOAs are the creation not of the sovereign, as cities are, but of markets and corporation law. They opt out of the polis and, as McCabe writes, "now outnumber cities 13 to 1" (p. 405). Through their covenants, conditions, and restrictions (CC&R) documents, HOAs regulate individual and collective behavior toward the "security of restricted collective preferences over the uncertainty of future, unpalatable individual choice (Heckathorne & Maser, 1990)" (p. 409). Thus the individual choice of admission involves a voluntary relinquishing of future choice, action, and speech, and these rules themselves are typically established by the developer prior to sale and subsequently difficult to change (pp. 415–418). Thus the gates promise security; the CC&Rs promise calculability and the regulation of lifestyle and behavior. However, given the proliferation of HOAs, the extent to which opting into these exceptional enclaves is voluntary becomes questionable.

Diken and Laustsen (2005), finally, illustrate how tourist enclaves like Club Med constitute the perverse opposite of the prison or detention center. In these "tourist camps" visitors are enticed to misbehave and abandon the conventions of and concessions made to the "normal" reality back home. They write, "Having left the social origin, stripped of former identities, the tourist occupies, or fantasizes to occupy, a sort of state of nature, in which tourists 'behave'—literally—like escaped convicts (Houellebecq, 2002)" (p. 111). The tourist industry enjoins us to leave "civilization" voluntarily and to return to a time before the pressures of modern society; it markets a reconstructed fantasy rooted in a state of nature in which the violation of inhibition and taboo is de facto *demanded* by the experience. It is a kind of superego injunction to "Enjoy!" (McGowan, 2004; Salecl, 2004; Zizek, 2000c). In these "exceptional" nonplaces, bodies become stripped of social and political predicates and obligations. We willfully become bare life, enjoined to surrender to pleasure, care-lessness, and pure animality.

When we see these spatial logics at work in "exceptional" spaces, we can then begin to see, as in the case of HOAs, how unexceptional the exception is actually becoming. We can recall that after September 11, 2001,

Americans were enjoined to fulfill their patriotic obligations through shopping and personal consumption (Williams, 2004). This demand to consume points to the very core of the state of the exception, the society of control, and the erosion of tradition. As sociologist Todd McGowan (2004) writes, traditional society is basically concerned with the preservation and success of the whole, and "the individual must give up her or his dreams of wholly individual achievement and fit his or her abilities into the structure of the team." Or, we can add, sacrificing for the People. As suggested in the section on choice and identity above, the breakdown of the world of representation shifts attention away from this goal, and people become more concerned with their own idiosyncratic, exceptional concerns and less worried about the "greater good." It is "no longer requisite that subjects accept constant dissatisfaction as the price for existing within a social order [i.e., sacrificing for the sake of the greater good]" (p. 3). Thus, while there may be some truth in analyses that interpret these changes as the retreat from public life, it is simply incorrect to view this "subjective turn" solely as selfishness or an apathetic retreat from the social world without taking account of the profound changes under way in the state of exception. As the exception becomes the rule, the very plausibility of a stable public sphere is attenuated; our conventional categories for organizing politics and our collective experience lose their efficacy; our experience of insecurity is amplified and mobilized to the ends of social (dis)ordering and the representational combat; and we come to relate to one another less in terms of the imposition of a single, qualified bios than in a relation of nonrelation. We are sovereigns in our own individualized, insecure worlds, shuddering in the shadows of indistinction between two camps.

Government as Constitutive Exclusion

Vanishing Referents and Antigovernmentalism

Strictly speaking, securitization and its toolbox of entrepreneurial, "securitorial" remedies have replaced public administration and its disciplinary, normalizing technologies. Though its tactics and strategies signal a state of crisis and vulnerability for this ontology, representation still continues to pursue the creation of a calculable, "safe and secure world" without disturbance. However, this unfolds not through disciplinary imposition but through the regulation of mobility and access. Individual subjects are less objects of coercion than we are induced by fears of insecurity and the denuded vulnerability of the "losers'" camp to self-regulate in accordance with our own individual security interests. On this terrain, government, too, becomes centrally concerned with the business of rendering secure. At the same time, however, rendering secure depends on the proliferation and production of the perception of threat and states of nature and the experience of vulnerability and isolation. In this way, control makes use of disorder and disintegration.

With regard to the crisis of legitimacy, two preliminary conclusions can be drawn at this point. First, to draw from the argument made above, an elementary contradiction in the rise and fall of the administrative state in part accounts for its legitimacy problem. The liberal constitution creates a government to serve the limited technical functions of calculation. Government is thought to be a neutral third party created to mediate disputes and preserve and/or realize order, an order from which it is separate rather than constitutive of. At the turn of the twentieth century, however, something changed when the exclusion, the excess, was internalized by the matrix of disciplinary society. Government was called upon to preserve the limits of representational order, but it was required to take positive action to discipline the bodies of the exclusion. The bind that the administrative state found itself in was that in taking positive disciplinary action, government appeared to violate the fiction of neutrality, as the disciplinary technologies on which it depended in order to sustain the neutral gaze of the fantasy and its materialized exclusion began to fail. It appeared to act on behalf of specific objects and not the natural order. It began to *appear* as *partial* and as an instrument of some particularity, some one specificity. Second, public administration is no longer legitimate for the simple reason that its theory and practice (discourse) are now archaic. Public administration existed and remained viable within a certain social topographical configuration that no longer exists. Governance in the mode of control has superseded it, and with this, ushered in the rise of the new public management. I do not wish, though, to exaggerate the novelty of the present, as some overzealous declarations of the passing of the past have (e.g. Barzelay, 2004/1987).[8] Public administration as defined and analyzed in chapter 5, however, *has* been superseded by a new mode of governing and biopolitical regime.

More to the point, however, the eroding efficacy of representation means that the very referent of political representation is not being produced; there is nothing for politics to represent. The People is not produced coherently in light of the individualizing and camping logics of the society of control since the very purpose of these technologies is to produce disintegration and disorder while maintaining the purported reassuring promise of oneness, the secure society, and the recovery of lost innocence. In the context of control, securitization, and the regulation of mobility and access, the exertion of governmental authority can easily come to be viewed as coercive, biased, or illegitimate since social regulation now focuses on access and mobility rather than fabricating "common" sense or technical neutrality. Authoritative representations made in the name of the People can be seen as hegemonic because in the individuated world of control there is no People. Or rather, it may be more precise to say that individualization against the backdrop of the People produces *individual representations of the People.* Here, again, we see the collapse of the mass into the individual. At the same moment, though, governmental authority seems boundless so long as it conforms to the symbolic universe of control and the telos of security. There appears to be both a retreat and an expansion. As I will argue next, understanding how these two dimensions of expansion and retreat operate in our state of exception is the key to understanding the contemporary terrain of governing.

Government as Constitutive Exclusion

As we are analyzing these extraordinary times, let me begin with an extraordinary text. In January of 2003, Governor Jeb Bush (2003) of Florida, brother to the U.S. president, made the following remarks at his second inaugural address:

> In the past, our response has been to raise more taxes, grow more government, and embrace the thin fiction that if only we can hire one more social worker or complete one more form then we can somehow reverse these corrosive trends and salvage these lives. But while these intentions may be noble these methods are folly. Government will never fill the hollowness of the human heart. It can only be filled by a like kind of substance. It can only be filled by another human heart. . . .

> In our most private moments alone, we should reflect on our unearned gifts and rededicate our lives to those around us. In a thousand ways we can be more accepting, more giving, more compassionate.
>
> And if we are, we can embed in society a sense of caring that makes government less necessary. There would be no greater tribute to our maturity as a society than if we can make these buildings around us empty of workers; silent monuments to the time when government played a larger role than it deserved or could adequately fill.

Certainly, we are all are quite familiar with this kind of antigovernment rhetoric. Nevertheless, Governor Bush's comments are remarkable. Most significantly, the *rejection* of government appears as kind of promise to realize the natural utopia lurking beneath the fabricated order of the social world. In spite of himself, Jeb Bush is articulating a striking and important paradox. The very breakdown in the capacity to produce the People and growing recognition that "the People" as such does not exist produces the opposite: the assertion that the People actually *does* exist. Now, the state of nature is not simply a regulative symbolic universe that denotes an element of irrationality but an *actual* lost place to which We the People can return. We the People can return to the natural (economic, moral, political) order and dwell under its Law. The *sovereign decision on the exception now works not simply to represent the Law through the mechanisms of positive, technical law, but to embody the Law directly.* In effect, there is no gap between the representation and its object.

This places government in a profoundly dangerous (and endangering) position. In the state of the exception, government itself comes to materialize the exclusion in order to sustain the fantasy of the People. It is, paradoxically, government, the supposed representation of the collectivity, which has moved into the position of fantasy$_2$. To make this point is not simply to argue that government is the scapegoat for social, group, and/or individual problems. Rather, the point is that government, that which marks the impossibility of the People, is now identified as the exceptional element that inhibits the authentic flourishing and realization of the People and, as such, occupies a critical structural position in the disintegrating representational world. As the story goes, "big government" has fractured the integrity—both moral and structural—of the People. As the contemporary machine begins to break down, it is *government as the constitutive exclusion* that emerges to occupy the position of fantasy$_2$. Government is the pathogen, the irrational element *both* inside and outside, the citizen and shadow, in the exceptional fantasy of the People. Indeed, echoing both Tom Paine and John Locke, Jeb Bush's statement suggests that the governmental is made of a *qualitatively different substance* than society—"Government will never fill the hollowness of the human heart. It can only be filled by a like kind of substance. It can only be filled by another human heart." Thus, while the bureaucrat might look like Us and talk like Us, she or he is literally not made of the same *stuff* as We the People is. I hasten to add that it is probably the case that when some denounce government, we all "really know" they are in fact denouncing terrorists, homosexuals, African American "welfare mothers." But it remains the case that *government* is the privileged term. Government serves to condense a broad array of social antagonisms that sustains the fantasy of the People and recomposes the battery of techniques and strategies for biopolitical struggle.

If we can say that government is the materialization of the exclusion, we have a strange state of affairs in which the technique is the same as its object. Rather than having government operate on society (or the People) and the exclusion, *government turns on itself,* a movement I will call simply *the Return.* This is a useful way to understand the discursive space within which contemporary enthusiasm for neoliberal new public management practices such as contracting out, outsourcing, and privatizing exists. These are techniques that aim ostensibly to put conventional government out of business, instruments for dismantling and redistributing governmental functions, which, by virtue of being returned to the domain of the social *cease to be coded as governmental.* To privatize is to return certain functions and capacities from the domain of politics into the allegedly natural, apolitical realms of the domestic and private.

Neoliberalism and the Double Movement of Antigovernmentalism

The obvious problem here is that the returning of antigovernmentalism is, of course, *not* antigovernmental at all, but rather deliberate and purposeful in redirecting the authority of government to the disintergrative ends of securitization. Taken at face value, the discourse of antigovernmentalism seems patently disingenuous. How can we understand this? Is it just crude, cynical rhetoric?

If the term *neoliberal* can be used to describe the confluence of free markets, social conservatism, and antigovernmentalism, we can conclude, in part, that

> Neo-liberalism managed to re-activate the skeptical vigilance over political government basic to classical liberalism, by linking different elements of the "rhetoric of reaction" with a series of techniques—none of them in itself particularly new or remarkable—that could render these criticisms governmental. Indeed one thing that is perhaps paradoxical about neo-liberalism is that, despite posing itself as a critique of political government, it retains the programmatic *a priori,* the presupposition that the real is programmable by authorities. . . . Neo-liberalism does not abandon the "will to govern": it maintains the view that the failure of government to achieve its objectives is to be overcome by inventing new strategies of government that will succeed. (Rose, 1997, p. 53)

To rephrase this, what the neoliberal position succeeds in doing is formulating its positive biopolitical project in "negative" decentralizing, antistatist terms. The success neoliberalism enjoys in this project, however, is not merely a matter of effective marketing or ideological deception. Rather, the force and success of neoliberalism derive from the mobilization of the fantasy of the People and the movement of government itself—the coincidence of object and technique in the Return—into the position of the constitutive exclusion. The paradoxical effect, however, is like throwing gasoline on a fire: the exacerbation of hostility toward *government* that thereby precipitates a *simultaneous reduction and expansion* to the core of the representational order on account of the way in which these trends structurally unfold. Here, again, neoliberalism succeeds in the face of its failure, producing the very conditions that justify its continued existence. Why, though, does this succeed?

The returning of government on itself codes governmental action in a fundamentally *restorative* or *naturalizing* manner. As Rose (1997) suggests, this itself may not be new, but the turning of government on itself now appears as a *re*turning of sovereignty to the People and, as such, manifests an *active construction of the domain of the natural* itself. These discourses and practices are distinguished from the interstitial disciplinary action of the administrative state in at least two important ways. First, the central distinction turns on administration's operation in a field in which the exclusion was materialized in the social field itself. What this meant was that there was recognition of the People's work and, by extension, the generation of relatively stable dominions of public and private action. Although the People was being reproduced in the private enclosures of discipline, the capacities to produce objects of public concern, that is, to decide on the exception, nevertheless produced the relatively autonomous realm of private life: a domain produced politically but nevertheless coded and lived as beyond the domain of politics. The returning of government and the rupture of the enclosures in the smooth space of control erodes these distinctions. Zones become indiscernible. Second, the internalizing mode of discipline made government itself the neutral domain and instrument for integration into the People-as-One. At present, however, the positioning of the government of Us as Other reveals the inherent *internal* antagonism within the category of the People itself, the gap between the supposed sovereign origin and representation. Government *cannot* ever be severely neutral, and it now becomes profoundly normative in its project of "resuscitating" or reconstituting the National Thing. It is in this moment that the process of the hegemonic articulation is itself revealed; the People is revealed as cracked, divided, and not-One. The authority to specify and decide on the exception is thus rendered highly problematic and contentious. Thus, here is the *reductive* solution—reduce the functionality of government to the apparent de minimus of security and thus preserve the underlying, fundamental ontological ordering. This unfolds not through the imposition of disciplinary molds but now through the segregating regulation of bodies and their mobility and access. By calling on the fantasy of the state of nature and the inherently problematic position of government, the oneness of the People is affirmed in the movement of the Return.

There is, at the same time, a radically *expansive* moment. As argued earlier, the danger in attempting to revive the National Thing on the topography of control is that *everything* potentially is or can be an exception, and renaturalization knows no bounds. The reason for this is that when the exclusion is not materialized in the social field, that is, when a specific zone and target of action are not specified, there is perforce *nothing* excluded from the domain of action. Where there is no materialization in the social field to define a domain of action, there is also nothing to define a domain *restricted from* intervention. On one hand this follows from the point on reduction. If government is in an actively restorative mode (in contrast to an integrative one), there should not be any domain exempt from restoration according to the specified terms. There can be no exceptions. Yet precisely the opposite is also true—everything is a potential exception because nothing can be specified. The lack of specification entails the concomitant failure to *limit* the scope of governmental action. This is a limitlessness, again, without territorial boundary. The only "limits" are the spaces of the Camp (where anything is possible) that define new states of nature and constitute foci for the immobilizing fear that produces the contemporary spectacle of the People. The coincidence of technique and exclusion allows for the effective renaturalization of the whole of the social. Further, this renders plausible the apparent abandonment of the apparatuses of government. This reductive moment cloaks the counter, renaturalizing expansion. Yet it all succeeds because of the peculiar nexus of the political ontology of the One, the fantasy of the People, and the contemporary terrain of the exception.

The returning of government upon itself and the ossification of the social field under the auspices of necessity are symptomatic of a radical passivity. Or, more precisely, symptomatic of an *active submissiveness.* The only "reasonable" move absent the capacity to define Our work is to shrink government in furtherance of the paradoxical injunction to increase the People's power. Thus we dwell in an eternal moment of a triumphant foreclosure: in this time of the "responsible," sovereign individual, our only choice is to return to a state of social, normative, and economic necessity and the denuded, deadened nonrelation of bare life and its practices of "camping." If necessity is our only choice, it goes without saying that we are left with no choice at all.

Conclusion

It is imperative to appreciate that the contemporary legitimacy crisis of government as well as the consolidating biopolitical regime of control and securitization emerge from the logic of popular sovereignty and the representation's underlying ontological commitment to the One. These are not deviations but rather emerge directly from the ontology upon which modern democracy rests.

Nevertheless, as I have argued here, our current condition manifests important points of divergence from the past, the most critical of which is the abandonment of the project of fabrication and the generative use of disorder, sovereign individuality, new social spatial configurations, and the relation of nonrelation to maintain the ontological ordering of representation. This shift marks a point of crisis and a destabilization of social relations and identity, one that is distinctive from the cycle of crisis that characterizes representation generally. This crisis of representation entails the erosion of the theoretical plausibility and practical efficacy of representation's primary mode of relationship (the model-copy). Both the ability to determine general terms of the model and collective capacities to recognize and concede to those terms are significantly compromised. As we move from a regimen of imposition to one of access and sovereign individualism, the production of the popular sovereign and the efficacy of political representation fail. The work of government changes from a prospective, fabricating imposition of the People and its fantasy to a regressive, renaturalizing return to a state of nature under the auspices of rendering secure. In this return and its spaces and moments of exception, we all exist potentially as bare life.

This naturalistic endgame is compounded by resistance to "grand theory" induced by both some "postmodern" currents and "third way" advocates which, together, constitute a "mental block which prevents us from imagining a fundamental social change, in the interests of an allegedly 'realistic' and 'mature' attitude" (Zizek, 2000b, p. 324). We are further confined by our conventional form of opposition, which takes the form of invocations of the People and visions of the seizure of power. Today, the proper attitude toward the People is to assert, "That's not the People! Here is the real People!" and simply contest the reigning hegemonic articulation of the fantasy and put another king on the throne (Farmer, 2005). Contest and questioning could take another form. Why must human relations be ones of representing and models and copies? Why an ontology of the One? If we desire a present with a future, we must begin to rethink the biopolitical relationship and the basic ontology of our human worlds.

7
A Politics of the Subject

Refusing Representation

The project of refusing representation is obviously not so easy since it requires the rejection of "the very fundamental *structural principle* of society, as happened with the emergence of the 'democratic invention'" (Zizek, 2000a, p. 93; emphasis in original).[1] This transformation must propose a new avenue of engagement and subjectivation that does not demand reference to the popular sovereign and replication of the model-copy relation.[2] Through this refusal, the ontology of representation and that of its political form, the People, are recognized for their internal and historical limitations as well as the limitations that this ontology imposes on the present. By no mean does this entail abandonment of the achievements of past contests over the terms of the model or of those that remain to be won since neither constitutionalism nor disciplinarity have vanished. However, this political ontology and the institutional arrangements that emerged in its furtherance and reproduction are not the final form of human worlds.

We must, again, raise the double *partiality* of the People: not simply for the partiality-as-universality it articulates and conceals, but for the way in which the People names a *particular way* in which we might live and be-together. The People does not merely insist on the imposition of a single way of life; it insists that it is the only way of being. However, representing is *a* way of living together; it is *a* way of constructing the categories, objects, and relations that sustain intelligible human interaction. It provides one answer to the questions of what life is and what life is for. To be as the People is not the only way to be-together, and hegemony names only one particular way of formulating the functionality and authority of government and the constitution of a political society.

In formulating the fundamental problem in terms of representation, I have tried to articulate a distinctive ground for a general *P*olitical transformation such that a new mode of governing and being itself might be postulated—a new political ontology. This transformation is grounded in a rejection not of *a particular* model of representation but of the *very idea* of a model, an order that authoritatively grounds the judgment of copies through imputation of positive, normative content to the mute structures of biological life and that, in its insistence on oneness, turns away from the fundamental indeterminacy of the void. In advancing this general theory of representation as a mode of social creation and reproduction, I have attempted, in turn, to justify a robust, expansive understanding of governing. On this new terrain, the avenues of transformation clearly are no longer restricted to the straits and narrows of conventional politics. A place for contestation appears anywhere a model of representation is deployed and the representational way of being is reproduced. Together, this primary concern for formal relations (the model-copy relation) rather than content (creating more accurate models) and its related topographical shift orients the reconceptualization of governing toward qualitatively changing the basic structuring principle of human relationship.[3]

By implication, future conducting of conduct might concern, fundamentally, the subjective constitution of those processes and how we make ourselves up. Governing might concern itself with the processes by which and through which truth, objectivities, and subjectivities are contextually produced, imposed, and sustained, rather than with the mechanisms that purport to represent a posited extant truth and its sovereign origin. While governing itself is recognized as a general human activity, this does not mean that government itself withers away. As we have seen, government is symptomatic of the nonexistence of the popular sovereign and the very absence of an object of representation. Government exists precisely because there is no self-regulating, autochthonous sociopolitical order devoid of imposition or ontological commitment. Government appears as a structural inevitability. The task is to theorize a government that does not exist to represent and replicate the division between those who rule and those who are ruled (either in the sense of the government ruling over the People or the People ruling over its representatives) or that rests on the fiction of a state of nature and a politics, both wistful and fearful, bent on creating an innocence always already lost. This is accomplished by rejecting the ontology of the One and its model-copy relation and by working through the possibilities that emerge from a new originary commitment.

In considering this kind of basic transformation, we express certain fidelity to the democratic invention, and from one perspective, of course, modern democracy has always been about the rejection of models. It is inextricably connected to the impulse to throw off the impositions of tradition, break away from the presuppositions of the past, and invent new futures. In this sense, democracy is the practice of transcending. The question, though, is—How has transcending and overcoming proceeded in the world of representation? Might it proceed differently? I have argued that transcending under representation unfolds as multiform combat to define the model for evaluating and judging copies. Transcending under representation is a struggle to redefine the model itself and to become the judge of others. Warring subjects struggle to position themselves in relations of hegemony that are an assertion not simply of political superiority but also of the abstracted correct mode of living itself, the biopolitical coincidence of a single qualified bios and zoë. So, in service of the We, we are set against one another since our very lives and identities depend upon securing domination over another and occupying the empty throne.

This war is waged against the backdrop of the basic ontological commitment to the One, a commitment that does not recognize the exclusion or exception as necessary to its constitution. The core problem in representation does not concern the generic issue of exclusion, the element that remains "outside" of a category or bounded domain of sense, since this exceptional moment is necessary for sense itself. Any category or context must be limited and limiting. The claims of representation and its model will never add up to One. The problem is that in its original commitment to oneness, representation denies its limits and so compels the excluded outside to be *materialized* or objectified as a target of political technology in order to pursue the impossible coincidence of the People and people. Paradoxically, it is representation's very commitment to unity that produces its most violent, destructive, and exclusionary effect. In the state of exception, the political discourse of all-inclusiveness and universality can no longer finesse or avoid the ontological necessity of incompleteness and indeterminacy.

Our tasks are to repeat the founding moment of the representational order itself at which the groundlessness of the world was exposed and to consider the structural principle by which conduct can be conducted. On what basis can we consider making authoritative and binding decisions on behalf of another? Deprived of the People and its ersatz normative neutrality, this can no longer proceed on the basis of a representation and appeals to the One. More contextually, denied the operative model, it cannot be on the basis of representational impositions here, either. Is there a mode of relating that can generate stability sufficient to sustain sense, subjects, and objects, yet one that functions with recognition of its inherent contingency and void such that it does not depend upon the materialization of the exclusion? These are the questions that the crisis of representation presses.

Though public administration holds unique possibility for engaging these questions, to do so requires acceptance of a difficult fact—public administration is dead. It has been surpassed and exceeded by a new regime of biopolitical production, one working within representation's failing ontology but in a new configuration (the society of control) and so deploying a distinct arsenal of technological weaponry (e.g., actuarialism, the Camp). In sustaining the fading world of representation, these weapons become more intensive, focused, particularized, and violent as the plausibility of maintaining representation's exclusionary unity is rendered more tenuous. For these reasons, it is a futile project to attempt to "legitimize" the enterprise of public administration through reference to a domain of sovereignty, be it of facts or values. More precisely, it is futile to attempt to challenge the reigning dominance of neoliberal governance without actively attempting to challenge the underlying ontology that generates the dimensions of the legitimacy question itself.

In spite of this obituary, the primary affirmation of this work opens us to another line of thought and action. We can affirm, again, the primacy and ubiquity of governing as a generic human activity, of which govern*ment* is a subcategory. Governing is *the conduct of conduct,* the production of mechanisms that constitute and sustain subjectivities and relationships among those subjects and their objects, and create the bounded contexts or contained spaces within which these appear. "Public administration," in this sense, is the general practice of making and sustaining human worlds, though this truth has been concealed by the political ontology of representation, which naturalized entire domains of human activity and neutralized the activity of governing in a narrow domain of politics. By rejecting a narrow view of governing as rendering calculable and secure, we might make a space that allows for the encounter of human subjectivities and permits the incalculable remainder of subjectivity to become the condition for world making rather than being that which impedes the realization of lost fullness.

A concern for the *conducting* of conduct, further, affirms the centrality of *how* we govern, the practices and relationships exercised and invented in the process of self-government and the governing of the self. *How* to govern more intimately and immediately concerns the matter of how we shall be-together rather than the immediate prescriptive determination of *what* we shall do next or *who* governs. Indeed, the *how* gains priority not least because it is ultimately *generative* of the *who* and the *what.* At the same time we can refuse the silent answer to the how—that is, representing—that has been diffused throughout the entire institutional, political, legal cosmology that underpins public administration's origins, practice and, ultimately, its demise. Our sense of vulnerability in the present should not tempt us to lament the passing of the administrative state or pine nostalgically for the safety and calculability of disciplinary society. Nor can we accept the world of the Camp.

Propositions for a Politics of the Subject

The ontology of representation began from a single commitment (the One), which inscribed a simple formula (model-copy relation). This formula was replicated like a virus throughout the many heterogeneous realms of human activity, producing a coherent, intelligible whole whose diversity and pluralistic ethos seemed to bear little resemblance to the originary formula. There is a lesson here—basic commitments about the structure and foundation of the world matter profoundly. Moreover, while we can accord these commitments different statuses, we cannot simply do without them since it is only by consciously affirming and advancing a distinct commitment or affirmation that relationships can be reconstructed. I want, then, to propose preliminary and general propositions of another political ontology. I will call this political ontology *the politics of the subject.*

Proposition 1: A relationship must be asserted between bios and zoë, and neither the imposition of single form of life nor the contemporary relation of nonrelation is satisfactory. Following from the analysis in chapter 3, we can assert the relationship of the void or empty set (∅).[4] That is, the ontology of the politics of the subject begins from the proposition that there is no natural or given relationship between political and biological and ecological existence yet states this as an affirmative commitment to a specific relationship between bios and zoë. We can write this as:

$$\text{Bios}_{\varnothing} \rightarrow \text{Zoë}$$

No positive attributes or descriptors naturally attach to human subjects as subjects of the political. Consistent with the indeterminacy of the social exposed by the democratic invention, what we can say definitively about being is that we cannot say anything definitely about being, save, again, its indeterminacy; this is a commitment that incorporates its own contingency and limit in order to form an affirmative proposition. No single form of life (either a general or local model) can represent Life itself. Rather, we can only create contestable constructions, none of which can be said to represent a unity behind appearance. What unity or continuity exists is an expressive product of possibility or creation, not a representation.

As representation's assertion of the One informed the development of political and scientific relations and objects, this originary commitment constitutes the terrain within which regional empirical, historical, and political inquiry can advance. Yet, unlike representation, this basic commitment allows for the recognition without hierarchy of regional ontologies and paradigms since no regional ontology can purport to speak for the One; each must simply be posited as a historical expression of possibility of knowledge and experience.

Proposition 2: A politics of the subject commits to the presupposition of *radical difference* in a double sense. First, collectivity is conceived as a disarticulated multitude (cf. Hardt & Negri, 2000) of what below I will call *compositions,* which does not entertain concepts of unity, such as the People or Nation, that belong to the realm of civic and political theology and the eschatological form of the Political. What compositions have in common is precisely the subjective void or empty set (∅), that which remains excessive to the domain of positive knowledge. This difference is universal but fundamentally differentiating. In this difference, there is no a priori, permanent basis for exclusion since no positive terms or predicates adhere to any collectivity; there is no model.

Difference in this sense serves as the ground for reconceiving democratic notions of equality and universality. Equality follows from the proposition that all human subjects are different, but that this subjective difference cannot be encapsulated or captured, not even by the complex vectors of risk management or technological surveillance. Something always escapes; as subjects, we never add up to One. Equality follows from the proposition that what is different cannot be subsumed within the presumptive terms of the model. Finally, as this analysis has suggested, equality follows from the immeasurable because only what is immeasurable can be equal since there is no implicit standard or model within which some particularity is counted twice—once as a particularity (copy) and once as the representative of the universal. On these conditions, a bios can be its own zoë (Agamben, 1998/1995, p. 188) and set its own limits for transcending. That is, each biological entity can define its own qualified form of life. It goes without saying, however, that this transcending is possible by virtue of being in relationship with other subjects who are also so enabled; and so a bios that can be its own zoë restates Marx's (1998/1848) proposition that "the free development of each is the condition for the free development of all" (p. 62).

Proposition 3: A politics of the subject concerns the generative, situational processes of subject constitution and the conduct of conduct. This politics gives primacy to the form of the act (the how). The question naturally arises, though, concerning the boundary of the situation itself, what belongs properly to the situation, and the relationship among/between situations. Following the path cleared by others (Badiou, 2006/1988; Follett, 1951/1924, 1998/1920; Fox & Miller, 1995; Hardt & Negri, 2004; Miller, 2005a, 2005b; Thayer, 1975), the situation and the operations of belonging must be more fully theorized. Though this cannot be worked out in detail here, let us speculate that a situation once produced and adhering to its own internal law is *composed* of singular subjectivities and their differences. If governing is the conducting of conduct, the intelligible situation can be viewed as a *composition.*

A composition cannot ignore the qualitative change precipitated by the arrival or departure of another subject. Moreover, a composition does not refer outside itself to an object of representation. Instead, it takes as an *object of common concern* the void of the composition itself, an object that is produced by the activity of composing and conducting conduct. Mary Parker Follett (1951/1924) provides an example of how a composition could produce an object of common concern. Follett argues that representation ignores the fact that something happens when a person from one group interacts with the members of another. People become involved in different patterns of activity and interaction that meaningfully change their understanding. Thus, that one fails to represent one's group does not perforce mean that one has betrayed that group; rather, in this interaction one becomes of both groups (p. 238). If there is a genuine meeting or "interweaving" of people in a composition there is no representation, only a production of something new that is in common (p. 239). "Doing something together creates a bond" (p. 244). The logic of representation arrests this creation of a new composition by tying people to objects outside the situation. This does not mean that people cease acting on behalf of communities or groups as spokespersons or delegates. Rather, as Follett writes, the central issue is "how to make the people I represent have a part in my own specific-response activity in the second group" (p. 245). The key question, in other words, concerns how different singularities come to belong to a composition.

Proposition 4: A politics of the subject rejects the quarantine of governing in the apparatuses of public institutions and embraces a robust understanding of governing that cuts across all composed domains of human experience. A politics of the subject does not posit sectoral boundaries of recognized operation but operates amid the collapse of our conventional categories of public and private, the political and the social, market and polis. This proposition permits an upending of the contemporary understanding of "privatization." Where we might see the Return of practices to the naturalized domain of the private, we can see the explicit expansion of the domain of governing into those naturalized domains. We can conceive of the Return as the explicit "publicization" and reappropriation of the naturalized spheres of representation. Though the language of publicization is itself problematic, it nevertheless articulates in our conventional political categories how the expansion of the naturalizing, necessitating logic of the Return produces the conditions for the rejection of the model-copy relation.

Proposition 5: In rejecting the quarantining of governing, a "public administration" as a politics of the subject embraces what David Farmer (2003a) calls the *death of the Practitioner.*[5] By and large, public administration has focused on the production of goods and services for an abstract figure of practice, the Practitioner. Specifying the face of the Practitioner has always been a difficult undertaking since we immediately encounter heterogeneity in the term—in diversity in learning styles, psychological type, pre-service versus in-service status, or employment in an analytical versus management position (Denhardt, 2001). There are further distinctions between staff practitioners and line managers (Cunningham & Weschler, 2002); and in the society of control's world of networks, third-party service delivery, and contracting, conceiving public administration in terms of the executive functionaries of government is an ever more tenuous assertion. In the figure of the Practitioner, differences become homogenized and reduced; at the same moment, practice itself must be abstracted in order that a proper "fit" be established between the Practitioner and the "real world" of governing.

To embrace the Practitioner's death, Farmer (2003a) writes, entails abandoning the vision of "the PA practitioner as hero of the PA story" (p. 32). The Practitioner is radically decentered and no longer viewed as the originator and narrator of public administration (PA) or the authoritative, privileged *position* from which to speak and judge in public administrative discourse. Indeed, the word *Practitioner* connotes not merely an abstract personage but also privileged access to administrative reality. To speak for the Practitioner is to speak to and about something real in the representational sense. It is to mistake oneself as the representative of public administration reality and, implicitly, to draw a line that hierarchically separates oneself from the useless, irrelevant, or impractical—as well as those people who represent those terms. The general account of governing offered throughout this text requires that the heterogeneity and difference subsumed by the Practitioner be recognized and that "practice" be considered in a more robust fashion.

We are all practitioners now.

Pedagogically, a different kind of academic relationship needs to be cultivated that takes into account a nonrepresentational relationship between the student and teacher. This implies a collaborative, seeking-together approach to knowledge production. As Deleuze (1994/1968) writes, "Our only teachers are those who tell us to 'do with me,' and are able to emit signs to be developed in heterogeneity rather than propose gestures for us to reproduce" (p. 23). While suggesting a problematic humanism, Denhardt's (2001) discussion of the "developmental perspective" in public administration education has provided the clearest indication of how a radically subject-oriented education that takes inventory of the radical difference of both teachers and students could work. Surveying the "big questions" in public administration education and concluding that these questions "may have to be answered by saying 'it depends'" (pp. 528–529), Denhardt writes that the "teaching/learning process of public administration is deeply bound up with issues of personal development for students and faculty" and, as such, "our answers to the big questions of public administration education must reflect both the intellectual and psychological needs and interests of our students—and our own" (p. 529). He goes on to identify three general facets of development (cognitive, linguistic/interactive, and psychosocial) as they intersect with the particular personal and professional trajectories of students. Critically, Denhardt notes that the trajectories of teachers must also be taken into account. "The developmental perspective presented here reminds us that, just as our students are growing and developing throughout their time in our programs, we are growing and developing as well. Faculty interests and orientations change over time, based on new substantive concerns that come to occupy us and on social and psychological changes in our own lives" (p. 532). He concludes: "Designing a faculty development program that not only nurtures and supports younger faculty, but attends to the changing needs and interests of mid-career and senior faculty is perhaps the best way to match the needs and interests of faculty with those of students. . . . Only in this way will we be able to design educational programs that meet the needs of our students, prepare them for involvement in the professional community, and utilize the full range of interests and skills of our faculty" (p. 533).

A similar attitude is required in the application or putting to work of scientific knowledge in public administrative contexts. The use of expertise and technical knowledge needs to be conceived as a part of a collaborative "doing with" in which science becomes closer and more deeply embedded in the fabric of self-governing.

Proposition 6: Finally, a practice of governing as a politics of the subject is governing that is *good for nothing* in a double sense. We can posit a governing that serves no purpose or end in itself: a governing that is good for nothing. This does not mean that governing or government is *useless* or without use—whatever popular claims to the contrary. Rather, governing would be *good for nothing.* This governing "minds the gap" in the composition of the situation; it is good for this nothing. The capacity for the situation to be sensible yet without rigid boundaries turns on its foundation on the recognition of the absence, the very limit that makes possible the sense of the composition and renders impossible its fantastic completion. Second, to be good for nothing entails a commitment to those subjects who have been reduced to their bodies and to bare life. Governing must be good for those who have been reduced to nothing and hominis sacres, stripped of all symbolic belonging.

I suggest that the figure of the midwife is a useful and appropriate figure for a governing that is good for nothing. Though more of a position than a figure, the midwife takes into account both the structural role of authority in human life and the ultimate groundlessness of that life. The figure of the midwife has been used many times before in public administration scholarship (e.g., Baer, 1977; Caldwell, 1975; Fox & Miller, 1995; Morgan & Kass, 1991; Stivers, 1993; Whitaker, 1980) to describe, broadly speaking, one who "facilitates the emergence of new possibilities by means of embodied and embodying action" (Stivers, 1993, p. 132). We can also turn to classical sources. Socrates announces early in *Theaetetus* (Plato, 1961) that his mother, a "fine buxom woman called Phaenarete," was a midwife, and asks Theaetetus, "Have you also been told that I practice the same art?" (149a).[6] The art Socrates practices is midwifery, or *maieutics.* What is a midwife? She is not simply one who assists in childbirth and cuts the proverbial cord but, as Stivers suggests, one who generally helps in bringing forth or bringing about. Midwives "can bring on the pains of travail or allay them at their will, make a difficult labor easy, and at an early stage cause a miscarriage if they so decide" (Plato, 1961, 149d) and have knowledge of who and who is not pregnant.

Socrates says his art is different in that his concern is not with the body but with the soul and, as such, his medium is speech. He maintains that he cannot bring forth knowledge himself. His task is to discern whether the offspring of a "young man's thought is a false phantom or instinct with life and truth. . . . The many admirable truths they bring to birth have been discovered by themselves from within. But the delivery is heaven's work and mine" (Plato, 1961, 150c, 150d). This delivery can be painful, and some find the pain too much and many leave too soon: "many who have not been conscious of my assistance but have made light of me, thinking that it was all their doing, have left me sooner than they should, whether under others' influence or of their own motion" (150e).

The midwife is to be distinguished from the physician, who aims at the cure. The midwife does not and cannot cure. Rather, she brings forth or dispenses with phantoms, with false births. Based on the discussion of representation, what could a "true" birth be? The truth brought forth is precisely the *truth of the void*—the truth of barrenness, the emptiness, or the lack at the center of being that representation reveals but disavows. The paradox is that the Socratic midwife assists in bringing forth "mere wind eggs and not worth the rearing" (Plato, 1961, 210b). True knowledge is barren as there is no treasure to bring forth. This recognition is the end of Socratic analysis. Socrates says as much to Theaetetus: "[I]if you remain barren, you will be gentler and more agreeable to your companions, having the good sense not to fancy you know what you do not know" (210c).[7]

Thus both self-governing and the governing of the self must be *good for nothing.*

Positions: The Logic of Subtraction

What kind of action can these propositions inform? Providing answers to this question requires substantial collaboration well beyond this conclusion, but let me sketch a subjective stance toward challenging representation in the state of the exception. Consistent with the theoretical analysis presented here about the dispersed nature of governing and creation of order, the transformations, initially, must be small ones that would occur in discrete relationships and contexts; they will unfold as a distinctly new mode of the creation of context itself. Indeed, if there is no One and if the presuppositions of the One (People, Law, Market, etc.) are what we are interrogating, the generation of a new relationship based on the propositions of the politics of the subject must proceed from the nonplace of the subject, for it is here that the fantasy of the One is actually sustained. It must proceed initially, in Jacques Lacan's (1999/1975) phrase, as a process of subtraction rather than biopolitical purification.[8] What does a logic of subtraction mean? Crudely, subtraction entails the act of positing one's own presuppositions or conditions of existence, that is, suspending the terms of one's own model of identification as well as one's emotional attachments to that model (a move ironically facilitated by the logic of control). This renders the subject "destitute" (Verhaeghe, 1999). In the field of rhetoric and pedagogy, Marshall Alcorn (2002) describes a similar working-through in his "work of mourning" and "libidinal withdrawal." Alcorn writes: "To disinvest social constructions, one must do more than use language or be rational, one must do the work of withdrawing desire from representation" (p. 117).

What would be a concrete instance of this subtraction? Consider it in the context of the everyday experience of "nonleaders" in a traditional organizational hierarchy. The leaders and nonleaders are locked in a representational relationship, a hierarchical relationship of model and copy. Nonleaders are in a position of being subjected to representations; leaders are the judges of representations as well as representations of the institution. As McSwite (2003) write, in this setting, the initial move "is refusal to grant deference to leaders [and] to drop all pretense that leaders do anything that is any more important than what non-leaders do" (pp. 195–196). This is more complex than a simple refusal to obey orders or do what one is told. In refusing deference, the refuser must find a way to subtract while fully remaining in the situation and avoiding producing a form of opposition that affirms and sustains the legitimacy of representation itself. All this is easier said than done, of course, and this subtractive move is typically easier for leaders, those in charge, than nonleading subordinates, for whom the consequences of subtracting are unknown and fraught with consequences. Likewise, for example, subtraction is easier for teachers than for students. Yet, as McSwite note, both representatives of models and copies are involved in the sustaining of the world of representation; we are all "implicated in the support of any social order of which [we] are a part" (p. 197). There then cannot perforce be any designation of final responsibility to either the leader/teacher/in charge or nonleader/student/subordinate series. The fundamental point is that subtractive action *can* be taken, a break from the past *can* be initiated, the effect of which, however, cannot be calculated or predicted.

In effect, what the stance of subtraction attempts is the "institutionalization of social lack" (Stavrakakis, 1999, p. 134) or the void, empty set.[9] A distinctive mode of governing might emerge here, a practice distinct from the administrator as implementing agent or technical expert. More generally, governing authority is no longer explicitly put to work instrumentally. Here, the function of the midwife in the composition is to produce a specific kind of texture of relationship, and to hold a unique position within it. What is distinctive about a subtractive practice is that its primary concern is this void and the way in which the production of composition, the conducting of conduct, proceeds. Yet this void is not materialized and instrumentally put to use for the People's ends; rather, it is prepared for as a possibility for redefining and reconstructing collectivity itself. Thus, the "first principle" of subtraction is that a positive identification with, for example, a decision, process, or policy must be preceded by an act of negation or destitution; a "clearing" must be created.

This discourse proposes that a composition is *produced,* initially, through singularization (or individuation), the unhooking from identification with the demand for and demands of representational models. In other words, a space for composition needs to be cleared that disputes the representational horizon of the People. From this space, shared understanding and sense-of-the-common can be generated. It is only then that anything prescriptive, like policies, can be made or lines of action decided upon, and scientific knowledge usefully introduced. Governing must be *good for this nothing.* The empty space, then, produced through subtraction and this modality of authority is the condition for a new composition.

I would emphasize that this event of subtraction does not enjoin anyone to commit conventionally "radical" political gestures—though these everyday, empty(ing) gestures of subjective destitution and refusal are often far more difficult than conventional political action. Since the field of the political is coincident with the fragmented terrain of human experience, small gestures and acts open up possibilities for being and experiencing the world. This politics of the subject concerns the generation of *conditions* beyond the conventional governmental that need *not* replicate representational imposition. Thus, as Thayer (1973) and Goux (1990/1973) intimate, homes, workplaces, classrooms, bedrooms, and boardrooms are potential locations of microtransformations that aim at achieving a qualitative change in human relationships and a displacement of representation. Again, easier said than done, especially considering the psychological and social peril that the refuser often puts him- or herself in. It is a strange paradox that the attempt to forge a collaborative compositional relationship potentially results in such isolation.

Here, we must conceive of an organizational supplement to subtraction. What is required is ongoing tactical *and* interpersonal support. Tactical support would respond directly to subtractive and compositional concerns in whatever site they were pursued. Experiences and insights could be pooled at the same time that the emotional, psychological, and physical strains of subtraction could be eased; the difficulties of detaching from the relation of nonrelation ameliorated by a reconnection in a qualitatively different relation. The group itself, though, embodies its own project and remains cognizant of the composition of a politics of the subject that is its non-end. The "goal," therefore, of the group is *not* the transformation of *another* group (e.g., the work unit) but ultimately the recomposition and expansion of *subjective* capacities to engage and connect beyond the insistence of the model and identity. What will be created is a context for being-with others differently—one that cultivates a different mode of being-with and being-together by breaking down the limitations imposed by identification with the model.

Provisions for a Dead Discipline

I have suggested a broad outline of a generic subjective and collective political attitude and general propositions that would inform a politics of the subject in a more theoretical way. What remains for the study and discipline of "public administration" in the conventional meaning of each? What is the attitude of the field, presumptuously proclaimed dead? First, public administrationists have always been right to insist on the *constitutive* function of administration in a democracy, that *how* one structures processes and interaction matters profoundly. In fulfilling the potential of this insight, a public administration that is committed to the politics of the subject and oriented toward the primacy of composition would make an explicit break from its own foundations. The positing not only of the inadequacy of the general model and the People but also of its impossibility suggests that administrative action is not the execution or actualization of representations but, as suggested above, that governing is the act that reconfigures the matrix of the model itself at the level of the subject or subject-group (Deleuze & Guattari, 1983/1972). The operation is not executive in the sense of carrying out; it is generative. Following the subtractive logic, if public administration historically has been preoccupied with a kind of utilitarian distribution of the Good, here we are concerned with the compositional processes that aim beyond the Good.

This "public administration" should also be distinguished from the conventional liberal and neoliberal critiques of political rationality and governmental omniscience in the name of individual rights and "natural" social processes, such as the market. Here the point is to challenge the liberal conception of the objectivity of the social with its natural prepolitical processes and to focus on the processes of composition. As I have argued, the representational mode of the political denies the constitutive moment that invents a political collectivity, thus ostensibly delimiting formal governmental functions to the "merely" regulatory, the making-regular, aspects of $fantasy_2$. A politics of the subject would insist on the constitutive moment of the political yet attempt to shift that locus of invention from the exclusivity and impossibility of the People's biopolitical project to discrete spaces of composition. This is a conception of an active and generative governing but one that does not insist that action be grounded in any positive foundation. Rather, like the practices of midwifery, the "governmental," broadly defined, is identified as a structural position that enables the subtractive suspension that allows for action and open composition, and that permits nonexclusionary belonging. Finally, while dispensing with the impositions of the People and popular sovereignty, the politics of the subject is moment of democracy. This core of democracy is difference, for only difference suspends representational judgment.

How can this conception of the political be actualized? I have suggested that this movement locally and singularly can be commenced now. As for "public administration" as a discipline concerned with government as a structural position in the politics of the subject, the subtractive logic similarly applies. Public administration can itself refuse the matrix of conventional politics and the timidity conditioned by its intellectual heritage and legitimacy problem. "Public administration" can renounce its renunciation, deny the sacrifice and identity crisis it has assumed on behalf of the People and, in effect, *deprive itself of its own organization of identity that is the legitimacy question.* Public administration will no longer be able to rely on its preordained position in the symbolic universe of representation. Indeed, it will see to it coming undone. "Public administration" could be the site of the coming politics of the subject; it could be the science of subtraction and composition; it could be the generic name of the group of tactical support. But it must make the first move.

Notes

Chapter 1

1. John Nalbandian (2005) has offered a variant of this formulation. Nalbandian suggests that the two dominant trends in governance are civic participation and administrative modernization.

2. In social science, these different ontologies are often called "paradigms." In *The Language of Public Administration,* David Farmer (1995) lucidly demonstrates how different language paradigms bring different ideas and objects into view and imply distinct limitations in what they can and cannot say about administrative realities. A text that elaborates the implications of ontological commitments for epistemology, method, and human organization is Burrell and Morgan's (1993/1979) *Sociological Paradigms and Organizational Analysis.* An excellent account of how an ontological commitment matters for political analysis is Hay's (2006) "Political Ontology." In this discussion, I do not have paradigms per se in mind but rather what could be called the "metaparadigmatic" commitment that organizes and distributes paradigmatic differences, what Hay identifies (discussed below) as regional ontologies. Thus in the spirit of Farmer's call for a "reflexive language paradigm" for public administration, this text's argument can be read as providing the conditions for such a reflexive "metaparadigmatic" position.

3. We need not accept a radically nominalist reduction of the world to an effect of signification to hold this view. Indeed, what I hope to show in this text is that we have mistakenly conceptualized constructivism (broadly defined) as questioning the materiality of the world behind appearances. Rather, what we should be calling into question is assumptions about the being of the world.

4. Other studies that have explored the relationship of ontology and the political include Pierre Bourdieu's (1991/1988) *The Political Ontology of Martin Heidegger,* Slavoj Zizek's (2000c) *The Ticklish Subject: The Absent Centre of Political Ontology,* and Philip Pettit (2005) "Rawls's Political Ontology." Pettit's argument also considers, via the thought of John Rawls, the ontology of "the people," a position I also (2005) have advanced. For other arguments about the political importance of returning to questions of ontology, see James (2005), Jones & Clarke (2006), and White (2000).

5. The impossibility of demonstrating the ultimate conditions for knowledge

and judgment is not a new, "postmodern" problem. This was a question with which Aristotle grappled in the law of contradiction (Fogelin, 2004). In brief, the law of contradiction (now *non*contradiction) states that one cannot hold contradictory or conflicting beliefs or propositions; it is thought to be the "most fundamental principle of rationality" (p. 18). As Fogelin writes it, it can take the form "It is not the case that something is both the case and not the case" (p. 19). The upshot of the law of noncontradiction is that a true statement is always produced even if the contents are somehow false. For example, "It is not the case that (both) lead is heavier than aluminum [which it is not] and lead is not heavier than aluminum" (p. 20). The problem that Aristotle articulated was that "because the law of noncontradiction lies at the basis of all demonstration, it was not . . . capable of proof or demonstration" (p. 33), a conclusion with which Fogelin substantively agrees. In other words, neither empirical nor rational, logical evidence can demonstrate the enabling conditions for empirical or logical demonstration itself. Rightly, Fogelin notes that the law of noncontradiction has been rejected by many who, to put it in crude contemporary terms, adopt a "postmodern" position. This rejection is based on the law's apparent disqualification of fundamental change and multiplicity. However, the law also works favorably in a poststructural/postmodern direction. For example, in Burrell and Morgan's (1993/1979) famous work, four sociological/organizational paradigms are described as incommensurable or "mutually exclusive" (p. 25). That is, one cannot hold simultaneously the fundamental assumptions of two paradigms that conflict at the level of ontology (e.g., radical humanism/subjectivism and radical structuralism/objectivism). What the "postmodernist" insists upon is that knowledge can occur only within bounded paradigms, the constitutive propositions of which must be held to be beyond logical or empirical demonstration: that is, simply taken for granted as the groundless/foundationless condition for demonstration. In this sense, the postmodernist adheres to a variant of the law of noncontradiction. The problem, of course, concerns the general relationship among paradigms. That is, what are the general conditions upon which one asserts a multiplicity of paradigms or regional ontologies? Here, postmodernists often find themselves in an awkward (albeit sometimes facile) violation of the law of noncontradiction, asserting—to take one common example—that "All truth claims are paradigmatically contingent." This is a statement that appears to contradict itself or implicitly make one paradigm first among equals—a move that replicates the logic of representation as outlined in chapter 3. To sort this out, I cannot help but believe that general, meta-paradigmatic or *ontological* commitments (rather than normative ones) are unavoidable in order to offer conditions for multiplicity and paradigmatic diversity and sidestep the problems of representation. From these commitments, we could recognize a profound, substantive difference between a naturalistic ontology of the One and an ontology of the void or lack that asserts itself as social and political construction and whose truth claims take account through internal paradox of the problematic nature of truth itself. I will elaborate these commitments in chapters 3 and 4.

6. An illuminating account of how the ideas of modernity diffused through the institutions and discourses of a "coalescing" new social order, the "modern social imaginary," appears in Charles Taylor's (2004) *Modern Social Imaginaries.*

7. An interesting presentation and analysis of this distinction between a "pure" and regional or "applied scientific ontology" is Jacquette's (2002) *Ontology.* Two major contemporary attempts to rethink ontology are Badiou's (2006/1988) *Being and Event,* which posits the proposition of "mathematics as ontology," and Deleuze's (1994/1968) *Difference and Repetition.* A well-known formulation of these questions is Heidegger's (1962/1926) project for a fundamental ontology. In brief, Heidegger argues that the "question of being" has been forgotten and that philosophy has focused on *ontic* questions, that is, the consideration of beings, at the expense of ontology, the question of what it means for those beings to be. Jacquette disputes Heidegger's claim, viewing his as more a contribution to the "ontic sciences" (p. 9), as well as Heidegger's proclamation that ontology is possible only as phenomenology. The basic orientation of this text is an acceptance of this distinction between a pure and "regional" ontology, that there is a distinction between the basic questions of what it means to be and the regional or applied domains within which objects, epistemologies, and methodologies are deployed. However, consistent with the general approach of Badiou and Jacquette, this pure ontology can be considered formally rather than phenomenologically. That is, the question of ontology cannot itself be grounded empirically in any kind of phenomenology (be it existential or positivist) or particular *regional* ontology. This naturalistic or empirical grounding for being constitutes the terrain of the People's biopolitical project.

8. In some sense, Ian Hacking's (2002) notion of "historical ontology" may be more appropriate than my use of "political ontology." Hacking claims to work from Michel Foucault's (1984) discussion of a "historical ontology of ourselves" in his essay "What Is Enlightenment?" As best as I can discern, Foucault refers in this essay (at least in this translation) to a *critical* ontology of ourselves (pp. 47, 50), but nevertheless Hacking's designation of this approach to ontology is appropriate. Foucault conceives of this critical ontology as a "historico-practical test of the limits that we may go beyond, and thus as work carried out by ourselves as free beings" (p. 47) and as "an attitude, an ethos, a philosophical life in which the critique of what we are is at one and the same time the historical analysis of the limits that are imposed on us and an experiment with the possibility of going beyond them" (p. 50). Foucault is concerned, in Hacking's (1999/1986) own terms, with how, historically and ontologically, we "make ourselves up" or constitute ourselves as human subjects. Hacking (2002) writes, "In thinking of constituting ourselves, we should think of constituting *as* so and so; we are concerned, in the end, with possible ways to be a person" (p. 2). Though this compactly describes this project, I have chosen to use *political* ontology, in part, to emphasize the political form of the administrative state and the necessity for thinking ontology in connection with political form, practices, and institutions beyond representation.

9. "Self-conscious" because interest in governmental administration is hardly a new concern, though the formulation of an academic field of study and professional training may be. As Mark Rutgers (1994, 1997) and Jos Raadschelders (1998, 2003) have detailed, conscious consideration of government administration extends well beyond Woodrow Wilson's retrospectively posited founding article. Indeed, administrative history may reach as far back as the Sumerians of 3000 BCE and ancient Egypt, or Babylonia's Code of Hammurabi, which provided that "the mason who builds a house which falls down and kills the inmate shall be put to death" (quoted in Shafritz and Russell, 2003, pp. 12–13). Aristotle's *Politics,* Plato's *The Laws,* and Machiavelli's *The Prince* are all texts quite consciously concerned with the governing of the state, and could very reasonably be included in introductory courses in public administration. Most significant, however, changes in the nature and role of the state during the Renaissance precipitated a focused attention on the administration of the governmental apparatuses of the state. This is seen in the emergence of "Cameralism" in Germany and Austro-Hungary, of the *science de la police* (policy or police science) in France, and "political arithmetik" (see Petty, 1690) in England. As chapter 4 illustrates, this police tradition was not merely a European phenomenon; it was alive and well in nineteenth-century America also. For a spirited discussion of how any attempt to grasp the reality of public administration is "intrinsically historical" and perhaps even at the core of the discipline, see Raadschedlers, Waganaar, Rutgers, & Overseen (2000). For other discussions of Cameralism and police science, see Foucault (1991/1979, 2000a/1983), Gordon (1991), Neocleous (2000), Novak (1996), and Raeff (1975).

10. These are exceptions to this general state of affairs, most notably O. C. McSwite (1997b), Jay D. White (1999), and Louis Howe (2006, 2003).

11. As Svara (1998) has argued, it may very well be the case that the strict dichotomy between politics and administration represented a significant departure from the original intentions of the early founders of public administration, such as Frank Goodnow and Woodrow Wilson and political reformers of the National Municipal League. These early theoreticians and practitioners, he shows, advocated "the insulation of administrators from interference by elected officials but not isolation" (p. 53). Svara (2001) argues for a model of "complementarity" rather than dichotomy. Harmon (2006, chap. 1) has provided an incisive criticism of this formulation, and the attitude of this text toward strict or "loose" forms of the dichotomy is that it is a difference without distinction.

12. It would be more precise to say, though, that the "rejection" of the politics-administration formula and other "conceptual shibboleths" (Gordon, 1947, p. 264) was characteristic not simply of Waldo but of his entire generation of public administrationists. In this "post-war dissent," the "assault on the politics-administration dichotomy" (Sayre, 1958, p. 103) was one of this generation of scholars' basic intellectual strategies. The period was marked by a renewed interest in the "public" in public administration (Martin, 1952, p. 668) and an emphasis on the political dimensions of administrative action (e.g., Appleby, 1970/1945). For example, Gordon

wrote of the growing recognition of the "entwining of 'legislative' and 'judicial' as well as 'executive,' elements in administration: the permeation with policy decisions of all but the most routine administrative actions; the function of administrative practice in reshaping policies 'laid down' by the normal 'legislative' or 'policy-making' authority" (p. 264). Arguably, Herbert Simon also participated in this dissent on the question of the dichotomy (Fry, 1989, pp. 185–186), though this position has been convincingly challenged by Harmon (1989b), who argued that Simon merely transposed the distinction between politics and administration into an epistemological dichotomy between values and facts. However, as I will argue here, Simon was not alone in leaving important dimensions of the dichotomy intact. For a contemporary theoretical analysis of the dissatisfied, dissenting mood of the entire postwar period, see Catlaw (2006d).

13. This is, in effect, simply a variant of the so-called naturalistic fallacy's conflation of "what is" with "what ought to be." In spite of his criticism, Waldo himself succumbs to what John Searle (1969) suggests is the "naturalistic fallacy fallacy," which assumes the actually-impossible separation of empirical, positive description, and moral judgment (pp. 132–136). Waldo writes, "moral laws purport to tell us *what ought to be true* and their 'meaning' lies in the fact of discrepancy between what ought to be true, and what is actually (generally or universally) the case. Physical laws purport to tell us what is *actually the case,* and they are 'laws' only if they describe or coincide with 'reality.'" This conflation allows for the positing of general laws of social and political development or progress that are "out there," independent of human creation, and "according to which any good and permanent society must be built" (p. 156). An excellent discussion of the fallacy and its relationship to questions of public administration appears in Harmon (2006, chap. 3).

14. Among the most explicit interrogations of public administration's relationship to political representation are Frederick Thayer's (1973) *An End to Hierarchy! An End to Competition!* Fox and Miller's *Postmodern Public Administration* (1995), and Mary Follett's *The New State* (1998/1920). I consider these accounts in chapter 3. I take McSwite's (1997b) analysis, however, to be more fundamental with regard to the ontological question and, additionally, more productive in opening toward alternatives; its limitations are substantial and are outlined in chapter 2. For contemporary considerations of the legacy of Waldo and *The Administrative State,* see Rosenbloom & McCurdy (2006) and the symposia edited by Frederickson & Marini (1997a, 1997b, 1997c).

15. As Redford (1969, p. 53) notes, elite theories (e.g., Mosca, 1939; Hunter, 1953; Mills, 1956; Pijl, 1984; Therborn, 1978) essentially are a gloss on this position. Castells's (2000) account of the globalized flow of "networkers" or Reich's (1992) more widely read account of "symbolic analysts" might similarly be read in this context. All these theories express fears of organizational structures and ruling cabals that are beyond the reach of the People. Note, however, that I am not therefore implicitly criticizing the elite position from the so-called pluralist position (e.g.,

Dahl, 1961). Dahl and others who share this view basically identify "the plural" as differentiated *interests* in pursuit of the common good or public interest, a form I connect to the logic of the People. A discussion of interests appears in chapter 3's discussion of Camilla Stivers and Ralph Hummel and in chapter 6.

16. Naturally, democracy has been actualized (or crystallized, to borrow a term from Mann [1993]) in various historical and national contexts according to various models (Held, 1996). Yet democratic theory and practice in the nineteenth and twentieth centuries, both in the United States and around the world, have relied on what Held (1997) has called certain "congruent" and "symmetrical" relationships between political decision makers and the recipients of those decisions, all of which, ultimately, depend upon the positing of a national People and its attendant apparatuses. It is a "mirroring" relationship, as discussed in chapter 3. The idea of government according to the will of a sovereign People is not merely central to contemporary democratic theory and practice but, as I argue, constitutive of it. Moreover, while the "legitimacy question" may be peculiar to the discourse of American politics, in particular public administration, the processes of legitimation pertaining to a People are not.

17. Readers familiar with Waldo's work might perceive a similarity in my Politics/politics formula and Waldo's use and subsequent abandonment of Public Administration/public administration to denote Public Administration as a normative, political enterprise and public administration as a technical one. From my point of view, this division is precisely the problem. It brackets the problem before we even begin. Public administration, be it PA or pa, cannot be anything but "technical" within the ontology of the People.

18. Analyses of the construction of collective identity, the construction, invention, or making up of the nation/people/state, have become widespread in theory and history, no doubt due in large part to Benedict Anderson's (1991) acclaimed work *Imagined Communities.* Other important critical examinations by scholars outside public administration include Bhabba (1994), Bourdieu (1990/1987), Hardt & Negri (2000), Laclau & Mouffe (1985), and Zizek (1991, 1993, 2002). An early influential discussion of the "so-called people" appears in Hegel's (1996/1821) *Philosophy of Right.* See also Marx's (1967/1843) *Critique* of Hegel's text. As discussed in chapter 3, the most direct challenges to the idea of the People in public administration are found in Sørensen (2002) and McSwite (1996), who made an analogous argument concerning the construction/production of the public interest amid postmodernizing conditions. However, as I show, the problem of the People may date back as far as Wilson's (1887) famous essay. An account that shares conceptual ground with the one presented here is Timothy Mitchell's (1991, 1999) Foucauldian analyses of the "state-effect." There also are many fine conventionally "historical" accounts on this score. In this work I make use, in particular, of Edmund Morgan's (1988) *Inventing the People.*

19. In this sense, the term *biopolitics* belongs to Foucault (1978/1976, 1994a, 2003/1997). Giorgio Agamben's (1998/1995) recent work has been influential in

extending Foucault's thought. Nikolas Rose (2001) has also influenced my understanding of the term and its practices. One of the differences between Agamben and Foucault concerns the question of whether biopolitics is a distinctively *modern* phenomenon. Agamben, following Hannah Arendt (1998/1958), suggests that the basic problem of biopolitics has been central to politics since ancient times and that, by extension, contemporary circumstances signal an exhaustion of the inheritance of classical thought; Foucault's more well-known texts suggest that it is a modern phenomenon associated distinctively with a concern with "the management of state forces" (Foucault 1994b, p. 71) arising in the seventeenth century. Diken and Laustsen (2005) point out, though, I think rightly, that Foucault's less widely read seminars (e.g., 2003/1997, only recently appearing in English) point to a position closer to Agamben's. My (2005) own view closely follows Agamben's.

While there is a stream of research in political science that draws from the biosciences to account for political behavior, the term has been used rarely in public administration. In a characteristically prescient 1973 chapter (originally published in 1964 in the *Yale Review*), Lynton Caldwell (1973/1964) introduces the term *biopolitics* as shorthand for "political efforts to reconcile biological facts and popular values—notably ethical values—in the formulation of public policy" (p. 24) in the face of the dual explosions of population and biological knowledge. This problem has two sides—whether what must be done politically can be justified bioscientifically, and whether what can be (or needs to be done) done bioscientifically can be done politically. The question is—Is an action biopolitically feasible? Caldwell is concerned with understanding how bioscientific knowledge can constructively relate to the social sciences and usefully be brought to be bear on public policy problems, such as environmental pollution. Drawing from contemporary biological theory and political science, Nancy Meyer-Emerick (2004) argues that concepts of critical theoretical analysis—such as hierarchy, authoritarianism, and submissiveness (pp. 1, 5)—actually may be grounded in human nature. There is a certain social and/or political disposition for which human beings are biologically predisposed. She contrasts this with Foucault's understanding, in which life and the biological existence of a population become an object of political power. This text rejects any attempt to ground politics in biology but assumes that politics cannot but exist in relation to the human as a biological entity and object. What I question here is the particular modern linkage of these two poles and the project of fabrication that follows from this posited relation. For a discussion of the relationship between these "poles," see Latour (1993/1991).

20. "Whole," that is, *not* in terms of a complete *positive* social field, but rather in the sense in which a political ontology diagrams the relation to the exclusion across the totality of the social field. This is to emphasize that the social world, as it were, has "no windows." There is no external (objective) position from which social reality might be viewed.

21. See also discussion in chapter 6 on neoliberalism.

Chapter 2

1. The use of "traditionalism" to describe Redford comes from White and McSwain (1990) and "neoconstitutionalism" to describe Wamsley and Rohr comes from Fox and Miller (1995). The remaining designations are either generally accepted in the literature or, as in "critical postpositivism," developed for this analysis.

2. For a lucid account of Ostrom's relationship to the general literature of Public Choice, see Schneider & Ingram (1997, pp. 38–51).

3. Rohr and his fellow authors of the "Blacksburg Manifesto" (Wamsley et al., 1990) write of *The* Public Administration as an "institution of government rather than of bureaucracy as an organizational form." They write, "*Bureaucracy* in its technical sense refers to a form of social organization that is not confined to the public sector. We carry no brief for any particular organizational form. Our focus is on the *functions* of government agencies and not on how they might be organized" (p. 34). For a related critique of Rohr, see Fox and Miller (1995).

Chapter 3

1. Here I have in mind, especially, Deleuze's (1983/1962) discussion of representation and Nietzsche in his *Nietzsche and Philosophy* and Heidegger's discussion of *Vorstellung* (see Jameson, 2002, pp. 42–75). The clearest discussion of the centrality of antirepresentationalism in "poststructuralist" thought appears in May (1994).

2. It bears noting that representation was purposefully selected as a form of government *in lieu* of democracy in order to safeguard against "factionalism." In Federalist Number 10 (Hamilton, Madison, & Jay, 1977/1787, pp. 61–70), Madison makes the case for "Union as a Safeguard against Domestic Faction and Insurrection":

> By a faction, I understand a number of citizens, whether amounting to a majority or a minority of the whole, who are united and actuated by some common impulse of passion, or of interest, adverse to the rights of other citizens, or to the permanent and aggregate interests of the community.
>
> There are two methods of curing the mischiefs of faction: the one, by removing its causes; the other, by controlling its effects. (p. 62)

Madison rejects the first option, arguing that it would either be tantamount to destroying liberty itself or be impossibly expecting that all men will come to think as a single mind. Faction, or difference, Madison concludes, with what appears to be a most sober realism, is inextricable from the terrain of liberty. Thus, controlling its effects remains. Madison presents two options. First, majority rule quells factionalism, but it is oppressive for those in the minority. "If the impulse and the opportunity be suffered to coincide, we well know that neither moral nor religious motives can be relied on as an adequate control" (p. 66). Madison links this problem to "pure democracy." The second option is republicanism—a form of government distinct from democracy in kind and scale. He writes, "The two great points of difference between a Democracy and a Republic are, first, the delegation of the Government, in the latter, to a small number of citizens elected by the rest; secondly, the greater number of citizens, and greater sphere of country, over which the latter may be extended" (p. 67). The two merits of republicanism largely amount to techniques of *diffusion.* Representatives diffuse passions because "as each Representative will be chosen by a greater number of citizens in the large than in the small Republic, it will be more difficult for unworthy candidates to practice with success the vicious arts, by which elections are too often carried; and the suffrages of The People being more free, will be more likely to centre in men who possess the most attractive merit, and the most diffusive and established characters" (p. 68).

The benefits of scale are enjoyed because "Extend the sphere, and you take in a greater variety of parties and interests; you make it less probable that a majority of the whole will have a common motive to invade the rights of other citizens; or if such a common motive exists, it will be more difficult for all who feel it to discover their own strength, and to act in unison with each other" (Hamilton, Madison, & Jay, 1977/1787, p. 69). Like many great thinkers, Madison turns vice into virtue by inverting the traditional conception of republicanism. The key rhetorical move Madison makes to counter the deeply held republican ideal that it is only in small communities that a republic could work. Indeed, he successfully argues that individual *liberty,* not *democracy,* is at stake and that the best protector of *liberty* is republicanism. Madison first draws this line between republicanism and democracy. Then, conjuring violent images, he argues that, contrary to common belief, small communities of "pure democracy" are not immune to factions or, by extension, oppressive majorities. Not only does republicanism check factions but, as it turns out, the bigger the republic the better. The diffused nature of the republic would allow consensus to form only around those issues of "true public good" (Rakove, 1996, 52).

3. Other notable recent contributions to the conversation about the public interest include Denhardt & Denhardt (2003), Goodsell (1990), Hart & Wright (1998a, 1998b), Marshall & Choudhury (1997), and Sarason (1986).

4. More recently, Miller (2005b) himself has offered a compelling critique of experience and the "residues of foundationalism" in classical pragmatism. An excellent and varied discussion of the Body in public administrative thought appears in the symposium edited by Patricia Patterson (2001). For a related discussion of the problems of collecting experience as qualitative data, see Silverman (2004).

5. For a discussion of the micro and macro as it pertains to the difference between McSwite and Miller, see McSwite (2005a, 2005b). A general discussion of differences between Fox and Miller, David John Farmer, and McSwite appears in McSwite (1997c).

6. For an exceptional discussion of Thayer's work, its reception, and the challenges of moving beyond entrenched dichotomies and theoretical commitments in public administration and social science, see White (1990). A related discussion of the problematic sociology in which public administration is embedded and which impedes transformation of governance appears in McSwite (2005b).

7. I acknowledge that, in Thayer's view, this is "only half the problem" (p. 80)—the other being economic competition. For a full-length treatment of this problem, see Thayer's (1984) *Rebuilding America: The Case for Economic Regulation.*

8. I think Sørensen would support this description. Sørensen and Jacob Torfing (2005), in an article on postliberal democracy, identify one of the three key theoretical commitments of postliberalism as "transgression of the ontological claims of the liberal theories of democracy" (p. 218). In questioning the status of the People and the efficacy of representation, Sørensen's work certainly transgresses the liberal ontology. For an excellent consideration of discourse theories that are relevant to the theoretical development of postliberal democracy and which inform Sørensen's work, see Torfing (1999).

9. It bears noting that Rorty himself may not be sympathetic to such an inquiry into "ontology" since, as Stephen White (2000) explains, ontological claims in our postmetaphysical world are, from Rorty's perspective, basically dressed-up ways of saying "my perspective" (p. 15). So, for Rorty, we should just say "my perspective" without all the philosophical jargon of ontology and its truth claims. However, as I want to suggest here—and as White describes—*not* analyzing ontologies leaves a lot unaccounted for and left taken for granted, such as liberalism's public-private distinction (p. 16) as well underlying substantial commitments that are inscribed into the fabric of everyday life and its institutions. So, while I make use of Rorty's critique, I do not subscribe to his pragmatic antiphilosophical position regarding ontology. Broadly speaking, though, I am in solidarity with Rorty's claims that "there is nothing which validates a person's or a culture's final vocabulary" (1989, p. 197) and that, following from this, the project then becomes to begin from where one find's oneself and commit to creating "a more expansive sense of solidarity than we presently have" (p. 196) and "an ever larger and more variegated *ethnos*" (p. 198). "All we can do is work with the final vocabulary we have, while keeping our ears open for hints about how it might be expanded or extended" (p. 197). For reasons I will elaborate, I am less confident than Rorty that liberal political subjectivity is quite up to this task. I also agree with his rejection of the notion of an identification with or solidarity grounded in "humanity as such," which he sees as "an awkward attempt to secularize the idea of becoming one with God" (p. 198)—though I see the People as simply a variant of this.

10. In August 1971, the Nixon administration closed the Treasury Department's gold window, effectively sounding the death knell of the international gold standard and the Bretton Woods institutions. By 1973, major national currencies began floating (Henwood, 1998, pp. 43–45). The year 1973 also marked the onset of a worldwide recession, the definitive end of the postwar economic expansion. The

breakdown of the gold standard signaled a "radical shift in the manner in which value gets represented as money . . . in the sense that [money] no longer has a formal or tangible link to precious metals (though the latter have continued to play a role as one potential form of money among many others), or for that matter to any other tangible commodity. . . . The world has come to rely, for the first time in its history, upon immaterial forms of money—i.e. money of account assessed quantitatively in numbers of some designated currency. . . . The de-linking of the financial system from active production and from any material monetary base calls into question the reliability of the basic mechanism whereby value is supposed to be represented" (Harvey, 1990, pp. 296–297). Indeed, paper money had been scandalous enough, yet at least it had the pretense of referring back to some *thing* of value, namely, gold, which made it convertible. Floating currencies refer to nothing but other currencies; they are "tautological voids" entirely subject to the forces of the market (Rotman, 1987, p. 89).

11. For further discussion of the role of the father in generating the general relations of authority in market or bourgeois society, see Horkheimer (1972).

12. For McSwite, grounding their work in Lacanian psychoanalytic theory, the central materialization asserted is "Woman," by which McSwite mean *not* the non-male gender but rather a particular subject position that by virtue of its materialization is both inside and outside the bounded domain. We need not accept, however, the elevation of "Woman" or sexual difference to the primary or privileged materialization of the exclusion *in general.* Indeed, the ontology of representation here is an attempt to break from the potentially arresting or essentializing logic of McSwite's Lacanian discussion of sexual difference. In my view, either the assertion of sexual difference relies on an empirical accounting of physical difference, which is highly problematic given the hybrid, intersexed bodies that inhabit the world between these poles, or sexual difference names structural positions, in which case I see no reason to essentialize them, specifically and universally, as sexual. In my view, McSwite's (2004) own work suggests as much. Following Lacan, they argue that a balanced Man/Woman dialectic is essential to the operation of language, the creation of meaning, and the sustaining of consciousness itself. When one function is overemphasized, worlds collapse. Viewing this in terms of sexual difference is useful in the specific analysis of Stivers's critique of the gender bias implicit at the founding of public administration, but, again, we need not code this general structure of "world-making" in sexed terms. To take a closely allied theory, anthropologist Victor Turner's (1969) account of structure and *communitas* closely resembles the Lacanian theory of sexual difference but conceptualizes in more generic terms.

13. In Hirst's (1999) text about Schmitt, we can see elements of Fox and Miller's analysis of the breakdown of the loop model of democracy. There is not a need, though, to blame "postmodern" conditions or interest group liberalism per se for this breakdown. Schmitt saw this occurring in the 1930s. He writes that the "situation of parliamentarianism is critical today because the development of modern

mass democracy has made argumentative public discussion an empty formality. . . . The masses are won over through a propaganda apparatus whose maximum effect relies on an appeal to immediate interests and passions. Argument in a real sense that is characteristic for genuine discussion ceases." In lieu of substantive argument, "the 'symbol' appears" (Schmitt, 1985a/1923, p. 6).

Chapter 4

1. It was, arguably, Vincent Ostrom's (1989/1973) analysis of the intellectual crisis of public administration that initiated the strong turn to law in public administrative thought. As shown in chapter 2, Ostrom presents a powerful examination of the legitimacy question (though he does not use the phrase) that is outlined essentially in terms of the mislaid foundation of public administration—management instead of law. John Rohr (1986) launches his critique from a similar starting point, though he frames his position more explicitly in terms of popular sovereignty, a notion Ostrom assiduously avoids. David Rosenbloom (2000a, 2000b) has described the project of "retrofitting" the administrative state to the regime of constitutional values and "recentering" Congress and the courts. Spicer (1995) described a tension between administration and the Constitution as representing a "conflict of world-views," a fundamental division between the powers and limits of reason, and his more recent work (2001) attempts to provide a constitutionally grounded account of administrative practice further warranted, in part, by the complex social fragmentation of postmodernity. In addition to the neoconstitutionalism prevalent in the field, law has received several other treatments. A broad discussion of the common law within and beyond public administration appears in Green (2002). Along quite different lines, Howe (2002) has offered a suggestive Foucauldian reading of administrative law that critically links constitutionalism with the field's many dichotomies. The most direct interrogation I have read of the bureaucracy's subservience to the law and political representation and the law's presupposed relation to legitimate and ethical action appears in Farmer (1995, pp. 77–85, 240–242).

2. The notion of a "split sovereign" borrows from Jacques Lacan's formulation of subjectivity as the "split subject" (barred-S). Bruce Fink (1995) writes,

> The subject is split between ego . . . and unconscious . . . , between conscious and unconscious, between an ineluctably false sense of self and the automatic functioning of language (the signifying chain) in the unconscious. . . .
>
> *The subject is nothing but this very split.* Lacan's variously termed "split subject," "divided subject," or "barred subject"—all written with the same symbol, S [barred-subject]—consist entirely in the fact that a speaking being's two "parts" or avatars share no common ground: they are radically separated (the ego or false being acquiring a refusal of unconscious thoughts, unconscious thought having no concern whatever for the ego's fine opinion of itself). (p. 45)

This split, as Dylan Evans (1996) explains, "denotes the impossibility of the ideal of a fully present self-consciousness; the subject will never know himself [*sic*] completely, but will always be cut off from his own knowledge" (p. 196). For Lacan, the movement that renders the identity of the ego and unconscious impossible is twofold. In the first movement, or *cut,* of alienation, an entity enters into language and what Lacan calls the Symbolic, sometimes also called the order of the Law or the big Other. Here the entity becomes a subject of language or the Law and submits to being represented by a signifier. In effect, a space is cleared for the emergence of a subject in the Symbolic order, the cost of which is subjection to the sovereignty of the signifier. The second cut, separation, "*involves the alienated subject's confrontation with the Other, not as language this time, but as desire*" (p. 50; emphasis in original). In this move, the subject comes to grips with the failure of the Symbolic order. That is, the *lack* of wholeness experienced confronts the lack in the Other, the incompleteness of the Law itself. It is at this juncture that a crucial third term emerges to mediate the relationship between the subject and the Symbolic order, which Lacan calls, variously, the Phallus, the signifier of the desire of the Other, or the Name-of-the-Father. Here the subject as such emerges (p. 59).

3. A book-length account of these issues, though written to rather different ends, is Hunt and Wickham's (1994) *Foucault and Law: Towards a Sociology of Law as Governance.* See also Kahn's (1997) *The Reign of Law: Marbury v. Madison and the Construction of America.*

4. In this section I rely heavily on two recognized classics of American legal history: Morton J. Horwitz's (1977) *The Transformation of American Law, 1780–1860* and Lawrence Friedman's (1973) *A History of American Law.*

5. The paradigm example is New York's Field Code of 1848. Of codification, David Dudley Field said, "The existence of a system of rules and conformity to them are the essential conditions for all free government and of republican government above all others. The law is our only sovereign. We have enthroned it" (Field, quoted in Subrin, 1987, p. 935). The idea was, in effect, to merge the flexibility that had been the hallmark of the equity courts before they had become too complicated with the stability and "sense" of the common law courts, yet these would be purged of the dangers of judicial discretion. This would be done through the written codification of the law and procedures, which would bind judges to the stated rules. The goal was certainly in the law (p. 939). We see a similar desire in the proliferation of rules and regulations to circumscribe administrative behavior.

6. It was on this score that the model of the capitalist market would prove effective (Appleby, 1984), for here was a model that would justify positive (corrective) action under the auspices of a naturally occurring system. Laws would represent the regulatory "invisible" processes of the market, and judicial decisions could be made to that end (Horwitz, 1977).

7. The crux of Novak's point has been made in other places, including the work of the *Commonwealth* history by Oscar Handlin and Mary Flug Handlin (1969) and, quite extensively in legal history, in particular the "Wisconsin School"

of law and society initiated by the work of James Willard Hurst (1956). Nevertheless, Novak makes an important point distinct from that literature by emphasizing the *continuity* with the liberal welfare state that followed the well-regulated police state. The core point is new (or at least underappreciated) in public administration. The issue, though, that Novak wishes to tackle with this project is rather different than the present one. He wishes to counter the claim that the law and state instrumentally promoted economic activity in the self-regulating market in the nineteenth century. Instead, he contends that law carved out a specific sphere of economic activity, thereby constituting an object for public management and regulation. In a way, given the tack taken here, these differences amount to one and the same problem; since what is at issue is not whether a "special" or "general" interest was served through technical law, but simply that technical law was *productive* of the People's order defined in and by Law. Regardless, though, it is an exceptional presentation of the various forms regulation took in the nineteenth century. It is a text that belongs in the public administration canon.

8. In his study of Locke, A. John Simmons (1993, pp. 12–13) writes of the *relational quality* of the state of nature for Locke. That is, people are in the state of nature always with regard to someone who is "in it." Thus, within a given society, some people can be in society and some in the state of nature, such as visiting aliens, minors under the age of consent, and those of defective reason. By extension and according to the argument here, the generation of the "common judge" is dependent upon maintaining classes of people in the state of nature.

9. The implicit theory of development in early public administration is not much different. For example, Goodnow writes, "Of course [man's] degree of intelligence, his ideas of right and wrong, at different periods of his development, are by no means the same, and form of government adopted at one stage of his development may have an important effect upon his later condition. But it is believed that the real political institutions of different peoples at the same stage of intelligence and morality will show great similarity, even where the external forms of government appear very different. This similarity is due, as has been said, to the fact that man is man everywhere and at all times, and that all political organizations of men must therefore adopt in a general way the same methods for their satisfaction" (1900, p. 7). We can see in this brief passage the full range of assumptions that sustain the discourse of "development." First, the appearance of specific institutions marks a specific state of collective intelligence and morality; this is underwritten by a linear conception of time. Second, there is the implicit humanist assumption of a universal human nature and, third, the related assumption that this common nature is ultimately oriented toward a single purpose or end state, largely irrespective of history or political content. Since western European bureaucracies are the point of reference for Goodnow, it is clear that other nations and cultures that are different and less developed are, by extension, perceived to be less moral and intelligent. While it may be tempting to dismiss this as more of Goodnow's Hegelianism (e.g., Rohr, 1986), as Gilbert Rist (1997) and other development theo-

rists have shown, there is a long tradition of this kind of thought in the West, and in the nineteenth century a broad consensus about "development" emerged on three essential points: "that progress has the same substance (or nature) as history; that all nations travel the same road; and that all do not advance at the same speed as Western society, which therefore has an indisputable 'lead' because of the greater size of its production, the dominant role that reason plays within it, and the scale of its scientific and technical discoveries" (p. 40). A thoughtful collection of essays on temporality is Waldo (1970).

10. Related to this was the skepticism concerning a woman's capacity for patriotic allegiance, which manifested itself, among other ways, in the asymmetrical naturalization laws (Cott, 1998).

11. The duration of disenfranchisement varied from state to state and changed over the course of the century. In some instances, pauperism was linked to permanent disenfranchisement; in others disenfranchisement was as temporary as the state of pauperism. Two other dimensions of pauperism bear note. First, as is the case with most forms of exclusion, there is an overlap between hostility toward immigrants and pauperism (Neuman, 1993), in part rising from the practice of England, and later France, of "pauper dumping." There also was economic cost associated with the responsibility of towns for aiding "settled" paupers. Thus many debates and controversies over pauperism in the nineteenth century turned on "settlement" issues.

12. Master-slave was, of course, another brutal form of "household" dependency. Emancipation required new strategies for maintaining dependence. See Van Tassell (1995).

13. In another dimension, this is the paradoxical process of the modern constitution that Bruno Latour (1993/1991) describes in *We Have Never Been Modern.* The attempts to produce purity actually increase the production of hybrids.

Chapter 5

1. Close to the arguments made by McSwite (1997b) and Stivers (2000), Porter (1995), in *Trust in Numbers: The Pursuit of Objectivity in Science and Public Life,* writes about the rise of "objective" discourse and the increasing importance of quantitative data. He also raises the important point of decision and authority: "To understand the circumstances under which quantitative objectivity has come into demand, we need to look not only at the intellectual formation of experts, but even more importantly at the social basis of authority" (p. 6). Likewise, he shows how "seasoned judgment" came to be rendered inadequate to the task of grounding political decision.

2. This notion of "efficient citizenry" is alive and well in contemporary debates over social capital. Consider the following statements from Robert Putnam's (2000) *Bowling Alone:* "a well-connected individual in a poorly connected society is not as productive as a well-connected individual in a well-connected society" (p. 20). "A

society characterized by generalized reciprocity is more efficient than a distrustful society, for the same reason that money is more efficient than barter." "First, social capital allows citizens to resolve collective problems more easily." "Second, social capital greases the wheels that allow communities to advance smoothly. . . . everyday business and social transactions are less costly" (p. 288). "The networks that constitute social capital also serve as conduits for the flow of helpful information that facilitates achieving our goals" (p. 289).

3. "Cartesian," that is, insofar as Descartes' revolution, in part, concerned the reconceptualization of physical bodies as *inert* objects moving through homogeneous, geometric space, as opposed to qualitatively changing by virtue of being in motion. See Koyré (1978/1966).

4. This schematic is inspired by similar diagrams in Agamben (1998/1995, p. 38). Thayer (1973, pp. 76–77) offers a related kind of diagrammatic presentation in his discussion of hierarchy and representation but does not offer an alterative visual expression for the topography of structured nonhierarchy. I thank Margaret Stout for bringing this similarity to my attention.

Chapter 6

1. Recall Waldo's (1980) claim: "I do not believe it is possible to 'solve' the problem of relating politics to administration in any way that is systematic and generally acceptable, in and for the United States, under present conditions and in any foreseeable future" (p. 77).

2. Here I am not saying, as perhaps Dreyfus and Rabinow do, that "political problems" are removed from the domain of politics and recast in neutral language precisely because the language of liberal democracy is always already both technical and (normatively) neutral. Liberal democracy is always a discourse of *reform*. Biopower marks a particular reconfiguration of the biopolitical project of the People.

3. In the film, Washington, DC, law enforcement officials possess "psychic technology" in the form of three precognitive, genetically altered humans. These "precogs" have visions of future homicides and provide the names of perpetrators to the police's "pre-crime" unit. A minority report refers to the case in which one of the precogs has a dissenting vision. The film is based on a short story by Philip Dick.

4. This is the case not only for the United States. For example, in the wake of the assaults in Beslan, Russia's Vladimir Putin has assumed the right to pursue terrorists anywhere in the world (Smith, 2006).

5. The related issue of the "privatization of public power" has been a particular topic of interest in international affairs. See, for example, Cutler, Haufler, & Porter (1999), Hall et al. (2002), and Rosenau (1992).

6. We can see this denuding to bare life even in cases that seem to run counter to this argument. For example, the proliferation of literal "boot camps" across the

country may appear to contradict this claim. On one level, though boot camps "typically include military-style drilling and quartering, ceremonies at entrance and exit, harsh verbal evaluations from correctional officers trained to act like drill sergeants, and summary punishments for disciplinary infractions in the form of physically taxing exercise" (Simon, 1995, p. 26), as well as embarrassing uniforms and harsh physical conditions, many have apparent "therapeutic" aspects as well. Indeed, many offer twelve-step type substance abuse programs, aftercare, and other rehabilitative and educational training (p. 27), which would signal continuity with modern forms of penalization. However, as John Simon suggests, this is deceptive and the presence of these camps may actually "[evidence] an end game of penal modernity" insofar as they exhibit postmodernity's "willful nostalgia" (p. 28). In other words, the very appearance of the boot camp signals the eclipse of its actual practice; it now serves as a screen upon which citizens' and politicians' fantasies of incarceration and imprisonment are projected. He writes, "much of the appeal of the boot camp lies not in its reference to a real set of social practices, i.e. the military, labor, or education, but its reference to modern penalty's reference to these external forces." Indeed, all these institutions are in crisis. Thus in the fantasy of the contemporary boot camp, it is not rehabilitation that is enacted, but rather a nostalgia of those declining institutions that is *re*enacted for a "middle-class television audience" (p. 36). The actual bodies in prison become role players in a reassuring nostalgic fantasy of wholesomeness and goodness. I thank Aaron Kupchik for alerting me to Simon's article and this dimension of the Camp.

7. For an interesting discussion of social regulation and the privatization of governing in the exceptional spaces of the shopping mall, see Passavant (2004).

8. For discussions in public administration about the continuity and discontinuity between the new public management and the bureaucratic paradigm, see Denhardt & Denhardt (2003), Lynn (2001), and Page (2005).

Chapter 7

1. For a discussion of the various dimensions of refusal, see the symposium edited by David John Farmer (2003b), "The Great Refusal."

2. While there are some affinities, there are differences in how I would configure and theorize those structures, topographies, and agencies in this *transformative* notion of the political as compared to, for example, the transformative *administration* of McSwain & White's (1993) and King & Zanetti's (2005) recent work. Nevertheless, there is a shared concern.

3. For a discussion based in Lacanian psychoanalytic theory on the use of formalism in understanding discourse and social relationship, see Catlaw (2006d).

4. The notion of the empty set comes from Alain Badiou's (2006/1988, pp. 52–69) *Being and Event.* I do not claim to adopt the whole of Badiou's system. Nevertheless, the mark of the empty set seems quite appropriate in naming another bio-

political relationship. The notion of "void" is here derived from the psychoanalytic theory of Jacques Lacan. For a discussion of Lacan's relationship to the void, see Catlaw (2006d).

5. For a longer analysis of the death of the Practitioner, see Catlaw (2006b). This passage draws from this article, which originally appeared in *Administrative Theory & Praxis,* and from Catlaw (2006d), "Performance Anxieties: Shifting Public Administration from the Relevant to the Real," published originally in *Administrative Theory & Praxis.*

6. It may be strange to invoke Plato at this point, sometimes considered the archphilosopher of the One. Yet, as Deleuze (1990b/1969) argues, we can also find in Plato the thinker of the simulacrum, the image that is the copy of the copy that has no primary referent of representation, and so undermines the model-copy relationship. See also Badiou (2006/1988, pp. 31–37).

7. For a discussion of the relationship between the figure of the midwife presented here and Lacanian psychoanalytic notion of the "discourse of the analyst," see Catlaw (2006a).

8. See Zizek (2002, pp. lxxii–lxxxviii) for an extended discussion of this point.

9. For an insightful discussion and critique of political theories based on this idea of "constitutive lack," see Robinson (2005). As exemplified in the work of Slavoj Zizek, Alenka Zupancic, Saul Neuman, Ernesto Laclau, Chantal Mouffe, and others, Robinson argues that this perspective is becoming "hegemonic" in political theory, perhaps second in influence only to the analytical/Rawlsian tradition.

References

Adorno, T., & Horkheimer, M. (1976). *Dialectic of enlightenment* (J. Cumming, Trans.). New York: Continuum.

Agamben, G. (1998/1995). *Homo sacer: Sovereign power and bare life* (D. Heller-Roazen, Trans.). Stanford, CA: Stanford University Press.

Agamben, G. (2002). Security and terror. *Theory & Event, 5*(4).

Albrow, M. (1996). *The global age: State and society beyond modernity.* Stanford, CA: Stanford University Press.

Alcorn, M. (2002). *Changing the subject in English class: Discourse and the construction of desire.* Carbondale, IL: Southern Illinois University Press.

Alexander, J. (1997). Avoiding the issue: Racism and administrative responsibility in public administration. *American Review of Public Administration, 27*(4), 343–361.

Althusser, L. (1971/1970). Ideology and ideological state apparatuses (notes towards an investigation). In *Lenin and philosophy and other essays* (pp. 127–188). London: Monthly Review.

Althusser, L., & Balibar, E. (1997/1970). *Reading capital.* London: Verso.

Amoore, L. (2006). Biometric borders: Governing mobilities in the war on terror. *Political Geography, 25*(3), 336–351.

Amoore, L., & De Goede, M. (2005). Governance, risk, and dataveillance in the war on terror. *Crime, Law & Social Change, 43,* 149–173.

Anderson, B. (1991). *Imagined communities* (Rev. ed.). London: Verso.

Appleby, J. O. (1984). *Capitalism and a new social order: The republican vision of the 1790's.* New York: New York University Press.

Appleby, P. H. (1970/1945). *Big democracy.* New York: Russell & Russell.

Arendt, H. (1998/1958). *The human condition* (2nd ed.). Chicago: University of Chicago Press.

Badiou, A. (2006/1988). *Being and event* (O. Feltham, Trans.). New York: Continuum.

Baer, W. C. (1977). Urban planners: Doctors or midwives? *Public Administration Review, 37*(6), 671–678.

Balakrishnan, G. (2000). *The enemy: An intellectual portrait of Carl Schmitt.* London: Verso.

Banta, M. (1993). *Taylored lives: Narrative productions in the age of Taylor, Veblen, and Ford.* Chicago: University of Chicago Press.

Barnes, H. E. (1917). Sociology before Comte: A summary of doctrines and an introduction to the literature. *American Journal of Sociology, 23*(2), 174–247.

Bartelson, J. (1995). *A genealogy of sovereignty.* Cambridge: Cambridge University Press.

Barzelay, M. (2004/1887). Breaking through bureaucracy. In J. M. Shafritz, A. C. Hyde, & S. J. Parkes (Eds.), *Classics of public administration* (5th ed., pp. 533–555). Fort Worth, TX: Harcourt Brace.

Bauman, Z. (1989). *Modernity and the Holocaust.* Cambridge: Polity Press.

Beck, U. (1992). *The risk society: Towards a new modernity* (M. Ritter, Trans.). London: Sage.

Beck, U., Giddens, A., & Lash, S. (1994). *Reflexive modernization.* Palo Alto, CA: Polity Press.

Bensel, R. (1990). *Yankee leviathan: The origins of central state authority in America, 1859–1877.* New York: Cambridge University Press.

Berger, P. L., & Luckman, T. (1966). *The social construction of reality: A treatise on the sociology of knowledge.* Garden City, NY: Anchor Books.

Bhabba, H. (1994). *The location of culture.* London: Routledge.

Bigo, D. (2002). Security and immigration: Toward a critique of the governmentality of unease. *Alternatives, 27*(Suppl. 1), 63–92.

Blakely, E. J., & Snyder, M. G. (1997). Divided we call: Gated and walled communities in the United States. In N. Ellin (Ed.), *Architecture of fear* (pp. 85–99). Princeton: Princeton Architectural Press.

Bolton, M. J., & Stolcis, G. B. (2003). Ties that do not bind: Musing on the specious relevance of academic research. *Public Administration Review, 63*(5), 626–630.

Bourdieu, P. (1990/1987). The uses of the "people." In *In Other Words: Essays toward a reflexive sociology* (Trans.) (pp. 150–155). Stanford, CA: Stanford University Press.

Bourdieu, P. (1991/1988). *The political ontology of Martin Heidegger* (P. Collier, Trans.). Stanford, CA: Stanford University Press.

Brown, B., & Stillman, R. J., II. (1986). *A search for public administration: The ideas and career of Dwight Waldo.* College Station: Texas A&M University Press.

Bumiller, E. (2001, October 30). Bush announces a crackdown on visa violators. *New York Times,* p. A1.

Burrell, G., & Morgan, G. (1993/1979). *Sociological paradigms and organizational analysis.* Aldershot, England: Ashgate.

Bush, G. W. (2002). *Iraq must disarm, says president in South Dakota speech.* White House. Retrieved May 24, 2005, from http://www.whitehouse.gov/news/releases/2002/11/20021105–1.html

Bush, J. (2003). *2003 inaugural address.* Executive Office of the Governor (Florida). Retrieved January 18, 2003, from http://aif.com/Article%20Archives/2003articles/2003InauguralAddress.htm?zoom_highlight=jeb+bush+inaugural

Butterfield, F. (2004, May 8). Mistreatment of prisoners is called routine in U.S. *New York Times,* p. A11.

Caldwell, L. (1973/1964). Biopolitics: Science, ethics, and public policy. In D. F. Paulsen & R. B. Denhardt (Eds.), *Pollution and public policy: A book of readings* (pp. 22–36). New York: Dodd, Mead.

Caldwell, L. K. (1975). Managing the transition to post-modern society. *Public Administration Review, 35*(6), 567–572.

Campbell, B. C. (1995). *The growth of American government.* Bloomington: University of Indiana Press.

Campbell, K. (2005). Nobody said it was easy: Examining the matrioshka dolls of citizen engagement. *Administration & Society, 37*(5), 636–648.

Castells, M. (2000). *The rise of network society* (2nd ed.). London: Blackwell.

Catlaw, T. J. (2005). Constitution as executive order: The administrative state and the political ontology of "We the People." *Administration & Society, 37*(4), 445–482.

Catlaw, T. J. (2006a). Authority, representation, and the contradictions of post-traditional governing. *American Review of Public Administration, 36*(3), 261–87.

Catlaw, T. J. (2006b). The death of the practitioner. *Administrative Theory & Praxis, 28*(2), 190–207.

Catlaw, T. J. (2006c). Discourse, decision, and the doublet: An essay on the crisis of modern authority. In G. Morçöl (Ed.), *The handbook on decision-making* (pp. 99–118). London: Taylor & Francis.

Catlaw, T. J. (2006d). Performance anxieties: Shifting public administration from the relevant to the real. *Administrative Theory & Praxis, 28*(1), 89–120.

Cavarero, A. (2002). Politicizing theory. *Political Theory, 30*(4), 503–532.

Cayer, N. J. (1975). *Public personnel management in the United States.* New York: St. Martin's Press.

Chambers, J. W., II. (1980). *The tyranny of change: America in the Progressive Era, 1900–1917.* New York: St. Martin's Press.

Chandler, R. C., & Plano, J. C. (1982). *The public administration dictionary.* New York: John Wiley & Sons.

Christie, N. (2000). *Crime control as industry: Towards gulags, Western style* (3rd ed.). London: Routledge.

Connolly, W. (1995). *The ethos of pluralization.* Minneapolis: University of Minnesota Press.

Conover, M. (1925). Merit systems of civil service in the states. *American Political Science Review, 19*(3), 544–560.

Corwin, E. S. (1928). *The "higher law" background of American constitutional law.* Ithaca, NY: Great Seal Books.

Cott, N. F. (1998). Marriage and women's citizenship in the United States, 1830–1934. *American Historical Review, 103*(5), 1440–1474.

Cunningham, R., & Weschler, L. (2002). Theory and the public administration student/practitioner. *Public Administration Review, 62*(1), 104–111.

Cutler, A. C., Haufler, V., & Porter, T. (Eds.). (1999). *Private authority and international affairs.* Albany: State University of New York Press.

Dahl, R. (1961). *Who governs?* New Haven, CT: Yale University Press.

Davidson, J. D., & Rees-Mogg, L. W. (1999). *The sovereign individual: Mastering the transition to the information age.* New York: Free Press.

Dean, M. (1999). *Governmentality: Power and rule in modern society.* Thousand Oaks, CA: Sage.

Deleuze, G. (1983/1962). *Nietzsche and philosophy* (H. Tomlinson, Trans.). New York: Columbia University Press.

Deleuze, G. (1988/1986). *Foucault* (S. Hand, Trans.). Minneapolis: University of Minnesota Press.

Deleuze, G. (1990a/1969). *The logic of sense* (M. Lester and C. Stivale, Trans.). New York: Columbia University Press.

Deleuze, G. (1990b/1969). The simulacrum and ancient philosophy. In *The logic of sense* (pp. 253–279). New York: Columbia University Press.

Deleuze, G. (1994/1968). *Difference and repetition* (P. Patton, Trans.). New York: Columbia University Press.

Deleuze, G. (1995/1990). Postscript on control societies. In *Negotiations, 1972–1990* (pp. 177–182). New York: Columbia University Press.

Deleuze, G., & Guattari, F. (1983/1972). *Anti-Oedipus: Capitalism and schizophrenia* (R. Hurley, M. Seem, & H. R. Lane, Trans.). Minneapolis: University of Minnesota Press.

Deleuze, G., & Guattari, F. (1987/1983). *A thousand plateaus: Capitalism and schizophrenia* (B. Massumi, Trans.). Minneapolis: University of Minnesota Press.

Denhardt, J. V., & Denhardt, R. B. (2003). *The new public service: Serving, not steering.* Armonk, NY: M. E. Sharpe.

Denhardt, R. B. (1981). *In the shadow of organization.* Lawrence: Regents Press of Kansas.

Denhardt, R. B. (1999). *Public administration: An action orientation* (3rd ed.). Fort Worth, TX: Harcourt Brace.

Denhardt, R. B. (2001). The big questions of public administration education. *Public Administration Review, 61*(5), 526–534.

Diken, B. (2004). From refugee camps to gated communities: Biopolitics and the end of the city. *Citizenship Studies, 8*(1), 83–106.

Diken, B., & Laustsen, C. B. (2002). Zones of indistinction: Security, terror, and bare life. *Space & Culture, 5*(3), 290–307.

Diken, B., & Laustsen, C. B. (2005). *The culture of exception: Sociology facing the camp.* London: Routledge.

Diner, S. J. (1998). *A very different age: Americans of the Progressive Era.* New York: Hill & Wang.

Dolan, J. A., & Rosenbloom, D. H. (Eds.). (2003). *Representative bureaucracy: Classic readings and continuing controversies.* Armonk, NY: M. E. Sharpe.

Dreyfus, H. L., & Rabinow, P. (1983). *Michel Foucault: Beyond structuralism and hermeneutics* (2nd ed.). Chicago: University of Chicago Press.

Evans, D. (1996). *An introductory dictionary of Lacanian psychoanalysis.* London: Routledge.

Fabian, J. (1983). *Time and the other: How anthropology makes its object.* New York: Columbia University Press.

Farmer, D. J. (1995). *The language of public administration: Bureaucracy, modernity and postmodernity.* Tuscaloosa: University of Alabama Press.

Farmer, D. J. (2003a). The allure of rhetoric and the truancy of poetry. *Administrative Theory & Praxis, 25*(1), 9–36.

Farmer, D. J. (Ed.). (2003b). The great refusal [symposium]. *Administrative Theory & Praxis, 25*(2), 173–298.

Farmer, D. J. (2005). *To kill the king: Post-traditional governance and bureaucracy.* Armonk, NY: M. E. Sharpe.

Feldman, A. (2004). Securocratic wars of public safety. *Interventions: Journal of Postcolonial Studies, 6*(3), 330–350.

Filene, P. G. (1970). An obituary for "the progressive movement." *American Quarterly, 22*(1), 20–34.

Fink, B. (1995). *The Lacanian subject: Between language and jouissance.* Princeton, NJ: Princeton University Press.

Fisher W., III, Horwitz, M. J., & Reed, T. A. (Eds.). (1993). *American legal realism.* Oxford: Oxford University Press.

Fogelin, R. (2004). *Walking the tightrope of reason: The precarious life of a rational animal.* Oxford: Oxford University Press.

Follett, M. P. (1951/1924). *Creative experience.* New York: Longman.

Follett, M. P. (1998/1920). *The new state: Group organization, the solution of popular government.* University Park: Pennsylvania State University Press.

Foucault, M. (1970/1966). *The order of things: An archeology of the human sciences* (A. Sheridan, Trans.). New York: Vintage Books.

Foucault, M. (1978/1976). *The history of sexuality: Vol. 1. An introduction* (R. Hurley, Trans.). New York: Vintage Books.

Foucault, M. (1984). What is enlightenment? In P. Rabinow (Ed.), *The Foucault reader* (pp. 32–50). New York: Pantheon Books.

Foucault, M. (1988/1961). *Madness and civilization* (R. Howard, Trans.). New York: Vintage Books.

Foucault, M. (1991/1979). Governmentality. In G. Burchell, C. Gordon, & P. Miller (Eds.), *The Foucault effect: Studies in governmentality with two lectures by and an interview with Michel Foucault* (pp. 87–104). Chicago: University of Chicago Press.

Foucault, M. (1994a). The birth of biopolitics. In P. Rabinow (Ed.), *Essential works of Foucault, 1954–1984: Vol. 1. Ethics* (pp. 73–80). New York: New Press.

Foucault, M. (1994b). Security, territory, and population. In P. Rabinow (Ed.), *Essential works of Foucault, 1954–1984: Vol. 1. Ethics* (pp. 67–71). New York: New Press.

Foucault, M. (1995/1975). *Discipline and punish: The birth of the prison* (A. Sheridan, Trans.). (2nd ed.). New York: Vintage Books.

Foucault, M. (2000a/1983). The subject and power. In J. D. Faubion (Ed.), *The essential works of Michel Foucault, 1954–1984: Vol. 3. Power* (pp. 326–348). New York: New Press.

Foucault, M. (2000b/1977). Truth and power. In J. D. Faubion (Ed.), *The essential works of Michel Foucault, 1954–1984: Vol. 3. Power* (pp. 111–133). New York: New Press.

Foucault, M. (2003/1997). *"Society must be defended": Lectures at the College de France, 1975–1976* (D. Macey, Trans.). New York: Picador.

Fox, C. J., & Miller, H. T. (1995). *Postmodern public administration: Toward discourse.* Thousand Oaks, CA: Sage.

Fox, K. (1977). *Better city government: Innovation in American urban politics.* Philadelphia: Temple University Press.

Frederickson, H. G. (1997). *The spirit of public administration.* San Francisco: Jossey-Bass.

Frederickson, H. G., & Marini, F. (Eds). (1997a). Bureaucracy and democracy: Essays in honor of Dwight Waldo. *Public Administration Review, 57*(3), 190–222.

Frederickson, H. G., & Marini, F. (Eds). (1997b). Modern comparative public administration: Essays in honor of Dwight Waldo. *Public Administration Review 57*(4), 323–353.

Frederickson, H. G., & Marini, F. (Eds). (1997c). The Waldo symposium. *Journal of Public Administration Research & Theory 7*(3), 389–487.

Friedman, L. M. (1973). *A history of American law.* New York: Simon & Schuster.

Fry, B. R. (1989). *Mastering public administration: From Max Weber to Dwight Waldo.* Chatham, NJ: Chatham House.

Galambos, L., & Pratt, J. (1988). *The rise of the corporate commonwealth: United States business and public policy in the 20th century.* New York: Basic Books.

Giddens, A. (1994). Living in a post-traditional society. In U. Beck, A. Giddens, & S. Lash (Eds.), *Reflexive modernization* (pp. 56–109). London: Polity Press.

Gignesi, A. L. (2004). *Relinquishing control: The married women's property acts in nineteenth century America.* Unpublished doctoral dissertation, American University, Washington, DC.

Goodnow, F. (1889). Local government in Prussia I. *Political Science Quarterly, 4*(4), 648–666.

Goodnow, F. (1890). Local government in Prussia II. *Political Science Quarterly, 5*(1), 124–158.

Goodnow, F. (1900). *Politics and administration: A study in government.* New York: Russell & Russell.

Goodnow, F. (1905). The growth of executive discretion. *Proceedings of the American Political Science Association, 2,* 29–44.

Goodnow, F. J. (1997/1895). *Municipal home rule: A study in administration.* Buffalo, NY: William S. Hein.

Goodsell, C. T. (1990). Public administration and the public interest. In G. I. Wamsley, R. N. Bacher, C. T. Goodsell, P. T. Kroneberg, J. A. Rohr, C. M. Stivers, O. F. White, & J. F. Wolf (Eds.), *Refounding public administration* (pp. 96–113). Newbury Park, CA: Sage.

Goodsell, C. T. (2004). American public administration's maturity: A profile. *International Journal of Public Administration, 27*(7), 471–480.

Gordon, C. (1991). Governmental rationality: An introduction. In G. Burchell, C. Gordon, & P. Miller (Eds.), *The Foucault effect: Studies in governmentality with two lectures by and an interview with Michel Foucault* (pp. 1–52). Chicago: University of Chicago Press.

Gordon, L. (1947). Public administration in perspective [Review of John Gaus's *Reflections on public administration*]. *Public Administration Review, 7*(4), 263–267.

Goux, J-.J. (1990/1973). *Symbolic economies: After Marx and Freud* (Jennifer Curtiss Gage, Trans.). Ithaca, NY: Cornell University Press.

Grant, R. W., & Keohane, R. O. (2005). Accountability and abuses of power in world politics. *American Political Science Review, 99*(1), 29–43.

Green, R. T. (2002). Common law, equity, and American public administration. *American Review of Public Administration, 32*(3), 263–294.

Gregory, D. (2004). The angel of Iraq. *Environment & Planning D: Space and Society, 22*(3), 317–324.

Gross, O. (2006). What "emergency" regime? *Constellations, 13*(1), 74–88.

Grossberg, M. (1985). *Governing the hearth: Law and the family in nineteenth century America.* Chapel Hill: University of North Carolina Press.

Hacking, I. (1983). *Representing and Intervening.* New York: Cambridge University Press.

Hacking, I. (1999/1986). Making people up. In M. Biagioli (Ed.), *The science studies reader* (pp. 161–171). New York: Routledge.

Hacking, I. (2002). Historical ontology. In *Historical ontology* (pp. 1–26). Cambridge, MA: Harvard University Press.

Hall, R. B., Biersteker, T. J., Smith, S., Brown, C., Cerny, P., Grieco, J., & Groom, A. J. R. (Eds.). (2002). *The emergence of private authority in global governance.* Cambridge: Cambridge University Press.

Hallward, P. (2003). *Badiou: A subject to truth.* Minneapolis: University of Minnesota Press.

Hamilton, A., Madison, J., & Jay, J. (1977/1787). *The federalist.* Franklin Center, PA: Franklin Library.

Handlin, O., & Handlin, M. F. (1969). *Commonwealth: A study of the role of government in the American economy, Massachusetts, 1774–1861* (Rev. ed.). Cambridge, MA: Belknap Press of Harvard University Press.

Hardt, M., & Negri, A. (2000). *Empire.* Cambridge, MA: Harvard University Press.

Hardt, M., & Negri, A. (2004). *Multitude: War and democracy in the age of Empire.* New York: Penguin Press.

Harmon, M. M. (1981). *Action theory for public administration.* New York: Longman.

Harmon, M. M. (1989a). "Decision" and "action" as contrasting perspectives in organization theory. *Public Administration Review, 49*(2), 144–152.

Harmon, M. M. (1989b). The Simon-Waldo debate: A review and update. *Public Administration Quarterly, 12*(1), 437–451.

Harmon, M. M. (1995). *Responsibility as paradox: A critique of rational discourse on government.* Thousand Oaks, CA: Sage.

Harmon, M. M. (2006). *Public administration's final exam: A pragmatist restructuring of the profession and the discipline.* Tuscaloosa: University of Alabama Press.

Hart, D. K., & Wright, N. D. (1998a). "The civic good": "The public interest" of civic humanism. *Administrative Theory & Praxis, 20*(4), 406–421.

Hart, D. K., & Wright, N. D. (1998b). The "public interest": What we are not leaving to our posterity. *Administrative Theory & Praxis, 18*(2), 14–28.

Harvey, D. (1990). *The condition of postmodernity.* Oxford: Blackwell.

Hay, C. (2006). Political ontology. In R. E. Goodin & C. Tilly (Eds.), *Oxford handbook of contextual political analysis* (pp. 78–96). Oxford: Oxford University Press.

Heckathorne, D. D., & Maser, S. M. (1990). The contractual architecture of public policy: A critical reconstruction of Lowi's typology. *Journal of Politics, 52,* 1101–1123.

Hegel, G. W. F. (1996/1821). *Philosophy of right* (S. W. Dyde, Trans.). Amherst, NY: Prometheus Books.

Heidegger, M. (1962/1926). *Being and time* (J. Macquarrie & E. Robinson, Trans.). San Francisco: HarperSanFrancisco.

Heidegger, M. (1977). On the essence of truth (J. Sallis, Trans.). In D. F. Krell (Ed.), *Basic writings* (pp. 143–188). New York: Harper & Row.

Held, D. (1996). *Models of democracy.* Stanford, CA: Stanford University Press.

Held, D. (1997). Democracy: From city-states to a cosmopolitan order? In R. E. Goodin & P. Pettit (Eds.), *Contemporary political philosophy: An anthology* (pp. 78–102). London: Blackwell.

Henwood, D. (1998). *Wall Street* (2nd ed.). London: Verso.

Hirshhorn, L. (1997). *Reworking authority: Leading and following in the post-modern organization.* Cambridge, MA: MIT Press.

Hirst, P. (1999). Carl Schmitt's decisionism. In C. Mouffe (Ed.), *The challenge of Carl Schmitt* (pp. 7–17). London: Verso.

Hobbes, T. (1991/1651). *Leviathan.* Cambridge: Cambridge University Press.

Hofstadter, R. (1955). *The age of reform.* New York: Vintage Books.

Holderlin, F. (1980/1802). *Patmos, poems, and fragments* (pp. 462–477). Cambridge: Cambridge University Press.

Horkheimer, M. (1972). Authority and the family. In *Critical Theory* (M. J. O'Connell and others, Trans.)(pp. 47–128). New York: Herder & Herder.

Horwitz, M. J. (1977). *The transformation of American law, 1780–1860*. Cambridge, MA: Harvard University Press.

Houellebecq, M. (2002). *The platform.* London: William Heinemann.

Howe, L. E. (2001). Civil service reform and the political culture of governmentality: Massachusetts, 1952–1981. *Administrative Theory & Praxis, 23*(2), 151–174.

Howe, L. E. (2002). Administrative law and governmentality: Politics and discretion in a changing state of sovereignty. *Administrative Theory & Praxis, 24*(1), 55–80.

Howe, L. (2003). Ontology and refusal in subaltern ethics. *Administrative Theory & Praxis, 25*(2), 277–298.

Howe, L. (2006) Enchantment, weak ontologies, and administrative ethics. *Administration & Society, 38*(4), 422–446.

Human Rights Watch. (2004). *The United States' "disappeared": The C.I.A.'s long-term "ghost detainees."* Retrieved April 23, 2007, from http://www.hrw.org/backgrounder/usa/us1004/

Hummel, R. P. (1994/1977). *The bureaucratic experience: A critique of life in modern organization* (6th ed.). New York: St. Martin's Press.

Hummel, R. (2002). Openness. *Administration & Society, 34*(1), 118–121.

Hummel, R. P., & Stivers, C. (1998). Government isn't us: The possibility of democratic knowledge in representative government. In C. S. King, C. Stivers, & collaborators, (Eds.), *Government is us: Public administration in an anti-government era* (pp. 28–45). Thousand Oaks, CA: Sage.

Hunt, A., & Wickham, G. (1994). *Foucault and law: Towards a sociology of law as governance.* London: Pluto Press.

Hunter, F. (1953). *Community power structure: A study of decision makers.* Chapel Hill: University of North Carolina Press.

Hurst, J. W. (1956). *Law and the conditions of freedom in the nineteenth-century United States.* Madison: University of Wisconsin Press.

Hyneman, C. S. (1950). *Bureaucracy in a democracy.* New York: Harper & Brothers.

Israel, J. I. (2001). *Radical enlightenment: Philosophy and the making of modernity, 1650–1750.* New York: Oxford University Press.

Jacobson, M. F. (2000). *Barbarian virtues: The United States encounters foreign peoples at home and abroad, 1876–1917.* New York: Hill & Wang.

Jacquette, D. (2002). *Ontology.* Montreal: McGill-Queen's University Press.

James, P. (2005). Theory and society in the shadow of terror. *Alternatives, 30*(3), 365–388.

James, W. (1977). Pragmatism's conception of truth. In J. J. McDermott (Ed.), *The writings of William James: A comprehensive edition* (pp. 429–443). Chicago: University of Chicago Press.

Jameson, F. (1981). *The political unconscious: Narrative as socially symbolic act.* Ithaca, NY: Cornell University Press.

Jameson, F. (2000/1984). Postmodernism; or, The cultural logic of late capitalism. In M. Hardt & K. Weeks (Eds.), *The Jameson reader* (pp. 188–232). Oxford: Blackwell.

Jameson, F. (2002). *A singular modernity: An essay on the ontology of the present.* London: Verso.

Jones, S. H., & Clarke, D. B. (2006). Waging terror: The geopolitics of the real. *Political Geography, 25*(3), 298–314.

Kahn, P. W. (1997). *The reign of law: Marbury v. Madison and the construction of America.* New Haven, CT: Yale University Press.

Kantorowicz, E. H. (1957). *The king's two bodies: A study in medieval political theology.* Princeton, NJ: Princeton University Press.

Kaplan, A. (1998). Manifest domesticity. *American Literature, 70*(3), 581–606.

Kennedy, R. (1997). *Race, crime, and the law.* New York: Pantheon.

Kennedy, S. S., & Jensen, L. (2004). Outsourcing patriotism: Privatization goes to war. *PA Times, 27*(9).

King, C. S., & Zanetti, L. (2005). *Transformational public service: Portraits of theory and practice.* Armonk, NY: M. E. Sharpe

Koyré, A. (1978/1966). *Galileo studies* (J. Mepham, Trans.). Atlantic Heights, NJ: Humanities Press.

Kuhn, T. S. (1996/1962). *The structure of scientific revolutions* (3rd ed.). Chicago: University of Chicago Press.

Lacan, J. (1999/1975). *The seminar of Jacques Lacan: Book 20. Encore, on feminine sexuality: The limits of love and knowledge* (B. Fink, Trans.). New York: W. W. Norton.

Lacan, J. (2006/1960). The subversion of the subject and the dialectic of desire. In *Ecrits* (Bruce Fink, Trans.) (pp. 672–702). New York: W. W. Norton.

Laclau, E. (2000). Identity and hegemony. In J. Butler, E. Laclau, & S. Zizek (Eds.), *Contingency, hegemony, universality* (pp. 44–89). London: Verso.

Laclau, E., & Mouffe, C. (1985). *Hegemony and socialist strategy: Towards a radical democratic politics.* London: Verso.

LaPorte, T. R. (1971). The recovery of relevance in the study of public organizations. In F. Marini (Ed.), *Toward a new public administration: The Minnowbrook perspective* (pp. 17–48). Scranton, PA: Chandler.

Latour, B. (1993/1991). *We have never been modern* (C. Porter, Trans.). Cambridge, MA: Harvard University Press.

Latour, B. (2004). Has critique run out of steam? From matters of fact to matters of concern. *Critical Inquiry, 30*(Winter), 225–248.

Lefort, C. (1986/1980). *The political forms of modern society: Bureaucracy, democracy, and totalitarianism.* Cambridge, MA: MIT Press.

Licht, W. (1995). *Industrializing America: The nineteenth century.* Baltimore, MD: Johns Hopkins University Press.

Lipset, S. M. (2003/1971). Bureaucracy and social change. In J. Dolan & D. H. Rosenbloom (Eds.), *Representative bureaucracy: Classic readings and continuing controversies* (pp. 80–83). Armonk, NY: M. E. Sharpe.

Locke, J. (1988/1689). *Two treatises on government.* Cambridge: Cambridge University Press.

Lowi, T. (1969). *The end of liberalism* (2nd ed.). New York: W. W. Norton.

Lynn Jr., L. E., (1997). *Public management as art, science, and profession.* Chatham, NJ: Chatham House.

Lynn Jr., L. E., (2001). The myth of the bureaucratic paradigm: What traditional public administration really stood for. *Public Administration Review, 61*(2), 144–160.

Lyon, D. (2001). *Surveillance society: Monitoring everyday life.* Buckingham, England: Open University Press.

Mann, M. (1993). *The sources of social power: Vol. 2. The rise of classes and nation-states, 1760–1914.* New York: Cambridge University Press.

Marcuse, H. (1964). *One-dimensional man: Studies in the ideology of advanced industrial society.* Boston: Beacon Press.

Marini, F. (Ed.). (1971). *Toward a new public administration: The Minnowbrook perspective.* Scranton, PA: Chandler.

Marshall, G. S., & Choudhury, E. (1997). Public administration and the public interest: Re-presenting a lost concept. *American Behaviorial Scientist, 41*(1), 119–131.

Martin, R. (2004). America as risk/securizing the other. *Interventions: International Journal of Postcolonial Studies, 6*(3), 351–361.

Martin, R. C. (1952). Political science and public administration: A note on the state of the union. *American Political Science Review, 46*(3), 660–676.

Marx, K. (1967/1867). *Capital: Vol. 1.* (S. Moore & E. Aveling, Trans.). New York: International Publishers.

Marx, K. (1967/1843). *Critique of Hegel's "Philosophy of Right"* (Joseph O'Malley, Ed. and Trans.). Cambridge: Cambridge University Press.

Marx, K. (1973). *Grundrisse* (M. Nicolaus, Trans.). London: Penguin Books (first Eng. pub; written 1857–61).

Marx, K. (1998/1848). *The communist manifesto.* London: Verso.

Massumi, B. (1992). *A user's guide to capitalism and schizophrenia: Deviations from Deleuze and Guattari.* Cambridge, MA: MIT Press.

May, T. (1994). *The political philosophy of post-structuralist anarchism.* University Park: Pennsylvania State University Press.

May, T. (1995). *The moral theory of post-structuralism.* University Park: Pennsylvania State University Press.

Mayhew, L. H. (1968). Society. In D. L. Sills (Ed.), *International encyclopedia of the social sciences* (Vol. 13, pp. 577–586). New York: Macmillan & Free Press.

Maynard-Mooney, S., & Musheno, M. (2003). *Cops, teachers, and counselors: Stories from the frontline of public service.* Ann Arbor: University of Michigan Press.

McCabe, B. C. (2005). The rules are different here: An institutional comparison of cities and homeowners associations. *Administration & Society, 37*(4), 404–425.

McCormick, J. P. (1997). *Carl Schmitt's critique of liberalism: Against politics as technology.* New York: Cambridge University Press.

McGowan, T. (2004). *The end of dissatisfaction? Jacques Lacan and the emerging society of enjoyment.* Albany: State University of New York Press.

McSwain, C. J., & White, O. F. (1993). A transformational theory of organizations. *American Review of Public Administration, 23*(2), 81–98.

McSwite, O. C. (1996). Postmodernism, public administration, and the public interest. In G. L. Wamsley & J. F. Wolf (Eds.), *Refounding democratic public administration* (pp. 198–224). Thousand Oaks, CA: Sage.

McSwite, O. C. (1997a). Jacques Lacan and the theory of the human subject: How psychoanalysis can help public administration. *American Behavioral Scientist, 41*(1), 43–63.

McSwite, O. C. (1997b). *Legitimacy in public administration: A discourse analysis.* Thousand Oaks, CA: Sage.

McSwite, O. C. (1997c). Postmodernism and public administration's identity crisis [Review of *The language of public administration: Bureaucracy, modernity, and postmodernity* and *Postmodern public administration: Toward discourse*]. *Public Administration Review, 55*(2), 174–181.

McSwite, O. C. (1998). The new normativism and the discourse movement: A meditation. *Administrative Theory & Praxis, 20*(2), 377–381.

McSwite, O. C. (2002). *Invitation to public administration:* Armonk, NY: M. E. Sharpe.

McSwite, O. C. (2003). Now more than ever: Refusal as redemption. *Administrative Theory & Praxis, 25*(2), 185–204.

McSwite, O. C. (2004). Creating reality through administrative practice: A psychoanalytic reading of Camilla Stivers' *Bureau Men, Settlement Women. Administration & Society, 36*(4), 406–426.

McSwite, O. C. (2005a). He did it again: A reply to Hugh Miller. *Administrative Theory & Praxis, 27*(3), 567–570.

McSwite, O. C. (2005b). Public administration post Fox and Miller: What we face now. *Administrative Theory & Praxis, 27*(3), 533–551.

McSwite, O. C. (2005c). Taking public administration seriously: Beyond humanism and bureaucrat bashing. *Administration & Society, 37*(1), 116–125.

Meyer-Emerick, N. (2004). Biopolitics, dominance, and critical theory. *Administrative Theory & Praxis, 26*(1), 1–15.

Miller, H. T. (2002). *Postmodern Public Policy.* Albany: State University of New York Press.

Miller, H. (2005a). Redescribing public administration. *Administrative Theory & Praxis, 27*(3), 469–483.

Miller, H. T. (2005b). Residues of foundationalism in classic pragmatism. *Administration & Society, 37*(3), 360–374.

Mills, C. W. (1956). *The power elite.* New York: Oxford University Press.

Minca, C. (2005). The return of the camp. *Progress in Human Geography, 29*(4), 405–412.

Mitchell, T. (1991). The limits of the state: Beyond statist approaches and their critics. *American Political Science Review, 85*(1), 77–96.

Mitchell, T. (1999). Society, economy, and the state-effect. In G. Steinmetz (Ed.), *State/Culture: State/formation after the cultural turn* (pp. 76–97). Ithaca, NY: Cornell University Press.

Montjoy, R. S., & Watson, D. J. (1995). A case for reinterpreted dichotomy of politics and administration as a professional standard in council-manager government. *Public Administration Review, 55*(3), 231–239.

Morçöl, G. (2002). *A new mind for policy analysis: Toward a post-Newtonian and postpositivist epistemology and methodology.* Westport, CT: Praeger.

Morgan, D. F., & Kass, H. D. (1991). Constitutional stewardship: Phronesis and the American administrative ethos. *Dialogue: The Public Administration Theory Network, 12*(1), 17–60.

Morgan, E. S. (1988). *Inventing the people: The rise of popular sovereignty in England and America.* New York: W. W. Norton.

Mosca, G. (1939). *Ruling class* (H. D. Kahn, Trans.). New York: McGraw-Hill.

Mosher, F. C. (1982). *Democracy and the public service* (2nd ed.). Oxford: Oxford University Press.

Mouffe, C. (1999). Introduction: Schmitt's challenge. In C. Mouffe (Ed.), *The challenge of Carl Schmitt* (pp. 1–6). London: Verso.

Nagel, T. (1986). *The view from nowhere.* Oxford: Oxford University Press.

Nalbandian, J. (2005). Professionals and conflicting forces of administrative modernization and civic engagement. *American Review of Public Administration, 35*(4), 311–326.

Negri, A. (1999/1992). *Insurgencies: Constituent power and the modern state* (M. Boscagli, Trans.). Minneapolis: University of Minnesota Press.

Neocleous, M. (2000). *The fabrication of social order: A critical theory of police power.* London: Pluto Press.

Neuman, G. L. (1993). The lost century of American immigration law. *Columbia Law Review, 93)* 93(8), 1833–1901

Nietzsche, F. (1967/1887). On the genealogy of morals. In W. Kaufmann (Ed.), *On the genealogy of morals and Ecce homo* (pp. 15–163). New York: Vintage.

Novak, W. J. (1996). *The people's welfare: Law and regulation in nineteenth-century America.* Chapel Hill: University of North Carolina Press.

Oakeshott, M. (1975). *On human conduct.* Oxford: Clarendon Press.

O'Malley, P. (1997). Risk and responsibility. In A. Barry, T. Osbourne, & N. Rose (Eds.), *Foucault and political reason: Liberalism, neo-liberalism, and rationalities of government* (pp. 189–208). Chicago: University of Chicago Press.

O'Malley, P. (2004). *Risk, uncertainty, and government.* London: Glasshouse Press.

Ostrom, V. (1989/1973). *The intellectual crisis in American public administration* (2nd ed.). Tuscaloosa: University of Alabama Press.

Page, S. (2005). What's new in the new public management? Administrative change in the human services. *Public Administration Review, 65*(6), 713–727.

Paine, T. (1976/1776). *Common sense.* London: Penguin Books.

Painter, N. I. (1987). *Standing at Armageddon: The United States, 1877–1919.* New York: W. W. Norton.

Passavant, P. A. (2004). The governmentality of consumption. *Interventions: International Journal of Postcolonial Studies, 6*(3), 381–400.

Patterson, P. M. (Ed.). (2001). Reinventing the public body: Embodiment, feminist theories, and public administration [symposium]. *Administrative Theory & Praxis, 23*(2), 175–251.

Pettit, P. (2005). Rawls's political ontology. *Politics, philosophy, and economics, 4*(2), 157–174.

Petty, W. (1690). *Political arthimetik.* Rod Grant, McMaster University Archive of Economic Thought. Retrieved June 15, 2006, from http://socserv2.socsci.mcmaster.ca/~econ/ugcm/3113/petty/poliarith.html

Pfeffer, J., & Sutton, R. I. (2006). *Hard facts, dangerous half-truths, and total nonsense: Profiting from evidence-based management.* Boston: Harvard Business School Press.

Pijl, K. v. d. (1984). *The making of an Atlantic ruling class.* London: Verso.

Plato. (1961). Theaetetus. In E. Hamilton, H. Cairns, & L. Cooper (Eds.), *The collected dialogues of Plato.* Princeton, NJ: Princeton University Press.

Porter, T. M. (1995). *Trust in numbers: The pursuit of objectivity in science and public life.* Princeton, NJ: Princeton University Press.

Postel, D. (2003). Noble lies and perpetual war: Leo Strauss, the neo-cons, and Iraq. In *openDemocracy.net:Conpendium edition 25, 13–19 2003* (pp. 1–7). Retrieved April 23, 2007, from http://www.opendemocracy.net/debates/article-3-77-1542.jsp

Powers, F. P. (1888). The reform of the federal service. *Political Science Quarterly, 3*(2), 247–281.

Preuss, U. K. (1999). Political order and democracy: Carl Schmitt and his influence. In C. Mouffe (Ed.), *The challenge of Carl Schmitt* (pp. 155–179). London: Verso.

Priest, D. (2005, November 2). C.I.A. holds terror suspects in secret prisons. *Washington Post,* p. A01.

Putnam, R. D. (2000). *Bowling alone: The collapse and revival of American community.* New York: Simon & Schuster.

Raadschedlers, J. C. N. (Ed.) (1998). *Handbook of administrative history.* New Brunswick, NJ: Transaction.

Raadschedlers, J. C. N. (2003). *Government: A public administration perspective.* Armonk, NY: M. E. Sharpe.

Raadschedlers, J. C. N., Waganaar, P., Rutgers, M. R., & Overseen, P. (2000). Against a study of the history of public administration: A manifesto. *Administrative Theory & Praxis, 22*(4), 772–791.

Raeff, M. (1975). The well-ordered police state and the development of modernity in 17th and 18th century Europe: An attempt at a comparative approach. *American Historical Review, 80*(5), 1221–1243.

Rakove, J. N. (1996). *Original meanings.* New York: Knopf.

Ramos, A. G. (1981). *The new science of organizations: A reconceptualization of the wealth of nations.* Toronto: University of Toronto Press.

Redford, E. S. (1969). *Democracy in the administrative state.* Oxford: Oxford University Press.

Reich, R. B. (1992). *The work of nations.* New York: Vintage Books.

Rich, A. C. (1986/1980). Compulsory heterosexuality and lesbian existence. In *Blood, bread, and poetry* . New York: W. W. Norton.

Rist, G. (1997). *The history of development: From Western origins to global faith* (Patrick Camiller, Trans.). New York: Zed Books.

Robinson, A. (2005). The political theory of constitutive lack: A critique. *Theory & Event, 8*(1).

Rodgers, D. T. (1982). In search of progressivism. *Reviews in American History, 10*(4), 113–132.

Rohr, J. (1986). *To run a constitution: The legitimacy of the administrative state.* Lawrence: University of Kansas Press.

Rohr, J. (1978). *Ethics for bureaucrats: An essay on law and values.* New York: Marcel Dekker.

Rorty, R. (1979). *Philosophy and the mirror of nature.* Princeton, NJ: Princeton University Press.

Rorty, R. (1989). *Contingency, irony, and solidarity.* Cambridge: Cambridge University Press.

Rose, N. (1997). Governing "advanced" liberal democracies. In A. Barry, T. Osbourne, & N. Rose (Eds.), *Foucault and political reason: Liberalism, neo-liberalism and rationalities of government* (pp. 37–64). Chicago: University of Chicago Press.

Rose, N. (1999). *Governing the soul: The shaping of the private self* (2nd ed.). New York: Free Association Books.

Rose, N. (2001). The politics of life itself. *Theory, Culture, & Society, 18*(6), 1–30.

Rosenau, J. N. (1990). *Turbulence in world politics.* Princeton, NJ: Princeton University Press.

Rosenau, J. N. (1992). The relocation of authority in a shrinking world. *Comparative Politics, 24*(3), 253–272.

Rosenbloom, D. (1999). *Public administration: Understanding management, politics, and law in the public sector* (4th ed.). New York: McGraw Hill.

Rosenbloom, D. H. (2000a). *Building a legislative-centered public administration: Congress and the administrative state, 1946–1999.* Tuscaloosa: University of Alabama Press.

Rosenbloom, D. H. (2000b). Retrofitting the administrative state to the Constitution: Congress and the judiciary's twentieth-century progress. *Public Administration Review, 60*(1), 39–46.

Rosenbloom, D. H., & McCurdy, H. E. (Eds.) (2006). *Revisiting Waldo's "Administrative State": Constancy and change in public administration.* Washington, DC: Georgetown University Press.

Rosenbloom, D. H., & O'Leary, R. (1997). *Public administration and law* (2nd ed.). New York: Marcel Dekker.

Rotman, B. (1987). *Signifying nothing: The semiotics of zero.* Stanford, CA: Stanford University Press.

Roy, W. G. (1997). *Socializing capital: The rise of the large industrial corporation.* Princeton, NJ: Princeton University Press.

Rutgers, M. (1994). Can the study of public administration do without a concept of the state? Reflections on the work of Lorenz Von Stein. *Administration & Society, 26*(3), 395–412.

Rutgers, M. R. (1997). Beyond Woodrow Wilson: The identity of public administration in historical perspective. *Administration & Society, 29*(3), 276–300.

Salecl, R. (2004). *On anxiety.* London: Routledge.

Salter, M. B. (2004). Passports, mobility, and security: How smart can the border be? *International Studies Perspectives, 5*, 71–91.

Sarason, S. B. (1986). And what is the public interest? *American Psychologist, 41*(8), 899–905.

Saussure, F. d. (1972). *Course in general linguistics* (R. Harris, Trans.). La Salle, IL: Open Court Press.

Sayre, W. S. (1958). Premises of public administration: Past and emerging. *Public Administration Review, 18*(2), 102–105.

Scheweber, H. (1999). The "science" of legal science: The model of the natural sciences in nineteenth century American legal education. *Law and History Review, 17*(3).

Schmitt, C. (1985a/1923). *The crisis of parliamentary democracy* (E. Kennedy, Trans.). Cambridge, MA: MIT Press.

Schmitt, C. (1985b/1922). *Political theology: Four chapters on the concept of sovereignty* (G. Schwab, Trans.). Cambridge, MA: MIT Press.

Schmitt, C. (1996/1932). *The concept of the political* (G. Schwab, Trans.). Chicago: University of Chicago Press.

Schneider, A. L., and Ingram, H. M. (1997). *Policy Design for Democracy.* Laurence: University of Kansas Press.

Schubert, G. (1960). *The public interest: A critique of the theory of political concept.* Glencoe, IL: Free Press.

Schwartz, B. (2004). *The paradox of choice: Why more is less.* New York: Ecco Press/HarperCollins.

Searle, J. (1969). *Speech acts: An essay in the philosophy of language.* Cambridge: Cambridge University Press.

Shafritz, J. M., & Russell, E. W. (2003). *Introducing public administration* (3rd ed.). New York: Longman.

Shamir, R. (2005). Without borders? Notes on the globalization as mobility regime. *Sociological Theory, 23*(2), 197–217.

Shpak-Lissak, R. (1989). *Pluralism & progressives: Hull House and the new immigrants, 1890–1919.* Chicago: University of Chicago Press.

Siegel, J. C. (1999). *Popular science: The sovereign constitution of polity.* Unpublished doctoral dissertation, University of Pennsylvania, Philadelphia.

Silverman, D. (2004). Who cares about "experience"? Missing issues in qualitative research. In D. Silverman (Ed.), *Qualitative research: Theory, method, and practice* (2nd ed., pp. 342–368). Thousand Oaks, CA: Sage.

Simmons, A. J. (1993). *On the edge of anarchy: Locke, consent, and the limits of society.* Princeton, NJ: Princeton University Press.

Simon, H. A. (1997/1945). *Administrative behavior* (4th ed.). New York: Free Press.

Simon, J. (1988). The ideological affects of actuarial practices. *Law and Society Review, 22*(4), 772–800.

Simon, J. (1995). They died with their boots on: The bootcamp and the limits of modern penalty. *Social Justice, 22*(2), 25–48.

Singer, P. W. (2005). Outsourcing war. *Foreign Affairs, 84*(2), 119–132.

Skowronek, S. (1982). *Building a new American state: The expansion of national administrative capacities, 1877–1920.* New York: Cambridge University Press.

Smith, K. K., & Berg, D. N. (1997/1987). *Paradoxes of group life: Understanding conflict, paralysis, and movement in group dynamics.* San Francisco: New Lexington Press.

Smith, N. (2006). Global executioner. *South Atlantic Quarterly, 105*(1), 55–69.

Sørensen, E. (2002). Democratic theory and network governance. *Administrative Theory & Praxis, 24*(4), 693–720.

Sørensen, E., & Torfing, J. (2005). Network governance and post-liberal democracy. *Administrative Theory & Praxis, 27*(2), 197–237.

Spicer, M. W. (1995). *The founders, the Constitution, and public administration: A conflict in worldviews.* Washington, DC: Georgetown University Press.

Spicer, M. W. (2001). *Public administration and the state: A postmodern perspective.* Tuscaloosa: University of Alabama Press.

Spielberg, S. D. (2002). *Minority report* [Motion picture]. United States: DreamWorks Pictures.

Stavrakakis, Y. (1999). *Lacan and the political.* New York: Routledge.

Steinfeld, R. J. (1989). Property and suffrage in the early American republic. *Stanford Law Review, 41.*

Stillman, R. J., II. (1991). *Preface to public administration.* New York: St. Martin's Press.

Stivers, C. (1993). *Gender images in public administration: Legitimacy and the administrative state.* Newbury Park, CA: Sage.

Stivers, C. (2000). *Bureau men, settlement women: Constructing public administration in the progressive era.* Lawrence: University Press of Kansas.

Streib, G., Slotkin, B. J., & Rivera, M. (2001). Public administration research from a practitioner perspective. *Public Administration Review, 61*(5), 515–525.

Subrin, S. N. (1987). How equity conquered common law: The Federal Rules of Civil Procedure in historical perspective. *University of Pennsylvania Law Review, 2007.*

Svara, J. H. (1985). Dichotomy and duality: Reconceptualizing the relationship between policy and administration in council-manager cities. *Public Administration Review, 45*(1), 221–232.

Svara, J. H. (1998). The politics-administration dichotomy model as aberration. *Public Administration Review, 58*(1), 51–58.

Svara, J. H. (2001). The myth of the dichotomy: Complementarity of politics and administration in the past and future of public administration. *Public Administration Review, 61*(2), 176–183.

Taylor, C. (2004). *Modern social imaginaries.* Durham, NC: Duke University Press.

Taylor, F. (1997/1912). Scientific management. In J. M. Shafritz & A. C. Hyde (Eds.), *Classics of public administration* (4th ed., pp. 30–32). Fort Worth, TX: Harcourt Brace.

Thayer, F. C. (1973). *An end to hierarchy! An end to competition! Organizing the politics and economics of survival.* New York: New Viewpoints.

Thayer, F. C. (1975). Organization theory as epistemology: Transcending hierarchy and objectivity. In C. Bellone (Ed.), *Organization theory and the new public administration* (pp. 113–139). New York: Allyn & Bacon.

Thayer, F. C. (1984). *Rebuilding America: The case for economic regulation.* New York: Praeger.

Therborn, G. (1978). *What does the ruling class do when it rules? State apparatuses and state power under feudalism, capitalism, and socialism.* London: New Left Books.

Thorne, K. (2004, June 10–12). *The dangerous case of the sovereign individual: How should we cultivate the civic in global cyberspace?* Paper presented at the Seventeenth Annual International Conference of the Public Administration Theory Network, University of Nebraska, Omaha.

Thorne, K. and A. Kouzmin. (2004). Borders in an (in)visible world: Revisiting communities, recognizing gulags. *Administrative Theory & Praxis, 26*(3), 408–429.

Tolbert, P. S., & Zucker, L. (1983). Institutional sources of change in formal structure of organizations: The diffusion of civil service reform, 1880–1935. *Administrative Science Quarterly, 28*(1), 22–39.

Torfing, J. (1999). *New theories of discourse: Laclau, Mouffe, and Zizek.* London: Blackwell.

Traynor, I. (2003, December 10). The privatization of war: $30 Billion goes to private military; fears over "hired guns" policy. *Guardian.* Retrieved July 6, 2006, from http://www.guardian.co.uk/print/0,3858,4815701–103681,00.html

Turner, V. (1969). *The ritual process: Structure and anti-structure.* Ithaca, NY: Cornell University Press.

Van Tassell, E. F. (1995). "Only the rule would rule between us": Antimiscegenation, the moral economy of dependency, and the debate over rights. *Chicago-Kent Law Review, 70*, 873–926.

Verhaeghe, P. (1999). Causation and destitution of a pre-ontological non-entity: On the Lacanian subject. In D. Nobus (Ed.), *Key concepts in Lacanian psychoanalysis* (pp. 164–189). New York: Other Press.

Verhaeghe, P. (2001). From impossibility to inability: Lacan's theory of the four discourses. In *Beyond gender: From subject to drive* (pp. 17–34). New York: Other Press.

Vogel, R. D. (2003). Capitalism and incarceration revisted. *Monthly Review, 55*(4), 38–55.

Wacquant, L. (2002a). Four strategies to curb carceral costs: On managing mass imprisonment in the U.S. *Studies in Political Economy, 69*, 19–30.

Wacquant, L. (2002b). Slavery to mass incarceration: Rethinking the "race question" in the U.S. *New Left Review, 13*, 41–60.

Waldo, D. (1948). *The administrative state: A study of the political theory of American public administration.* New York: Ronald Press.

Waldo, D. (Ed.). (1970). *Temporal dimensions of development administration.* Durham, NC: Duke University Press.

Waldo, D. (1980). *The enterprise of public administration.* Novato, CA: Chandler & Sharp.

Wamsley, G. L. (1990). The agency perspective: Public administrators as agential leaders. In G. L. Wamsley, R. N. Bacher, C. T. Goodsell, P. S. Kroneberg, J. A. Rohr, C. M. Stivers, O. F. White, & J. F. Wolf (Eds.), *Refounding public administration* (pp. 115–162). Newbury Park, CA: Sage.

Wamsley, G. L., Goodsell, C. T., Rohr, J. A., Stivers, C. M., White, O. F., & Wolf, J. F. (1990). Public administration and the governance process: Shifting the political dialogue. In G. L. Wamsley, R. N. Bacher, C. T. Goodsell, P. S. Kroneberg, J. A. Rohr, C. M. Stivers, O. F. White, & J. F. Wolf (Eds.), *Refounding public administration* (pp. 31–51). Newbury Park, CA: Sage.

Weick, K. C. (1993). The collapse of sensemaking in organizations: The Mann Gulch disaster. *Administrative Science Quarterly, 38*(4), 628–652.

Whitaker, G. P. (1980). Coproduction: Citizen participation in service delivery. *Public Administration Review, 40*(3), 240–246.

White, J. D. (1999). *Taking language seriously: The narrative foundations of public administration research.* Washington, DC: Georgetown University Press.

White, O. F. (1969). The dialectical organization. *Public Administration Review, 29*(1), 32–42.

White, O. F. (1990). Reframing the authority-participation debate. In G. L. Wamsley, R. N. Bacher, C. T. Goodsell, P. S. Kroneberg, J. A. Rohr, C. M. Stivers, O. F. White, & J. F. Wolf (Eds.), *Refounding public administration* (pp. 182–245). Newbury Park, CA: Sage.

White, O. F., & McSwain, C. J. (1990). The phoenix project: Raising a new image of public administration from the ashes of its past. In H. D. Cass & B. Caytron (Eds.), *Images and identities in public administration* (pp. 23–59). Newbury Park, CA: Sage.

White, S. K. (2000). *Sustaining affirmation: The strengths of weak ontology in political theory.* Princeton, NJ: Princeton University Press.

Wiebe, R. H. (1967). *The search for order, 1877–1920.* New York: Hill & Wang.

Williams, B. (2004). *Debt for sale: A social history of the credit trap.* Philadelphia: University of Pennsylvania Press.

Williams, W. A. (1969). *The roots of the modern American empire: A study of the growth and shaping of social consciousness in a marketplace society.* New York: Random House.

Wilson, W. (1887). The study of administration. *Political Science Quarterly, 2*(2), 197–222.

Woodruff, C. R. (1908). The national municipal league. *Proceedings of the American Political Association, 5*, 131–148.

Yanow, D. (2003). *Constructing "race" and "ethnicity" in America: Category-making in public administration and policy.* Armonk, NY: M. E. Sharpe.

Zizek, S. (1989). *The sublime object of ideology.* London: Verso.

Zizek, S. (1991). *Looking awry: An introduction of Jacques Lacan through popular culture.* Cambridge, MA: MIT Press.

Zizek, S. (1992). *Enjoy your symptom! Jacques Lacan in Hollywood and out.* New York: Routledge.

Zizek, S. (1993). *Tarrying with the negative: Kant, Hegel, and the critique of ideology.* Durham, NC: Duke University Press.

Zizek, S. (1996). "I hear you with my eyes"; or, The invisible master. In R. Salecl & S. Zizek (Eds.), *Gaze and voice as love objects* (pp. 90–128). Durham, NC: Duke University Press.

Zizek, S. (1998). The seven veils of fantasy. In D. Nobus (Ed.), *Key concepts of Lacanian psychoanalysis* (pp. 190–218). New York: Other Press.

Zizek, S. (2000a). Class struggle or postmodernism? Yes, please! In J. Butler, E. Laclau, & S. Zizek (Eds.), *Contingency, hegemony, and solidarity* (pp. 90–135). London: Verso.

Zizek, S. (2000b). Holding the place. In J. Butler, E. Laclau, & S. Zizek (Eds.), *Contingency, hegemony, universality* (pp. 309–329). London: Verso.

Zizek, S. (2000c). *The ticklish subject: The absent centre of political ontology* (First paperback ed.). London: Verso.

Zizek, S. (2002). *For they know not what they do: Enjoyment as a political factor* (2nd ed.). London: Verso.

Index